The Nixons

Books by Edwin P. Hoyt

Jumboes and Jackasses: A Popular History of the Political Wars
The Vanderbilts and Their Fortunes
The Guggenheims and the American Dream
The House of Morgan
The Peabody Influence
The Goulds
The Tempering Years (1930–1940)
A Matter of Conscience

The Nixons
An American Family

Edwin P. Hoyt

Random House   New York

ISBN: 394-47324-8
Library of Congress Catalog Card Number: 74-37052
All pictures are White House Photographs except as individually
noted.

Manufactured in the United States of America
by the Colonial Press, Clinton, Mass.

24689753
First Edition

For
Jessamyn West

Author's Note

This is the story of an ordinary American family, and if the story has validity and importance in the fabric of history, it is because one member of that family rose out of the ranks to become a celebrated political figure, and finally to become President of the United States.

The career of Richard Milhous Nixon is a triumph of perseverance in a very old American tradition. By his own statements, that career was shaped by the philosophy he acquired at the Nixon home in California. And the philosophy and way of life of that Nixon household in Yorba Linda and later Whittier, were in turn determined by a combination of events and the backgrounds of the Nixons and of his mother's family, the Milhouses. It is valid, then, to examine the Nixons and the Milhouses in search of their relationship to the man who would be called the "most powerful in the world" in his time, and who, in his own words, had "drunk too deeply of the stuff which really makes life exciting and worth living to be satisfied with the froth."

During the months of research for this book, many people were of invaluable help. Herb Klein was continually cooperative in lending me materials, and opening doors for me. So was Rob Odle, then one of Mr.

Klein's assistants. Rose Mary Woods was helpful in a dozen ways, and so were members of her staff, especially Mrs. Marge Acker. Other members of the White House staff were also of great assistance, in preparing the way and arranging for me to see President Nixon. Mrs. Constance Stuart, Mrs. Nixon's press secretary, and her staff gave me materials and arranged for me to have time with Mrs. Nixon. And, of course, I am indebted to the Nixons, very busy people in the swirl of public life, for having taken the time to talk to me about what must have seemed to them such peripheral affairs as family background. Mrs. Nixon even lent me certain private papers, and Miss Woods arranged for me to have others. Noble Melenkamp of the White House correspondence staff gave me many papers and materials relating to the family and the background.

Among these I found an opening point with the various genealogical studies of the Nixon and Milhous families, starting with that by Emily Emerson Lantz, assisted by Amy E. E. Hull, which dealt with early Nixon history in England and Ireland. Then came the massive and remarkable genealogy of the Nixon lines (Nixon, Wadsworth, Milhous, and Burdg) conducted over more than twenty years by Raymond M. Bell of Washington and Jefferson College in Washington, Pa. Other genealogical notes came from Mrs. W. L. Ashby of Atascadero, Calif.; Mrs. Helen B. Kithcart of Mt. Pleasant, Ohio; Mrs. Marvin H. Puckett of Oxford, Ohio; Joseph C. Snyder of Martinsburg, W. Va.; Claude Hardwick of Rock Island, Ill.; James Gotch, of Detroit; Harry McLaughlin of York, Pa.; Frederick D. Anderson of Los Angeles; Harry Themal of the Wilmington (Del.) *New Journal;* Mrs. Horace McSwain of Macon, Ga. Philip Meyer of the Chicago *Daily News* did a most valuable article, based on Professor Bell's studies, partly, in which he interviewed a number of Nixon cousins. (The Ohio Nixons, for example, got together at the Hocking county armory one day in 1969. There were nearly a hundred of them.) *The New Yorker,* on March 15, 1969, had an interesting note in Talk of the Town on the Nixons. And Jack Rugh of Coal Valley, Ill., sent the President a study of his investigations into the fate of George Nixon, the Revolutionary War soldier who died in 1842 in Henry county, Ill.

Here a note on procedure is in order: mine is *not* a genealogical study of the Nixon family, for it deals only with the Nixon and Milhous lines. The soldiers of Women's Lib will undoubtedly dismiss me as a male chauvinist for not investigating the backgrounds of the wives of the Nixon males, and for my approach to the Milhouses. But I quite arbitrarily limited the book to the Nixon and Milhous families, from the beginning, on the basis that these are the two dominant strains in the making of the President, genealogically speaking.

I am indebted to the Republican National Committee for making available the film *Nixon: a Self-Portrait,* which was used in the 1968 campaign, and for providing a script, which was very useful in showing the

President's self-analysis. Then there were scores of individuals who either talked or wrote about the Nixons and the Milhouses. Chief among these must be Jessamyn West, President Nixon's cousin, who lent me materials on the Milhous family and spent many hours with me discussing the family and the Quaker background. Among the family, other members very helpful were Merle West, of Whittier, Calif., the President's cousin and brother of Jessamyn, Mrs. Jane Beeson, of Lindsay, Calif., and Mrs. O. O. Marshburn of Whittier (both aunts on the Milhous side), Mrs. Roy Nixon and Roy Nixon, Jr., of McArthur, Ohio, cousins, and Mrs. Nixon's brother Thomas Ryan of Glendale, Calif. Friends and associates who contributed a good deal of information were Raymond Arbuthnot of La Verne, Calif.; Harrison McCall of South Pasadena; Dr. Paul S. Smith of Whittier; Mrs. Thurmond Clarke of Corona De Mar, Calif.; Mrs. George C. Brock of Los Angeles; O. W. Richard of Newport Beach, Calif.; Herbert W. Kalmbach of Newport Beach, Dr. John Lungren of Long Beach; John B. Reilly of Whittier; Clinton O. Harris of Whittier; France Raine of Los Angeles; Robert H. Volk of Los Angeles.

I am extremely indebted to Miss Loie Gaunt, a long-time member of President Nixon's staff and now associated with the Nixon Foundation in Los Angeles, for searching through the Nixon family papers, and for making contacts and helping arrange appointments in Southern California. Dr. Benjamin Whitten, librarian of Whittier College's Wardman Library, was most helpful in finding materials relating to Mr. Nixon's college days and later when he was associated with the college as a trustee. Dr. O. O. Marshburn, the President's uncle-in-law, was also helpful in lending materials. Mr. and Mrs. Jack Drown of Rolling Hills, Calif., shared experiences involving the Nixons over the years. Mrs. Evelyn Dorn, former secretary to Nixon's Whittier law firm, opened some doors and gave me material about the Nixons. Earl Adams, of Adams, Duque and Hazeltine, told me a very great deal about Mr. Nixon's early political career and his association with the Adams law firm in 1961. Hoyt Corbit of Yorba Linda, the Nixon birthplace, spent a good deal of time telling me about early Yorba Linda days.

I am in debt to many librarians. Those at Whittier made available much information, including the files of the Whittier *News* and *Register.* Librarians in Yorba Linda have made a collection of Yorba Linda history that is most valuable. The City of Whittier Historical Committee has produced studies and pamphlets of interest. Librarians at the Ohio Historical Society were most helpful, especially Mrs. Marion Bates. I am also indebted to Alberta Marsh of North American House in Vernon, Jennings county, Ind., for information and material. Mrs. Nellie Howell, one of Mr. Nixon's cousins, made arrangements for Fermin Boring, Recorder for Vinton county, Ohio, to check certain records for me. I am grateful to them both. Mrs. Hallie Durvin, curator of the Washington

County (Pa.) Historical Society, steered me to many histories and documents of interest. Librarians at the Pennsylvania Historical Society in Philadelphia made much information available about early Quakers and the Milhouses. Joanne Mattern of the Historical Society of Delaware copied documents and gave me histories of the state and the Revolution that were useful. Librarians at the Indiana Historical Society in Indianapolis were helpful, and so were those of the North Vernon Public Library in North Vernon, Ind.

Mrs. Nixon's cousin, Ned Sullivan, of Mt. Kisco, N.Y., gave me information about the Ryans in the early days. John H. Corcoran of the Cerritos, Calif., Chamber of Commerce, was helpful in finding material on the Ryans in Artesia. And some information came from as far afield as Richard Hardt, the Bürgermeister of Ober-Rosbach in Germany (Mrs. Nixon's mother came from Germany).

Murray Chotiner, long-time political associate and campaign manager, was also of assistance. Mr. Chotiner, like Earl Adams and Harrison McCall and Raymond Arbuthnot, gave me good insights into the Nixon character.

The reading, of course, was voluminous, for when a man remains in public life as long as Richard Nixon has been there, and becomes President of the United States, the amount of written information about him is immense.

For my purposes (largely historical) I found the Earl Mazo biography of Richard Nixon most useful. The Nixons and their associates recommended the Bela Kornitzer biography, *The Real Nixon,* but that book, while revealing, sometimes erred. Jules Witcover's *The Resurrection of Richard Nixon,* is an impressive work about the political comeback, and so is Garry Wills' *Nixon Agonistes* for a sharp appraisal of the man and his political problems. Other books ranged from *The Delaware Continentals* by Christopher L. Ward, to histories of the various counties in Delaware, Pennsylvania, Ohio, Indiana, and California in which the Nixon and Milhous families lived, the History of the 73rd Ohio Volunteer Infantry Regiment, and a thesis by Andrea Durham Lentz on the Columbus, Ohio, street railway company.

The facts, then, are as accurate as research can make them, and they have been checked for accuracy by members of the White House staff. As for the conclusions and opinions, they are my own.

Edwin P. Hoyt
Annapolis, December 1971

Contents

The Nixons

1

James Nixon and the Ordinary Name

Nixon is an old American name, but a very ordinary one. Like most American families, its members' lives were so commonplace that for two hundred years the name seldom appeared in the newspapers or in public records, except in a few encounters with officialdom, mostly in the disposition of property.

And yet—a Nixon helped to settle Delaware, a Nixon was with Washington at Trenton and Princeton and fought at the battle of the Brandywine. This same Nixon spied for the Americans against the British in Philadelphia. A Nixon fought through the western campaigns of the Civil War and died a hero's death at Gettysburg. Nixons heeded the movement to the West, and gradually made their way from Delaware to the last frontier in California. And there, the Nixon family produced a man who would be President of the United States.

On his mother's side, this man could boast a distinguished line in another way. His mother's name was Milhous, and although the Milhouses shared the reticence of Quakers, they were a proud and useful people in the story of this country. They founded meeting houses and helped to operate the Underground Railway, led in the cultural development of the areas where they lived, and established and carried forth a tradition of good works whose effects have been strongly felt throughout America.

To be sure the Nixons are an ordinary American family, and in their very commonality lies a story that is very old, but one that many of us tend to forget. We can sneer and call it the Horatio Alger syndrome, if we wish—and many sophisticates like to do just that. But the fact is that the American dream still existed in the 1970s, when a man of a very ordinary American family was President of the United States, his election itself proving a reenactment of the American dream that any man (and someday any woman) can aspire to high office and even the leadership of his nation.

There is any amount of speculation among genealogists as to the origin of the Nixon name and family. As early as 1273 the names of Henry Nix and William Nix appeared in the records of the county of Oxford, England. In 1379, the name Margaret Nikeson was registered. A Nicson paid the poll tax in the West Riding of Yorkshire; a Robert Nikkeson appeared in Nottinghamshire in 1309; a John Nickeson in Warwickshire in 1332; and a John Nyxon in Cambridgeshire in 1450, and there was a famous prophet and seer in Cheshire named Robert Nixon.

There were other Nixons abroad in these early days, in Scotland, where William Nycson flourished in the last half of the fourteenth century in Ermyldoune, in the Bewcastle area of Cumberland. Various coats of arms and seals have been established, undoubtedly by different Nixons whose interrelationship is very cloudy. But one thing seems clear: sometime in the seventeenth century, one or more of the Nixons joined Cromwell's armies of the Commonwealth in the invasion of Ireland, and the Nixons became established there on lands granted by the government after they were seized from the unlucky natives.

What happened to one John Nixon, born in 1616 in England, gives a good indication of the reason for the American emigration of Nixons. This John joined Cromwell and went to Ireland to fight. At the end of his war service he claimed a grant of land in Kilkenny and was given the lands. He came home, gathered his family around him and emigrated to Ireland to become a man of property. But times changed, and so did politics, as they always do. It was not many years before he was deprived of his estates by a new English government under what were euphemistically called the "Acts of Settlement." Naturally Nixons coming to Ireland under these conditions were not very popular with the Irish, and while that stigma continued, after a few years they were subject to the same persecutions as the native-born—and had trouble from both sides. Small wonder that the New World looked good to the Nixons of the British Isles. John had brothers named James, George, Thomas, and Richard—and this is what leads to the suspicion that he was a part of the Nixon family that produced the man who would one day become President of the United States.

It was hard to go from the landed gentry to the ranks of the hoi polloi. For in England the family was not wealthy, not well known at all. They had lost their lands in Ireland. Had this John stayed home he would have had to share with his brothers in a father's meager English estate: a house, a cottage, two gardens, an orchard, and only eight acres of tillable land, five acres of meadow, and one acre wood lot.

But now there were Nixons in Ireland, chafing though they might be. John's brother James leased some lands in Bohmean, County Meath, and bought some more in Killamagh in County Mayo, where he died in 1694. His son James had five children (and the names George and James were there again. It does not prove much, does it? And yet

the constant recurrence of names in a family indicates
something.) This James died in 1701, leaving a son George
and lands in Kilmeena and Killamagh.

Whether or not these were uncles or cousins of the Nixons in whom we are here interested, their story follows the
pattern we know of the progenitors of Richard Milhous
Nixon: the next generation brought the emigration. Now,
other English and Scotch and Irish families had been coming to America for nearly a century, beginning with the
Virginia colonies, and the Pilgrims. But the Nixons did not
come until after the turn of the eighteenth century. The first
to come apparently was James Nixon, and he may well
have been a scion of this family; there is record of a James
who was born May 16, 1690, and settled as a young man in
New Ross, County Wexford. Then James Nixon appeared
on April 3, 1731, across the Atlantic in Brandywine Hundred, New Castle county, in the colony of Delaware. That
day he bought a hundred acres of land from Joseph and
Mary Cox, land located a little distance from the road that
ran between Concord and Willing's Town, about four miles
from what is now Wilmington. Other Nixons came to the
New World too at about this time; thousands of people were
moving in from Ireland then. Some went to New Jersey,
and some went to the New England colonies. Three Nixon
brothers of this family settled in Virginia. One lived in Lou-
don county, one joined the Virginia Colonial Militia as a
sergeant, and received a Virginia land grant of two hundred acres a little later; and one moved to Maryland. Nixons were spreading out around the Colonies, and some of
them would become distinguished citizens of Boston, Philadelphia, and Virginia. George Nixon of Virginia became a
plantation owner, with a thousand acres of land, a number
of houses, gristmills, sawmills, and many slaves. The Nixons
of Maryland fared well enough, establishing an estate called
Poor Stony Hill in Prince George's county.

But these others were not our Nixons—not the direct
line to the man who would become President. James, who

bought the land from the Coxes and was the first of the direct line, began life in America as a cooper, a relatively humble if useful trade.

The land to which James Nixon came was the farthest north of the three counties of Delaware, bounded on the north by the line of Pennsylvania, on the east by the Delaware River and bay, and on the south by Duck Creek and a line that runs west to Maryland. It was a part of the Piedmont plateau, and the land was notable because it contains the highest elevation in all Delaware—five hundred feet above sea level. Brandywine Hundred, where James found his land to purchase, was notable for its dark-blue hard rock, called Brandywine granite.

It was a promising area, with plenty of rivers and creeks to irrigate the land, feed the stock, and provide power to run the mills. Brandywine Hundred got its name from a man named Andrew Braindwine who settled there around 1670. Originally it had been called Fish Falls. But whatever it was called it was fine land, and James Nixon could see with half an eye that it would produce for him crops to put the old lands of Ireland to shame. Here he could plant peaches and apples and other fruit trees, maize would grow well, and other grains, and crops, large and small.

Henry Hudson had stopped here in 1609 on his search for a route to the East Indies in behalf of the Dutch East India Company. He had sailed into Delaware Bay, thought it to be a river, and named it South River. Captain Samuel Argall, a British sailor employed by his own government, was the next to come to the area, and he was impressed because he found the Lenni Lenape Indians very friendly. Then came Captain Cornelius May, who named the famous cape for himself. The settlement had come from the Swedish West India Company, which sent two shiploads of settlers to land near the confluence of the Brandywine and Christina rivers. Peter Minuit, a Dutchman, working for the Swedes, led the expedition. The original colonists had not been a very prepossessing bunch. Sweden's government had found little enthusiasm for colonization among its people, and so soldiers who had committed various offenses were transported (along with their families). Finns who had been found guilty of cutting timber and cultivating land in the state forests (which was most of the land) were also sent to the New World. The Dutch conquered the Swedes in time, but the Swedes had been there long enough to introduce their marvelous invention, the log cabin, and it was with such cabins as this, the logs fastened together with clay to keep the weather out, that most settlers began their lives in the New World.

The English had won control of this land and that north of it in battle with the Dutch, about a half-century before James Nixon came. The Duke of York had given Delaware to William Penn on August 31, 1682. But lest one believe that it was a placid, simple community, let him know that the banks of the Delaware were lined with Indians growing more unfriendly every year, and the waters themselves were the homing place of pirates, even when James Nixon came there. Were that not enough, by 1700 the colonists of Pennsylvania and Delaware were at dagger's points. The men of Delaware insisted on their independence from the larger, richer colony to the north, with such verve that in New Castle county representatives had refused to attend the assembly. In 1704 Governor John Evans agreed to a separation. Two years later the men of New Castle built their own fort and made all vessels sailing up river stop and pay their respects and ask for permission to go up to Philadelphia. That was an indication of the relationship between the Delaware colonists and the Pennsylvanians. Over this affair, Governor Evans was eventually discharged by Penn, an action which left more smoldering fires.

The area was growing nicely when James Nixon came. Gristmills and flour mills were flourishing on the banks of the Brandywine and had been for a dozen years. Just recently a furnace had been built on the Christina, and shipbuilders were beginning to ply their trade along the rivers. The Christina was to become famous as the home of sturdy little coasting vessels.

And of course the combination of shipping and the manufacture of flour started a trade that again brought more profit and more ideas to the people along the rivers. That same year that James bought his farm from the Coxes, there was a flurry in the colony, when Thomas Willing of Philadelphia announced grandiose plans to create a town, which, of course, he would call Willingtown. Willing had married the daughter of Andres Justison, one of the richest men in the colony, and had thus come into possession of a large tract of land on the north shore of Christina Creek. But he was not the man that his father-in-law was, and while James Nixon, in his own way, prospered as he planted his wheat and corn and fruit trees, Willing did not get along very well with his greater plans. In fact, James Nixon did so well that in 1734 he was able to approach Jacob Vandiver, one of the settlers from an old Dutch family, and contract to buy another hundred acres of land for £140. He was extending himself, he could not pay for it all at once, but he could use it and he could afford to make the payments on a land contract. Willing faltered and his town came to nothing until a Quaker named William Shipley came to the area from Ridley, Pennsylvania, and bought up most of the land. Shipley was a persuasive fellow, and a year or so after James Nixon bought his second farm, Shipley had brought Quaker friends in, and thirty-three houses had been built in the town, which was about three miles away from the Nixon place. Shipley widened the streets, built more of them, and put up a market house at Fourth Street, where farmers like Nixon could come and sell their produce in exchange for what they needed from town. Soon the town had a charter, but not as Willingtown. The governor changed the name to

Wilmington, after an English Earl, to remind the colonists that influence and authority lay on the other side of the Atlantic.

James Nixon continued to do well, and built a substantial stone house on his new property. Perhaps one reason for his success was association with the Vandiver family, who were very prominent in the area. A Dutchman had settled on an island in Brandywine Hundred opposite the site of Wilmington in the seventeenth century, to practice the cooper's trade, then the island came into the hands of Jacob Van de Vere, and soon the family name was Americanized to Vandiver. He and his family had acquired hundreds of acres of land before they sold to Nixon, with frontage on the King's road, and a Vandiver had built the bridge that replaced the ferry across the Brandywine. (It was later replaced by the Market Street Bridge.)

There was a good deal of buying and selling of lands, as newcomers arrived and offered high prices to the descendents of the old families. For example, nearby, Morgan Druitt had received five hundred and thirty-two acres from William Penn around 1683, and just before James Nixon bought his land, the Druitts sold their holdings to Reuben Ford. There the difference showed: the Druitts had been landholders, the Fords were farmers who would work the land: three years after James Nixon bought the Vandiver property, Reuben Ford turned over 93 acres to one son, 73 to another, and 115 acres to a third. That was the way of the land in the new country for those farmers who came in at the right time, and managed to get enough land so they could arrange to keep their families around them. There was, of course, a rub. In these days, because of the high incidence of child death due to typhus and typhoid and other killing diseases, and when contraception was basically as unknown as it was unholy, men had big families. And if the children survived, or most of them did, it took a grand effort and a good deal of luck to amass enough land to keep them all by the hearth.

James married, and his wife bore six children who lived. There may have been more, but the scanty records of the time do not seem to indicate so. Four of the children were daughters: Elizabeth, who married James Hannah (the Hannahs were a family from nearby Mill Creek Hundred); Mary, named after her mother, who married John Latta; Catherine, who married Samuel Donnald; and Jean, who was still unmarried at the time of her father's death.

The boys were George, born in 1752, and James Junior, born in 1755. Tradition, even in the New World, dictated that the daughters would get love, and money, and household furnishings. The sons would get the land. That was how James Nixon planned his estate, too.

The Nixon place grew. James bought another seventy-eight acres to the north from Thomas McCracken, and now his farm was quite respectable in size, although he had not yet paid entirely for the Vandiver tract.

As the years of the eighteenth century rolled along, the Nixons prospered with the colony. Wilmington began to grow into a real town and New Castle county developed as an industrial center of the central Colonies, with its iron ore, mills, and good supply of water power. In 1740 a good-sized ship, the *Wilmington*, was launched and put out to sea to head for Jamaica with a cargo of flour and barreled beef. Sloops began to ply from the harbors of Delaware up and down the coast carrying goods and bringing profits. There were half a dozen flour mills in the area, taking all the local grain they could get from James Nixon and the other farmers.

As long as the farmers stuck to their fields, there was no trouble. But when they began shipping American goods in American bottoms to the Caribbean colonies, eyebrows began to raise in England, and the continued industrial prosperity of the little American colonies seemed to become a cause for alarm in London. New Castle county soon began to feel the pinch of British repressions along with the other prospering places in the Colonies.

2

The Nixons
of Delaware

The two sons of James Nixon were dutiful boys, and they worked their father's land summer and winter. In the spring they hitched the horses to the plow and furrowed the land, then planted the corn. They slopped the hogs and lambed and sheared the sheep and kept the rail fences in repair with timbers from their big woods. Although they grew strong and straight and healthy, neither boy thought of early marriage. James proudly called himself "yeoman" now, which meant small landowner, but it would be a hardship to break up the family holdings; land in that area was too valuable and too hard to come by; otherwise James might have bought land for the boys, even though he had sold, or agreed to sell, that seventy-eight-acre piece he had bought from McCracken to Daniel McBride. There was, however, very little land to buy at a reasonable price. Besides, the two-hundred-acre farm took pretty much the efforts of all the family if it was to be farmed economically.

James aged, and after the winter of 1772 he was feeling his mortality so intensely that in the spring he decided to draw his will, and called in neighbors McBride and James Day to witness it. George and James would inherit the land and James, as the younger, would be bound to take care of his mother as long as she lived. It was a common enough arrangement, with the understanding in any reasonable family that the eldest son would help out as much as he could, although it was his right to be freed first from obligation to the parents, and this year he was twenty-one years old.

Two years later, in June 1775, James Nixon died, and the will went to probate in New Castle county on the twenty-sixth of that month. The children then learned their father's decisions, which were to be carried out by Mary, his widow, and George, as executors.

Mary was to have £60 in cash, which had been put out to James McCorkle. (It was not unusual for a farmer to lend his cash or entrust it to some commercially minded neighbor for investment; it was a long way to any large banking institution, and money drew nothing while sitting around the house.) Much more important, Mary was to have one-third interest in the income of the plantation, as James called it, as long as she lived, and it was simply assumed that she would stay on in the big stone house until her death. She was to own outright her bed and bedding and furniture for one room of her own.

George inherited the first landholding, the tract bought in 1731, which James referred to still as the John Reily plantation, although he had held it for forty years. The exact amount of land was 106 acres, and with it George was to have £70 in cash.

The daughters received just what they expected, their father's remembrance and not much else, for the husbands of three of them were expected to provide, and Jean, the youngest, who must have been now in her early twenties, might still catch a husband. She was to have £60 in cash, which was held by a schoolmaster named Robert Smith, who ran an academy in Pequea, Lancaster county. She would also have a horse of her own, a saddle, and a bed which would be kept in the big stone house.

Elizabeth, the first daughter, and her husband James Hannah would have £10 in cash. Mary, the second daughter, and her husband John Latta would have £20. Catherine, the third daughter, and her husband Samuel Donnald would have £15. Perhaps these varying figures represented degrees of affection James held for his girls and their husbands, but more likely they represented his appraisal of the financial condition of their husbands.

When all the bequests were made, James disposed of the home plantation, which would go to James, Jr. He would have the hundred prime acres here, the stone house, and the two black slaves, the man Ned and the woman Nance. Yes, this first American ancestor of Richard Milhous Nixon was indeed a slaveholder. So the Nixons share the great guilt of White America in a very personal way. Not only that, unmentioned in the Nixon chronicles, they share the guilt of the French and Indian wars, which had flared during James Nixon's husbandry. In the beginning, when James first came, the colonists were still using old Indian paths, and the Indians hunted in the lands near theirs. But as the colonists settled the lands and built their fences, the Indians were driven north and west, becoming angrier and more determined to fight for their rights as they moved away. Brandywine Hundred did not suffer from the massacres of whites and Indians; these were safely out of sight in the woodlands and frontier lands of western Pennsylvania and New York, but troops of soldiers were raised to fight the Indians, and did not James Nixon share in the responsibility if not in the soldiering? These Delawares, peoples of the Algonquin and Iroquois nations had called themselves "the original people." Now they were driven from their homeland.

But by the time James Nixon died, such matters were given scant philosophical consideration, save perhaps by the

Quakers in the area. The political matters that interested the Nixons and the other citizens of Delaware in the 1770s involved relations with Mother England.

By 1764 the British at home were actively seeking to make the American Colonies support the armies that had been sent to protect them from the Indians and the French, and to make the prospering Americans pay a part of the cost of wars in Europe, too. The growing number of ship-owners and traders on Delaware Bay took violent exception to the attempts to set up and enforce customs laws, and of course, what hurt Delaware business hurt the people of New Castle county; farmers, too. Money was hard enough to come by, and London made it harder by canceling the right of the Colonies to issue their own paper money. Then came the Stamp Act, which taxed James Nixon's reading matter: any newspapers, almanacs, and pamphlets, as well as any legal documents.

The Nixon boys, then, grew up in a new political atmosphere. James had come to an America where the enemy, if one might call it that, was nature—and the Indians. Politically life had been relatively serene in the early years, for Delaware was not wracked with religious controversy, and men working the land for their livelihood were not inclined to sit around the taverns, glass and stemmed pipe in hand, worrying over political affairs. Leave that to the townspeople, the politicians, aristocrats, and business-men.

But when the tax began to hit home, on leather goods produced from Nixon hides by the local tanneries and shipped abroad, and when they found that anything they wanted that came from France or Spain would cost them dear and that the money was going to George III and his ministers, then the farmers began to take a different attitude. The Stamp Act was the most obnoxious, because anyone who could read felt it. When young George was but thirteen years old, representatives of the Colonies met in New York to see what they could do to end the Stamp Act.

Ben Franklin and other representatives of the Colonies were fighting in London against the act too, and their reports were often in the papers here at home. Delaware's representatives to what became known as the Stamp Act Congress were unofficial ones, to be sure, but the papers reported what was done and said, and people became more aroused. The Stamp Act was repealed the next year (1766) but Parliament did not give up its declared right to tax the Americans whenever it wished. Intellectuals worried about that, not simple farmers, and there the matter stood for a time.

One of the reasons for pain in Delaware had been the high tax on sugar from the West Indies, and of course sugar was one of the principal imports the ships of Delaware Bay brought back from their island trade. It was also a staple that the Nixons could scarcely do without, and its taxing had been a very personal matter indeed. But the British regulation of commerce now began again in extra measure, harsh and unreasonable from the Delaware standpoint, and by 1768 the British had made the mistake of using force in New York and Boston. Of course, the Delaware papers reported every instance, and the tempers of young and old, city and farm people rose again.

In 1768 colonists in Delaware and elsewhere began to say that if the British wanted to be difficult, they could be too, and the leaders of the rebellious element advocated "nonimportation." On the farm, that meant hardship of a sort, for the Nixons would have to get along without new shears and rakes and other implements of iron that came from England, but the fever was in the air: by the end of 1769 nearly everybody was refusing to "buy British," and that summer people in Wilmington and the other towns drew up formal papers for colonists to sign, pledging themselves to import no British goods until the taxes were all repealed. There was no doubt that it hurt in London: imports to America dropped just about in half. The British gave a little, and although the hotheads argued, the colonists dropped the idea of nonimportation—but the quarrel left ashes.

There was more violence in Boston and New York in 1770 and 1771—one might say that George and his younger brother James Nixon grew up in an atmosphere of rebellion and violence. One could not drive the team the three miles to Wilmington without hearing of some new evil the British were committing, in New York or Boston for the most part. The Battle of New York over the Quartering Act, and the Boston Massacre of 1771 were known everywhere. But it was not only in the North; there was trouble in North Carolina, and in Rhode Island, and elsewhere; in the spring that old James Nixon died, several of the Colonies had formed Committees of Correspondence, through which the leading radical leaders reinforced their grievances and publicized them. Feeling was growing higher in Delaware, even on the farms.

Later that year came the Boston Tea Party, and then in 1774, Ben Franklin, who was still in London, was dismissed from a job as Deputy British Postmaster General for America. It was a slap in the face to the Colonies as well as to Franklin, and because he came from neighboring Pennsylvania there was a good deal of attention given this act in Delaware. Things went from bad to worse, and the agitators of Philadelphia picked up steam, which led to the calling of the First Continental Congress. It would be nice to think of the Nixons as deep in the councils of the colony as it struggled with growing impatience of the British and the anger of the people at what they called repression. But in 1774, when the Congress was held, James Nixon had died, and his sons were barely men. The representatives of New Castle county and the area were rich and prominent businessmen and landowners, not simple farmers in homespun. Thomas McKean, George Read, and Caesar Rodney went to the

Congress in Philadelphia. The Nixon boys stayed home, like most Americans, and read about the Congress in the newspapers.

George Nixon had more weighty personal matters on his mind. As proprietor of his own "plantation," yet without all the equipment and the slaves from the mother place, he had to scurry to make ends meet. And further, he was interested in a young woman named Sarah Seeds, who was the daughter of a comfortably fixed family in Wilmington. The crisis was drawing near in New England, but Massachusetts was a long ways away, and even had George Nixon been violently involved, life and love went on. The battle of Lexington and Concord came to the Colonies; men marched in the North; the Second Continental Congress convened in Philadelphia that spring while George Nixon tended his crops. The Congress named George Washington to lead its armies—that was in June—and George Nixon courted Sarah Seeds. The Colonies began talk about raising an army, and on August 17, George and Sarah were married in Holy Trinity Episcopal Church and went forthwith to live on the farm his father had left him. The war was raging in the North, but not around Brandywine Hundred, and there was a great deal to be done, with very little help. Setting up a new household took most of a man's energy if he had also to cultivate his farm. So George contented himself with planting his crops and caring for his animals, and next door James did the same, for he had his mother and sister Jean to care for now that James was gone. Survival came before patriotism, and the war seemed very far away.

3

The Nixons at
Trenton and Princeton

By the end of 1775, the American war began to take on a different tint, as seen from New Castle county. Rebels had been fighting in Virginia against forces raised by Governor Dunmore. And that winter Thomas Paine's voice rose loud in the land from Philadelphia, where he published *Common Sense*, a personal attack on George III that any farmer could understand. Still it was an indeterminate war, fought in anger and to redress grievances. It was not until the summer of 1776 that the war assumed the character of a struggle for independence, with the declaration of July. Caesar Rodney of Delaware could be said in a way to have settled that matter, for he arrived in Philadelphia just in time to vote for independence and help throw the weight of the Nixons' colony that way.

But even then the Nixons were not yet directly involved in the struggle.

Delaware's involvement in a military way began in

1775, when a battalion was raised to help fight the war, and the conditions of that battalion's service became, generally speaking, those of the colonists who would go to war thereafter. A private received five dollars a month, an ensign fourteen dollars, and a lieutenant eighteen. A company consisted of seventy-six men with two drums or fifes, and the men found their own arms but received shoes and stockings and a felt hat. Later, they were to have more formal uniforms. As for their provisions, they would have a pound of beef or three-quarters pound of pork or a pound of salt fish every day, a pound of bread and a pint of milk, and a weekly allowance of beans or other vegetables. They also got rice and cider or spruce beer, and molasses, candles, and soap. Of course that was in theory. As the war continued and the men began to move ahead of the wagons, they seldom had all and sometimes none of the theoretical allotments.

Colonel John Haslet headed the Delaware battalion, which was able to count eight companies by April 1776. The Delaware regiment was to have fine uniforms. The coats were blue, faced and lined in red, and the men wore white waistcoats. Their breeches were of buckskin, and they wore white woolen stockings that came up to the knees and black spats over their shoes. The officers' uniforms had gilded buttons, and the men's buttons were pewter with the initials D.B. on them. They had small high peaked leather hats, which bore the inscription in front: "Liberty and Independence, Delaware Regiment."

The Delaware men set an example for all the colonists in these early days of organized fighting. They were handsomely accoutered, well-armed (courtesy of the Congress in Philadelphia), and they comported themselves bravely in the initial battles. They were together under General Stirling with the Marylanders and at the battle of Long Island. Washington later wrote that "they behaved with great bravery and resolution, charging the enemy and maintaining their posts from about seven or eight in the morning till two in the afternoon, when they were obliged to attempt a retreat, being surrounded and overpowered by numbers on all sides."

It was quite a beginning for others to live up to.

Having men in the field made a vital change in the attitude of people in Delaware. The war was their war now, and if in Sussex county to the south there was a plethora of Tories, such could hardly be said of the more northern counties. After this battle Wilmington and other towns in the colony were enraged by tales of the murder—slaughter —of Americans who tried to surrender to surrounding British troops. The fact that the tales were at best highly exaggerated made no difference. War is war, and one of its prime instruments is the horror story. Some Americans were bayoneted; there was no question about that, but the number was not two thousand, as the story had it, but only a few.

The war continued: New York, Harlem Heights, Mamaroneck, White Plains, and the people of New Castle had the news—long after the fact—of the ebb and flow of the struggle against the ever-more-hated British.

Still, there was a good deal of feeling among the farmers of Delaware that the war was somebody else's business. In the fall of 1776, since the American army was busy in the North, Congress called on New Jersey, Delaware, and Maryland to raise and equip ten thousand men of the militia, who would serve until December 1, to protect the Middle Colonies.

Samuel Patterson, a miller who kept his gristmill on the Christina above the village of that name, was appointed colonel of the Delaware contingent.

He was to raise eight hundred men to form a battalion. In order to do so he was given the right to offer a bounty of twenty dollars to each noncommissioned officer and private, plus a promise of one hundred acres of land to those who served during the war, or to their children if they were killed.

This first attempt to raise militia on a short-term basis

was not very successful. Some of Nixon's neighbors went, but the effort was very nearly doomed. The men discovered that their officers were scarcely better informed about military matters than they themselves, and they began almost immediately to grow discontented. The troops trained for a while, and then were sent to Philadelphia. There about half of them laid down their guns because they discovered that the Pennsylvania militia was getting more money. They would not go a step further until they got the same pay as the Pennsylvanians, they vowed. Colonel Patterson threatened to send for two battalions of troops from outside to arrest the Delaware men and hold them in prison. That solved the problem, or seemed to. He marched the men down to the wharf, where they would embark in vessels for New Jersey. Those men went quietly enough, but one company did not have all its arms, so the colonel kept them ashore one more night. During the night, the whole company deserted except eleven men. The colonel said his officers were worse than none, and as for the men, they were a mixed bag. "In my opinion, they had better have stayed at home."

The fall continued that way for Colonel Patterson. From New Brunswick he wrote that half the men were deserting, and ordered them arrested so they could not steal the battalion's funds and sell its guns. He was particularly upset with the troops from Kent and Sussex, and wrote from Amboy that he would not again consider bringing up men from the southern part of the state. So the militiamen of Delaware got a bad name that they were never to live down completely.

The enlistment of this levy of men expired on December 1, 1776, which was just about the time that George and James Nixon decided they would go to war for their country, and joined the company of Captain George Evans. They trained, received a poor substitute for the handsome uniforms of the Delaware regulars, and then made ready for battle.

This winter the Delaware militia consisted of one brigade of three battalions. New Castle county's battalion was now under Colonel John McKinly. Caesar Rodney commanded the Kent battalion and John Dagworthy led the Sussex men. (McKinly also happened to be chairman of the Delaware Council of Safety, which was the nearest thing to an executive that the state possessed.)

When the call came for troops to march north in December, the militiamen were scarcely ready, either physically or morally, to fight. No one in Delaware quite knew where the British were, except that they were in New Jersey—somewhere around New Brunswick. That did not seem so very close to some of the men. And others were not willing to sign up for the six weeks that the colonial government was asking of them. But some of the New Castle militia behaved quite differently, and George and James Nixon were among them. They joined the unit of Major Thomas Duff, who with three companies slipped away to fight without arguing with Colonel McKinly, who was prone to endless discussion without action. On about the twelfth of December, Duff and his men set off for Philadelphia, not waiting for a call to action. Action would not be long in coming.

Duff's militiamen marched north, and from the south marched other militiamen of Delaware under Captain Thomas Rodney, the aristocratic Caesar Rodney's brother.

On their way, the Nixons and the other militiamen passed members of Congress hastening on their miserable way to Baltimore. Philadelphians of little heart jammed the roads, their possessions in carts and on their backs. On December 16 the Nixons, in the first contingent of militiamen from Delaware, arrived in Philadelphia, to be greeted by the silence of Tories skulking in the streets, waiting for the great day when the British would arrive, and to march past the empty houses of half the town. Even the Tories lay low, the streets were windblown and lonely, ghostly and cold, and in one public house where the officers of the regiment adjourned, no one appeared save the proprietor himself.

General Israel Putnam was in the town, and his regular troops kept such order as remained in Philadelphia, and he ordered the Nixons and all the other militiamen to assemble at his house. On December 21, George and James Nixon marched through the streets of a Philadelphia that looked as though it had already been sacked by an enemy force, doors hanging open and the litter of desertion everywhere. But they saw hundreds more militiamen coming in from every direction, and they took heart as they marched over snowy roads to Red Lion. On December 22, the Delaware men reached Bristol, where they joined the brigade of General John Cadwalader. Captain Rodney, as a gentleman and officer, was quartered in a house on Neshaminy Creek and dined with the general. The Nixon brothers, privates, huddled around their campfires in their scanty uniforms and burrowed into blankets for warmth. Rodney learned that General Washington was planning an attack against the British outposts on the other side of the river on Christmas night. The Nixon brothers learned nothing as they shivered in the snowy cold.

Lord Howe had established his line of posts from Staten Island to Princeton. One was located at Amboy, one at Brunswick, and one at Princeton. And along the river, from Bordentown to Burlington, Colonel von Donop, the Hessian leader, commanded some three thousand men, mercenaries and troops of the 42nd Highlanders. Perhaps fifteen hundred of these were at Trenton, with the others at Bordentown, six miles away.

On Christmas day the plan was ready. The objective would be Trenton. The Americans would cross the river at three different places.

At both ends of the town the British forces were routed, and by nine o'clock the next morning the battle was over and about five hundred British were running to escape, while nearly nine hundred were captured.

It was victory, but there was a brassy taste in Washington's mouth because his flank troops had failed him.

But the victory at Trenton had another effect, it cemented Washington's leadership of the army, which had been waning in the constant retreat and the ambitions of his subordinates to supplant him. It also raised the spirits of James and George Nixon and the other militiamen who comprised the fresh troops on which Washington must count for further victories. The militia were now eager to fight; having beaten the British once, they thought they could do it again.

The British were moving south, but slowly. Washington planned to cross the Delaware again, and this time to make a fight of it for New Jersey. The Nixons and other militiamen crossed, and marched for Trenton. The word came: the British were marching on the town, and were determined to drive the Americans out of it.

Howe sent General Cornwallis to Princeton, and here he had eight thousand troops against perhaps five thousand Americans around Trenton. Cornwallis left twelve hundred men in Princeton and moved, carrying twenty-eight field guns with him.

George and James Nixon were with the main Washington force now, deployed along with the other Delaware militia and thousands of others on the high ridge of the south side of Assanpink Creek.

It was growing dark, the afternoon was wasting away, and the British grew impatient. They tried to force the bridge across the creek, but now the American artillery behind could open up and did; the British troops were forced back three times by gunfire, and loud yells arose from the American lines on the ridge each time the enemy was repulsed.

Since George Nixon's Delaware farm neighbors were not trained soldiers, not all of them behaved very well in this fight. Thomas Rodney was forced to discipline his men to keep them in order. The enemy came to force the bridge just after sunset, and it looked like they might succeed on one of these attempts in spite of the gunfire. Rodney's men were ordered to move down to protect the bridge at all costs, and he led them. He stopped and motioned them forward. A man named Martinas Sipple was ten steps behind the man in front of him, and Rodney drew his sword and threatened to cut off Sipple's head if he did not close up and keep ranks. Sipple closed up and Rodney moved back to the head of the company. The gunfire increased, and soon the British began to retreat, so Rodney led his men back to the woods of the ridge, where they camped and built up their fires for the night. He had the roll of his men called, and discovered that Sipple was missing. His lieutenant informed him that just after Rodney had moved back to the head of the column Sipple had fled the field, and now was nowhere to be found.

It was a desperate time, and such cowardice was blameworthy, but it was also understandable, because the militiamen like George and James Nixon had scarcely a week of real training. Many of them knew how to handle a gun only as farmers and woodsmen do.

With nightfall, the British stopped their attack, ready to renew it in the morning. Above the Assanpink George Nixon this night served as an ensign, or subofficer, and carried a sword and half-pike. Later he recalled the fires of the ridge south of Assanpink Ridge. He was there, waiting with the others for what might come the next day.

On the Assanpink, Washington was worried. The British had more men, and Washington knew only too well that among his own troops there were hundreds if not thousands only a shade removed from the state of mind of Martinas Sipple. Like the Nixon brothers, undisciplined, untrained, they were fighting on personal courage, their faith in themselves, and their faith in Washington's leadership. None of these qualities could be counted on among untrained men in a moment of crisis, and the general knew it.

Someone came up with an audacious plan. Let them

withdraw, all right, during the middle of the night, but not go down the river and face the British there. Instead, they would march around the British left flank, avoid the outposts, and strike the British where they least expected it—at Princeton. Then, they could go straight along to Brunswick, where the British kept a large supply of stores, capture the arms, ammunition, and food.

Once the decision was made, Washington's officers went into action. The Nixons and others were sent to tear up fence rails and be sure that all the fires along the ridge were brightly lit. Meanwhile a party of men was set to digging entrenchments so the British would hear the noise, and at midnight the fires were raised with more rails. At one o'clock the baggage train moved out; the march to Princeton was begun.

George and James Nixon stoked the fires, and when they were told to move they did so. A rear guard was left to keep the fires going until nearly dawn, then to retreat swiftly and silently and follow the main force. No lesser officers, Thomas Rodney or other commanders, knew the plan, but they knew that excitement was in the offing, and they responded. The wheels of the gun carriages were wrapped in rags, and orders were given in whispers.

The troops took a rough new trail to Sandtown, stumbling and falling over the roots and stumps, and sometimes the guns had to be heaved and horsed to keep them moving over the rough trail. At Sandtown they could take the road to Quaker Bridge. All went well, except that at one point militiamen from Philadelphia panicked when they thought they were surrounded by Hessians. They fled in disorder, but the Nixons' unit kept on, turned at Quaker Bridge and swung northwest on a road to Princeton.

At this point the Delaware men were to fight a delaying action if Cornwallis was pursuing the Americans down that road.

The Americans did not know that Cornwallis had left three regiments in Princeton overnight, and that two of them were setting out that morning on the road to Trenton to reinforce the British there. Lt. Col. Charles Mawhood was leading the British, and he had just crossed the stone bridge on his pony, and come to the top of a little hill, when he caught sight of the reflection of sun on metal. A band of men was emerging from the woods before him.

The Americans saw the British at the same time, and both sides made a dash for an orchard that rose above the level of the plain near the bridge. The Americans reached it first, and moved behind a hedge.

The enemies faced each other then, in lines of battle about a hundred twenty feet apart. Both sides fired. The Delaware men retreated in confusion, and the British pursued them, until they saw another American force coming out of the woods. The British moved into position with their guns, and the fight began again.

The Americans were threatening to break, when Washington arrived on his big white horse, and waving his hat at his men, urged them to stand and fight the enemy. He moved to within thirty paces of the British line, and his aides thought he was surely done for, but he emerged from the smoke of a volley unscathed, and then another, and Washington was still urging his men. Their response was very feeble, again training was telling and the British stood like rocks as compared to the withering Americans. But regular troops came up now, to follow their leader.

Some of the Delaware men moved into the thick of battle. Rodney's force crossed from right to left and took a position to protect the American artillery.

". . . the enemy's fire was dreadful and three balls . . . had grazed me; one passed within my elbow nicking my greatcoat and carried away the breech of Sergeant McKnatt's gun, he being close behind me, another carried away the inside edge of one of my shoesoles, another had nicked my hat and indeed they seemed as thick as hail. . . ."

The American regulars came whooping on, giving

heart to the Nixons and the other militia, and as more Americans came up, they managed to surround the British troops. With one desperate charge Mawhood led his men through the American lines, across the bridge, and retreated toward Trenton where Cornwallis lay. Other British forces retreated into Princeton, where they holed up and were captured (Captain Alexander Hamilton played an important part in that action) and still others retreated toward Brunswick. The Americans had won the day, and later George Nixon was to claim modestly that he had borne his share of the battle to the best of his skill and understanding of the arts of war. No one could fault the farmer-militiamen for failing to have training no one had given them. All Washington could ask was that they fight as best they could, and the Nixon brothers had done that, along with their neighbors and hundreds of other farm boys from Delaware and Pennsylvania.

4

George and James
at Morristown

The actions of the past two days had strained the farmer-militiamen to their limits, and Washington knew it. Instead of marching against the British at Brunswick and seizing all those coveted stores, the commander-in-chief stopped to think. His men had been in movement for forty hours in the coldest of winter weather. They had had no sleep. They had not been able to cook a hot meal. They had marched sixteen miles in darkness and had fought a hard battle. He looked around him and saw men dropping off to sleep on the frozen ground, and realized that his army could not go on to another action. If he had but been given another six hundred or eight hundred fresh men he could have sent them to destroy enough British stores so that he felt Cornwallis would be unable to continue the war. But it was not to be. He turned for the hilly wooded country around Morristown, where he had earlier decided he would winter if he could.

So they marched—George and James Nixon and the rest—to Rocky Hill, where they took the road to the left that led to Morristown rather than that to the right which led to Brunswick.

Instead of following the Americans along the left road at Rocky Hill, Cornwallis suspected Washington might be trying to confuse him, and he took the right road to Brunswick to protect his stores.

The Americans reached Somerset Court House that evening as night began to fall. They had no cooking equipment, no stores, and few even had blankets, for the baggage had been sent away to safety from the ridge above Trenton. But so tired were the soldiers, regulars and militiamen like the Nixons, that they cast themselves upon the ground, finding what shelter they could or huddling together, and slept the sleep of the exhausted.

Next morning they were up at dawn. But today the march was a straggling affair. The strong went ahead, but at Pluckemin their officers had to stop them. A thousand men were unable to keep up. There had been no food for the army for two days, and marching men could not forage, especially when they knew the British might be close behind them. Thomas Rodney had been placed in charge of the vanguard. The Delaware men were relatively fresh, for they had come lately into the battle, and men like George and James Nixon were well-nourished from their lives on the farm, while the troops who had been fighting with Washington down from New York were tired and weak.

The army rested there for two days, and recovered its provisions while Washington went about the business of a commander, sending word to Philadelphia of the victory he had won. The word quickly spread home to New Castle and Wilmington and further, that the Americans had won a great victory. The colonists were heartened, really much more so than the soldiers themselves, who were too tired to give more than quick consideration to what they had done.

Thomas Rodney was chosen to command the whole

regiment of militia light infantry and on January 6 his group led the army into Morristown, where the Rodney infantry was quartered in a big two-storey house. Because the Nixons and the other Delaware men had clean, matching uniforms, they were chosen to be Washington's guard, an honor that did not seem to impress many of them, for within a few days most of the Delaware militia were agitating to go home. They had enlisted for thirty days, the time was up.

Among the militiamen from Rodney's Dover company almost all seemed determined to go home.

Back home in the Nixons' New Castle the reluctance of the farmers to fight was even more marked. Here is a list, compiled by John Clark, the sheriff of New Castle, who was trying then to enroll recruits for the militia to be sent to Washington. He polled the men called and compiled their responses:

Names	Responses
Slator Clay	Will not march
Richard Janvier	Will not march
John Powell	Ready and willing to march
David Morton	Same
George Read	Same
Thomas Cooch, Jr.	Same
Robert Wiley	I'm damned if I march
Edward Sweeny	Family in distress
James Wilson	Hired one in his place
John Booth, Jr.	Substitute in Continental army
Joseph Tatlow	Will not march
Daniel Smith	Son in his place
James Faith	Will not march
William Hazlett	I never will march
Thomas Nodes	I'm damned if I march

Of a total of sixty-three men called for this militia company with the obligation to the government of Delaware to defend their colony as called—for every able-bodied man was a militiaman unless specifically excused—only twenty-two agreed to go to war. If nearly two hundred years later President Nixon was troubled by the flat refusal of men in Vietnam to undertake military action in which they did not believe, then at least it could be said that the tradition went back a long way in American history.

The Nixon boys stayed on in this winter at Morristown as enlisted men. Other Nixons were serving, too, men of wealth and substance from different parts of the Colonies. Colonel John Nixon of Pennsylvania would become a general in Washington's army, and Thomas Nixon, of Dover, would be a colonel. But in spite of the moment of glory at Princeton when he carried the sword and spontoon (half-pike) of an ensign, George's service with the Delaware militia in this enlistment was as a private, and it was as a private that he was paid. For reenlisting he and James received a bounty of six dollars; James got his on February 2 while the army moved quietly about the camp in the village of Morristown.

Even with the bounty, Congress and the Colonies were having difficulty in getting troops, and Delaware was possibly the worst-recruited ground of all. The banks of the bays were loaded with Tories who traded with the enemy and made small effort to conceal their contempt for the revolutionary movement. But a worse problem was apathy on the part of farmers who thought in terms of their annual crops and not of freedom. Congress offered twenty dollars to each recruit who would enlist for three years or the duration of the war, plus a hundred acres of land. But in Delaware the offer went begging. Thomas McKean and the Rodney brothers agitated for independence up and down the colony, but for every word they uttered the Tories had another, and there was a large body of "appeasers," who would have preferred to settle affairs with Britain rather than seek independence. Colonel John McKinly represented the most conservative kind of thought. He had failed so miserably to get the Delaware militiamen to Washington in December, and now in February he would be honored by being elected as President of the new government under its first constitution. Thomas Rodney wrote his brother despairingly that the General Assembly could not have chosen a man more suited to represent the Tories.

In this atmosphere George Nixon's neighbors did not do at all well by their country. Late in January Caesar Rodney raised a force of 238 militiamen and sent them to Princeton under Major Duff and another officer. There they were dispatched by General Putnam as guards for a wagon train carrying supplies to feed the soldiers at Morristown, George Nixon among them, but they behaved so badly on the road and in camp that Washington sent them back to Putnam, who dispatched them home as completely useless.

The army was in very serious condition that winter, and it is a tribute to the Nixon brothers that they stayed in service when others were deserting by the scores. Food was so short that the men went hungry. There were no replacements for uniforms, and the soldiers suffered particularly for want of shoes and leggings. Congress failed to secure supplies for Washington, so he sent his soldiers out around the countryside, where they commandeered beef, pork, flour, and liquor if they could get it. Smallpox broke out, and the men were inoculated, which made them so sick that at one time a thousand of his three thousand men were down with the effects of inoculation.

Slowly the army deteriorated. The Nixon brothers grew restive with the approach of spring, for they had obligations back in Delaware; two families were waiting on the plantations they had inherited from their father. The spring plowing must be done, and who would do it if they did not? James could not rely on his mother or his sister Jean alone, and even the Negro Ned would find difficulty in doing all the work. George had a new wife of less than six months when he answered the call to arms, and he too had work to do on the farm. So in March the Nixon boys were ready to go home to Delaware, along with most of the army. On March 14, Washington reported dolefully to Congress that he had fewer than three thousand troops at Morristown, and that more than two thousand of these were militia, whose enlistments were running out every day, and who were moving homeward. Unless something was done, said Washington, he would have no army with which to fight when the British broke camp in a few weeks. He had only a handful of true soldiers, and these from Jersey, Pennsylvania, and Virginia. On this day there was just one man from Delaware whose enlistment had not expired. The Nixon brothers had headed home.

5

The Nixons at Brandywine and Beyond

The Nixon brothers went back to their farms for the summer, and planted their fields with wheat and rye. They could not afford to lose their crops, and their neighbors felt the same way; indeed some of their neighbors who had not gone to war earlier now refused to go. David Sullivan said he had two crops of wheat to care for and would not go into the militia. William Berry avowed that he would not leave his harvest for anyone, and even Richard Reynolds, a sergeant in the militia, said he could not go without losing the proceeds of his farm that year, and he did not choose to do so. Most of these people were not as well off as the Nixons, who had slaves, for there were very few blacks and almost no indentured servants in Brandywine Hundred. Nor could a man hire labor easily, for nearly everyone in Delaware outside the cities was a farmer and had his own ground to care for.

Except for imminent threat of invasion, then, the farmers of Delaware wanted at most to be winter fighters.

By summer that invasion seemed to be coming. Lord Howe's fleet sailed away from Sandy Hook in the north, and Washington feared that it might be heading south, carrying the British army. The general appealed to Congress for more troops, and Congress passed the word—and the buck—to Delaware authorities. Colonel McKinly, president of Delaware, first ordered the removal of all livestock from the area around the bay so the British would not get them if they landed. The colony's Board of War called on Caesar Rodney, who was now the general of the militia, to bring together and arm as many militia as he could, and for a time it appeared that Rodney had the weapon he needed to bring the farmers to arms: fear of imminent invasion. But the British fleet did not appear in June or July, and the farmers talked much, but actually went about their agricultural business.

Then came August, and the word that Howe and his fleet were in Chesapeake Bay. In the manner of men of indecision, McKinly now panicked and called on Rodney to bring out the militia immediately to prevent the enemy from plundering the inhabitants. As usual his view of the war was a very narrow one.

The call came again on August 21, and although the harvest was not yet in, George Nixon put on his uniform and joined other soldiers in defense of colony and country. He was still with George Evans' company, but now Evans was promoted to major and head of the regiment.

Again many of the militiamen refused to move or to fight, but George Nixon had an excellent reason to obey orders. The enemy were moving in a direction very near to his farm, and Washington was going to try to stop them in what would be called the battle of the Brandywine. The battle would be another British victory.

Meanwhile the Delaware militia had been stationed at

Christina Bridge and Noxontown. Washington had hoped before Brandywine that the militia might serve him by interposing themselves between the British forces and their ships and creating havoc among the soldiers of a retreating army. It was a pleasant dream, no more. Most of the militia, at least, were nowhere near the battle of the Brandywine. And yet, George Nixon's tombstone notes the dates August 21, 1777—when the Delaware militia were reformed—and October 6, 1777, which marked the end of the battle of Germantown. Considering his willingness to fight (which is demonstrated in his record) it seems likely that somehow George found his way with the army; otherwise the October date is meaningless. For the Delaware militia, faced with the occupation of Wilmington and much of their state, simply disappeared after Brandywine. The farmers began driving their horses and cattle away from the British, knowing the animals would be taken if they did not. And the men of the militia went where they could to salvage what they might and keep their military records from the knowledge of the British.

Washington and the British marched and maneuvered in September in the vicinity of Valley Forge; the British outfought and outmaneuvered the Americans, and began to move on Philadelphia toward the end of September while Congress fled to Lancaster. On September 26 the British captured Philadelphia. Washington was camped at Pottsgrove, his troops resting after having marched and fought over 140 miles in eleven days, losing their equipment and wearing out their precious shoes.

Still the Americans were determined to fight, the Nixons in the Delaware regiment among them. Washington moved against Germantown, a village on the road that led from Philadelphia to Reading, where Howe set up his headquarters.

It was a near thing—nearly a victory—but the timing did not work. The Delaware regiment lost three men killed, twenty-six wounded, and nine missing. Obviously it had been in the thick of the fight. Two days later it was October 6, which marked the end of George Nixon's service for the time.

George's anxiety was intense, for the British were over-running his area of Delaware. He feared for his wife and his family. On October 12, Ambrose Serle, secretary to Lord Howe, entered Wilmington, and on October 14 he went to New Castle, where he walked around the town. He found the "principal houses" utterly abandoned by rebels, but managed to find some old men, Quakers, and Tories to talk with him.

Delaware's militia were still active, although now behind the enemy lines. Next day Serle was very nearly captured by a band of some sixty militiamen who came out of the woods and captured several British sailors. So the Americans were still fighting, and although they had taken northern Delaware, given the spirit shown by the Nixon boys, the British could not feel secure.

6

George Nixon and
the Westering Fever

Again in the winter of 1777 George Nixon went home, and
now he served in various capacities in the irregular army of
the interior of Delaware. The militia was formed again in
October, and George Nixon was involved. On October 29
the council of state authorized the raising of six hundred
militia, three hundred of them from New Castle, under
Caesar Rodney, who was now a major general of militia.
George Latimer was put in charge of this group, but George
and James served under David McKee, who was first a lieutenant and then a captain.

The battle had passed Delaware by, but the redcoats
were in the state, in the port towns and lying offshore in
their warships. The job of the militia was clear enough: they
must fight the British when they could catch little groups,
kidnap and kill, and above all give them no peace and prevent them from enjoying the fruits of their victory in the colony. It was rough, dangerous work, that of night riders and

guerrillas and spies. George became a sergeant in this company, and young James continued as a private. Later, George was promoted to lieutenant.

George Nixon saw no more active service with Washington's armies, then. The war finally drew to a close in 1782, and the farmers of New Castle county could begin anew to raise animals and crops without fear of their loss to the armies. It had been a difficult time for everyone, but the brothers George and James Nixon had survived. It was a commentary on the life of those war years, however, that George and Sarah Seeds Nixon did not have children during that time. Their first son, George Junior, was born in 1784, the year after the formal peace treaty was signed and the infant American government was left in peace to work out its destiny.

Delaware grew. Three years after young George was born, the new states met in Congress in Philadelphia to strengthen or amend the faltering government that existed under the Articles of Confederation, and draw up the Constitution of the United States. George Washington was elected President, and Delaware was the first state to ratify the new Constitution. Delaware then drew up a new state constitution of its own in 1791.

Business in the colony began to boom. Wilmington became an iron fabricating center. Ships brought iron from Sweden and Russia, and the artisans of Wilmington made it into nails and other necessary tools. The leather industry prospered anew. And these industries led to the development of a brisk coastal trade, with sloops of thirty tons and more, and then ships twice as large. Shipyards now lined the Christina River, and ocean-going vessels moved between America and the West Indies, England, and Ireland. In 1787 John Fitch was granted what amounted to a state patent on a steamboat.

The state attracted many new people. Yellow fever broke out in the cities of the east coast, and sent thousands of people to Wilmington and other parts of Delaware, some of whom decided to stay. In 1791 the blacks rebelled against the French in the island of Santo Domingo (creating the nation of Haiti), and a good number of whites fled to Delaware, where they saw opportunity.

All this activity buzzed about the head of Farmer George Nixon, who continued to plant his crops on the 106-acre farm and raise his family. A second son, Seeds, was born in 1792, and a third son, Francis, was born in 1796, and three daughters were born to the family. When the census taker came around in 1800, George was living on the farm with his wife and two sons and three daughters. One boy must have been living with a relative; it was common practice for the children of big families to go where they were needed to help with the work, and brothers and sisters were close enough in those days to raise each other's children without the lift of an eyebrow.

George Junior was very nearly a man, and should be able to expect from his father what George had received from James, an honorable start in life. But land was growing dearer and harder to come by, as never before. The rich city merchants bought suburban houses and created estates. Along came a Frenchman named Eleuthère Irénée Du Pont, in the summer of 1802, who bought up a little stone gristmill on the Brandywine from the heirs of Jacob Broom, and began the manufacture of black powder. His business flourished, adding to the scarcity and value of land in that area. Other powder companies, paper mills, and snuff mills sprang up in and around Wilmington, and the city sprawled ever northward toward George Nixon's farm.

George faced a great American dilemma: how could he provide for his growing family in a land where men were free and equal (some of them)? He and his brother James could see merchants in the cities who had started out as low as themselves and had acquired great lands and huge wealth. There seemed little chance for him in Delaware; a man could not work hard enough on 106 acres to raise a family and put aside the wherewithal to buy a new tract, prices were too badly inflated.

But there was opportunity on the frontier, and the statesmen of Delaware were among the leaders in pushing its opening to all. Early in the Revolution Delaware and other states whose colonial boundaries gave them no western lands had moved to limit the western boundaries of all the states. The move had failed but the politics of it continued, and one by one the states ceded their claims to extend west across the continent, and Congress took control of the lands. Speculators were buying lands in the West for a few cents an acre, huge grants were inveigled by other speculators on delicate pretenses, and in 1796 Congress passed its Land Act, which provided for the division of lands into townships (units six miles square) and the division of the townships into sections of 640 acres each. Western lands would sell for two dollars an acre, payable within a year.

Eyes turned west with the development of Ohio, and the establishment of land offices there. In 1800 the land laws were modified, making it easier to obtain credit, and each year came new activity in the west and anent western lands that made the opportunity seem greater to those who were left behind in the scrabble for fortune in the East.

By 1803 changes had come to the household of George Nixon. His wife Sarah had died, and he had married a woman named Martha. George Junior had nearly reached his majority, when he could do as he pleased with his life. George Nixon, Sr., then made the fateful decision to move west and seek the family fortune. He was not willing to take the whole jump—to abandon the settled society of the states for the wild, Indian-ridden life of a territorial settler, or even to go into new lands where there were few roads and churches and fewer schools. One might say that George was ambitious but not adventurous, and his story bears out this contention: he sold the 106-acre farm to William Young, packed, and moved to the village of Washington, in the west end of Pennsylvania, where he bought a farm of 224 acres. The prices tell the story. George sold his 106 acres for two thousand dollars and bought his 224 acres for sixteen hundred dollars. After nearly half a century of farming, most of it spent in hard work, he had managed to approximate the situation his father had reached much earlier in life, but only by moving west with the country.

7

Washington, Pennsylvania:
Early 19th Century

The name of this new town in Pennsylvania was Bassett, when the place was laid out and first settled in 1781, but at the end of the Revolutionary War there was a spate of emotionalism in which Americans chose to honor their heroes (it was to become part of the American tradition). Bassett, like scores of other places, gave up its lowly name and became Washington in this bath of patriotic zeal.

It had originally been largely three pieces of land called Catfish's Camp, Grand Cairo, and Martha's Bottom, but these had all come into the hands of one David Hoge in the days before the Revolutionary War when land was cheap.

Originally it was a part of Spottsylvania County, Virginia, which was named more reasonably, for Alexander Spottswood, who had been the first to find a decent passage over the Appalachians in 1721. There he encountered the

Kuskuskee Indians, whose hunting grounds occupied the territory between the Allegheny Mountains and the Ohio River.

For a long time the Pennsylvanians had a good record in their dealings with the Indians they were pushing west, and they made treaties with the Kuskuskees which seemed to indicate that all would live in peace and plenty forevermore. In 1759 the chief of the Kuskuskees, who was named Tingoocqua or Catfish, went to Philadelphia and met with the governor and his council to make his own peace with the white men following the general treaty with the Delawares, signed at Easton in 1758.

Catfish was still around the area when David Hoge began his speculative venture. The place didn't seem good for much, it was a thicket of black and red hawthorn, laced with wild plums, hazel bushes, shrub oaks, and briar. In fact, the whole area was forest, except for a few glades, until the white man came with his ax, and where the courthouse was to stand was an especially fine patch of hazelnuts. Hoge was obviously a speculator, for lots fell into the hands of such unlikely settlers as Robert Fulton, the steamboat inventor, who held quite a parcel for several years. So while the town was laid out in "streets" they were not built immediately, except for the boundaries, which were Walnut, on the north, College, on the east, Maiden, on the south, and West Alley. When the streets were built they matched a Westerner's dream—they were sixty feet wide.

To Hoge's disappointment, the town did not grow rapidly, and even in 1788 old Catfish still had a hunting camp inside the town. But the whites did come, and he moved, first a few miles away, and then deep in the woods, and finally across the Ohio to get away from them.

By that time Washington had a log courthouse (which burned down two years later) where among other things, the Rev. Thaddeus Dodd kept a classical school for youth. After the courthouse burned, the townspeople agreed to build a brick building instead. The Presbyterians were strong here among the first settlers, and they had services occasionally in the courthouse when supply ministers came from the church at Chartiers, near Canonsburg. Then, just after the new courthouse was built, a church was put up.

The Nixons arrived at the height of a religious controversy, which must have been important to them because there are indications that George Nixon grew up a Presbyterian. Many of the Scotch-Irish who came over from Ireland were of that protestation, and when old James, his father, died, the money he left behind in the hands of Dr. Smith, the educator, indicated a Presbyterian leaning, because Dr. Smith was of that persuasion.

In 1800 a group within the Presbyterian persuasion here decided to bring into town as their minister the Rev. Thomas Ledlie Birch, a famous preacher who had made his reputation in Ireland. The Presbytery in Philadelphia endorsed the selection, and the Rev. Mr. Birch came to Washington. But here he found changes, and a challenge to his interpretation of the religion. In January 1801, the Presbytery at Cross Creek examined the Rev. Mr. Birch, and found him wanting in his interpretations and knowledge of the Scriptures. Still, he returned to Washington and his pulpit. Washington was then a growing town, and he received six hundred dollars a year for his work, plus another hundred for preaching in the little town of Pittsburgh up north. Things went from bad to worse, and soon the congregation was completely split, with one faction making representations to the General Assembly to get a new minister, while Birch's supporters did the same to keep him. The Presbytery appointed supply ministers who came from afar to preach to the dissidents, while Mr. Birch stubbornly held his pulpit with the applause of his supporters.

The Birch-haters secured the use of the school, the new Washington Academy, in 1802, and declared this to be the true Presbyterian church in the area, and brought in ministers. Poor Mr. Birch gave up, and finally died, but still the struggle continued, with the Birchers outlawed by their brethren, and that is how matters stood in the fall of 1803 when the Nixons arrived on the scene.

The Nixons did not come to live in town, for they were farmers; they found their farm in Canton Township near Washington village and there they settled down. George was fifty-one, George Junior was nineteen, Seeds was eleven, and Francis was seven years old. The girls were apparently younger, and probably children of the second marriage to Martha.

There would have to be schools for the little ones, and this was still frontier country, although the farms were established, and the Indians mostly gone. For these frontier schools the neighbors would get together and find a man who could read, write, and cipher well enough to teach someone else. If he was willing, they would employ him, take a piece of ground, cut logs and build a rude cabin. Instead of a window, one log might be kept out for an entire length, to serve the same purpose. The chimney was made of logs and clay and rocks. Seats were made of split trees cut twelve feet long, the flat side smoothed with an ax; legs were inserted into the round side. The floor was dirt.

But as time went on, Washington schools became more sophisticated, and when the Nixon girls were growing up, Mrs. Good opened a school in town to teach young women embroidery, sewing, painting, drawing, and reading—the arts and crafts of young ladies.

Around 1806, George Nixon, Jr., began courting the daughter of Washington blacksmith William Wilson. Her name was Hannah, and they shared at least a Delaware background, for the Wilsons had come to western Pennsylvania from Delaware a few years before the Nixons. George Junior and Hannah were married, and settled down in their own house, on the family farm a little way from George's place, and began raising their family.

Exciting events showed the temper of the times. For example, on June 10, 1810, Captain John Bavington of

Washington tried to cross the Ohio River at Kelley's Ferry at the mouth of Harman's Creek on a flatboat with a wagon loaded with whiskey and flour and four horses. The horses became frightened and began stamping their feet, which loosened the planking of the boat. The boards separated and the boat sank, and the captain and the ferryman were drowned. Life in the West was dangerous.

War came again in 1812, and many young men of Washington county enlisted, most of them to serve under General William Henry Harrison. There is no record of George Junior volunteering for his service, and it is quite understandable. He was twenty-eight years old, and very much a family man. He and Hannah were active in the Methodist church, she as a stalwart member of the women's class which met on Friday afternoons, and he as a member of the country class which met on Sunday after church. But even though the Nixons did not go to war this time, they were not immune to its effects. On August 24, 1812, news came that a force of British troops and Indians estimated to number five thousand men had landed at the mouth of the Yuron River and were marching on Cleveland, after which they would march against Pittsburgh. The invasion never came, but it caused a grand stir in Washington county. Messages were sent out to all the villages and centers in the area, and people crowded the town, while the young men of the area cried that they would volunteer to defend their homeland. A committee of arrangements was quickly appointed to provide wagons and provisions for the force, and the women opened a small factory for making knapsacks and hunting shirts for the troops. Even little children were put to work scraping lint from cloth to make bandages. Wilson's blacksmith shop began turning out tomahawks and knives instead of horseshoes and fire tongs, and the town carpenters fitted them into handles.

In a few hours all was ready, and the volunteers took up the march, crossed the Ohio River, and then learned that the enemy was not coming—so they stayed in camp for a day or so, and then struck their tents and went home to finish the harvest.

The shocking news of the war came to western Pennsylvania bit by bit, carried by express riders who endangered life and limb rushing through the countryside. The surrender of General Hull at Detroit was called "despicable," and when Captain William Sample and his volunteers came back from Buffalo early in 1813, they told of the disorganization of the American forces.

In the summer of 1814 British Admiral Cochrane landed an army that marched on the national capital city of Washington, and burned the Capitol and much of the city. The namesake town in Pennsylvania was up in arms, and men were ready to march again, but they were not called, not needed. And finally the war ended, as far as Washington county was concerned, with the resounding victory of Andrew Jackson at New Orleans.

George's second son, Seeds Nixon, was married in the fall of 1815 to Sarah Waller, and he built a house for himself on the farm. Daughter Sarah married Andrew McGowan in the summer of 1817 and moved away from home, and the third son, Francis, married Ann Kennedy that same year.

Next year came an event that was to have far-reaching consequences for the nation and the Nixons—the building of the great highway called the National Pike, which was to run from the sea at Baltimore across country, up hill and down valley, around mountains and over the streams, from the shore to the uncrossable Mississippi River, which stood on the frontier of the Western world.

The road was built across Washington county from east to west, and passed not far north of the Nixon farm. With its building, the West was opened anew to travelers, this time by stagecoach and Conestoga wagon, each drawn by six or eight horses, hauling four to five tons of merchandise to the West at $4.25 per hundred pounds from Baltimore to Wheeling. The coaches began running regularly through Washington to the East that year, making the round trip three times a week. The fare, from Wheeling to Philadelphia, was twelve dollars.

George Nixon was not one to flaunt himself or seek acclaim, but like his father lived the simple life of a countryman. He had concerns, but they were the concerns of the farmer and family man; like his father he never sought public office nor leadership in the community. He celebrated one great day each year, the Fourth of July, at which time the whiskey barrels were rolled out, and the speakers stood tall on their platforms as they enunciated the glories of the Revolution, and more, the War of 1812. Someone would speak of Oliver Perry, the Hero of Erie, and of the "late lamented Lawrence," of Washington and Jefferson and Alexander Hamilton, John Adams and Andrew Jackson, of the yeomen of the area and the ladies of the township, the people of the United States, "may victory be their watchword, and liberty their inheritance," and even of the state of Ohio—"a few years since the dreadful haunt of the savage —now the peaceful abode of the American."

The West still beckoned, with the building of new roads, and the people of Washington county saw and appreciated the opportunity of their new land, where for white men the future was then bounded not so much by luck as by ambition and adventurousness.

As for the nation, in these years, the issue was whether and how much to spend on internal improvements. Should the people build a vast network of roads to connect the states, marketplace and farm, port and manufactury? Some said yes and some said no; it depended on who you were and what you did for a living.

In the spring of 1817 George Nixon and his neighbors had the uncommon honor of a visit from President James Monroe, who was traveling about, cementing the "Era of Good Feelings" in the nation. He came to Washington on May 4, accompanied by aides, including Governor Lewis Cass of Detroit, and they were escorted into town by a company of militia, to put up at Morris's hotel in the center of town.

That same year, with the coming of the National Pike, the Nixons and other Washingtonians became very much aware of the problem of internal improvements which was to become an issue at the end of Monroe's Presidency and even more so in the term of John Quincy Adams. The National Pike came to Washington county and with it a general agitation for more and better roads to connect with it.

The pike brought with it new public houses, excitement, and a new rough element, the wagon men. There were a number of taverns in the town and around it, the oldest being one called The Sign of the Swan in those days, which was notable for having exhibited Columbus, the first elephant ever to be seen in this part of the country, but other men kept other public houses, and the most successful were those that appealed to the wagon men and travelers along the pike.

One of the most popular places was the Mansion House, where farmers and townspeople gathered, as well as overnight guests, in the big barroom over which John N. Dagg presided. The Mansion House boasted one nicety— no one wore his cowhide boots inside, but every man was shown the bootjack, and given a pair of slippers to wear inside. Then, when the guests chose to leave, they found their cowhide boots had been cleaned and polished for them.

There were more than a thousand people in Washington, and what was then called "the western country," where once Catfish's hunting grounds had laid, numbered some forty thousand.

What was needed, cried the advocates of improvements, was a grand national effort to pull America forward. "What avails it if we have renounced our allegiance to George 3rd if we still succumb to the mercantile monopoly of Great Britain and are held in bondage by her manufacturing ascendancy?" So in the summer of 1817 wrote a neighbor of Nixon's who signed himself "Seventy Six," and the object of his writing was to promote the building of a turnpike from Washington to Bedford so that more Western people could take advantage of the new roads.

The roads were changing life very rapidly in the West. In one short year, as flour, hides, and whiskey moved back to the Atlantic seaports in the Conestoga wagons over the new road, the Westerners found themselves much better off. ("We have seen. . . . the discount on our country money fall 10 and 12 to two percent.") There was hope, said old Seventy Six, that if the roads were more complete, the West would soon be in an equal position with the moneyed East.

There was also now a plan for a road from Washington to Pittsburgh, for the citizens of Washington needed to go to that port for salt, castings and machinery, and above all, coal. George Nixon and his neighbors now paid ten cents a bushel for coal, but with the development of a direct road overland, it was estimated that the price could be dropped to seven cents a bushel, so every man would save.

The coming of the pike brought entertainments to Washington for the first time. In 1817 the local paper, *The Examiner*, was carrying advertisements for strictly homespun theatrical productions:

"In Rehearsal and will be Performed next week, at the Office of the Western Register, 'Impudence and Verbosity,' or, 'Jack Pudding in a Rage.' A new fantastic, comic, ludi-cro-bombastic farce. The part of 'Harlequin' to be performed by Thomas Morgan, Wm. Duane's son in law. . . . He will also play 'Sylvester Daggerwood' with all his 'ludi-crous contortions' in character."

But the next year, as the traffic was established along the road, Washington began to get traveling shows, as in October 1818, when a traveling show called The Museum appeared in town at the house of Captain Wilcox. It brought "a panorama view of the city of Rome" and "the Ruins of Ancient Rome" plus an exhibition of wax figures of Andrew Jackson, Commodore Stephen Decatur, and Commodore Oliver Perry.

After viewing the exhibits the amusement seekers would settle down to frozen scenes:

CINCINNATI & KENTUCKY BEAUTIES

A LADY WITH HER FAMILY

CAPT. MONTRAVILLE AND CHARLOTTE TEMPLE

THE GODDESS OF LIBERTY

SUPPORTING THE AMERICAN STANDARD.

All was accompanied by music played on "an elegant organ," and children of the farmers and townspeople were admitted at half price.

Or, now, there were minstrel shows and other entertainments at the dining room of the Valentine House in town; once an African lion was exhibited in town; and later another elephant showed up, one who would "lie down and get up at command, draw the cork from a bottle and manage it in such a manner as to drink the contents."

And soon such single exhibitions gave way to circuses, which traveled the open road.

The society was changing in many ways early in the 1820s. There was always violence in the community, too, and in the summer of 1822 there occurred a particularly celebrated murder, involving a neighboring farm family named Crawford.

William Crawford had been a British soldier during the War of 1812, and he had deserted and remained in the United States, but he still called himself Old Britannia, to the amusement of the farmers around the area. He had a son named Henry, and he worked that son very hard, so that Henry resented it. Further, old William was a martinet who mistreated his wife, so that she and Henry left the house one day and went to live elsewhere. But they still worked the same land because that was their living.

One day old William held a "manure frolic," which is to say he called in his neighbors to help him get rid of the pile of manure in his barnyard. It was the custom in the county for farmers to help in such chores, as in harvesting and plowing and building a house—and the favor would always be a debt to be repaid.

When the work was done that morning, the farmers gathered round the house with a jug of whiskey, and Henry hung around the place, much to his father's annoyance. The old man threatened to kill the young whippersnapper if he did not get out of there.

Henry Crawford was not dismayed, because he had broken his father's gun. (He did not know that the old man had gotten it repaired.) The festivities continued, and Henry stayed around. Some of the farmers came to warn him about the old man's growing anger, but he laughed. There was one thing that Henry did that annoyed his father more than anything else: that was to sing a patriotic song of the day called "The Blackbird." Toward evening Henry moved up near the house, while the men inside were drinking, sat himself down on a log and began singing "The Blackbird." The old man did not say a word, but picked up his gun, and just as Henry started the second verse, William Crawford shot him dead.

In a few moments old William was disarmed and headed for Washington county jail, where on November 21 he was brought to trial for murder. It was a celebrated trial, with thirty-four jurors called before a jury could be found, and the town buzzed with the excitement. But the case was simple enough and was concluded on the afternoon of the next day, after the jury went out, and in an hour and ten minutes brought back a verdict.

"Guilty of murder in the first degree."

Old William was sentenced to be hanged. They kept him in prison for several months, and in the fashion of prisoners before and since, he wrote a story of his life, which was published in *The Examiner*. Then he tried to starve himself to death, while his lawyers fought the case through the state courts, but he got too hungry and gave in. Finally, late in January all the legal recourses had been exhausted, and the governor sent the death warrant to the sheriff, and the time had come for Washington to have its first execution for murder. On February 21, 1823, execution day, Sheriff Robert Officer harnessed a horse to his sled—it was cold, and the ground was covered with snow. They put the coffin on the sled, and old William Crawford rode beside it, unrepentant, peeling an apple and talking to the boys who ran alongside, telling them not to hurry, as the hanging would not take place until he got there. They rode through a huge crowd, for it seemed that everyone from the county had come to see the execution. And finally the procession reached Gallows Hill, the crowd looping behind and following.

Old William gave them a show all the way. When the Baptist minister exhorted him to forgive his enemies he refused. When the minister urged him to pray he told the man of God to mind his own business.

"Crawford was placed over the trap door, and the rope was tied around his neck, after which those on the gallows, with the exception of the sheriff, bid him farewell and descended to the ground. When Sheriff Officer asked him if he wished the execution delayed to the last minute allowed by the warrant, he replied that he wished it over with, as he wanted to give his friends time to take him home that night. The black cap was drawn over his eyes by the sheriff, who shook hands with him, and picking up a hatchet, cut the cord that held the trap, and plunged the soul of William Crawford into eternity."

The new national road brought roughnecks and sometimes violence, but most important about the roads was the way they looked and beckoned West, and as George Nixon worked his farm he encountered the drivers and travelers heading West along them to adventure and perhaps to fortune.

But the enthusiasm for building roads affected the Nixons directly. In 1825 promoters in the county decided to run

a road through the Nixon farm. George and George Junior
and Francis all went to court to protest the road, because it
would run directly in front of the senior Nixon's house and
cut off his fields. Furthermore, since his house was located
on an embankment, the building of the road might cause
danger to the Nixon house foundations.

The protest was successful, and the route of the road
was changed so that it did not upset the Nixon way of life.

But George Nixon was feeling the westering fever once
again. In 1824 he sold off two pieces of his land to William
Wilson, who was the father of George Junior's wife, Hannah. The year of the road controversy he transferred two
pieces of land totaling forty-five acres to George Junior. He
had done just about half as well by his eldest son as his father had done by him.

Washington was growing, and George Nixon, Jr., did
not feel the pioneering urges of his father, but considered
Washington county his home. The town itself was sprawling
out, and the public buildings around Main and Beau streets
were being changed and even rebuilt to be "creditable to
the county and have all the conveniences which the wants
of the people required." The market house was on the corner of Main and Beau, and next to it was the engine house.
Across the alley was the sheriff's house, which led to the jail,
and next to that was the prothonotary's office, where important public business was transacted, and next to all was the
big brick courthouse. South of it was the clerk's office, and
that of the register of deeds, and next to them was a small
shop owned by Alfred Galt, a watchmaker who was thought
to be either crazy or a genius, depending on the point of
view, and then three offices which were rented to lawyers
and merchants.

The area began to boom, which meant again that land
prices rose, and since George Nixon showed none of the attributes of a businessman, he did not share in the growing
wealth.

The glories of other days were brought back to George

Nixon in the spring of 1825, when the Marquis de Lafayette returned to the United States to visit, and then began a tour of the nation. Lafayette came to Washington on May 25, and they say that twenty thousand people came from the farms and villages around and from the back country to see the old general and pay their respects. It was the greatest celebration in the history of the town.

A new element was added with the increase in the black population—a special school for the black children. It was unthinkable that the blacks be educated with the whites, for although Washington was in a free state, the sentiment in these years was overwhelmingly proslavery, and continued so, although the abolitionists gained a foothold here.

That sentiment led to another big trial that rocked Washington county in 1828, a case that began on the morning of February 1, with the discovery of the body of a white man on the National Pike west of Washington.

The murdered man was identified as Robert Carlyle, a "Negro drover" who had passed through Washington a few days earlier bound south with a number of runaway slaves. One, named Christian Sharp, had escaped, and leaving the others under guard at Wheeling, Carlyle had come back, found the slave, recaptured him, and headed back for Wheeling on the westbound mail stage. He had stopped at Briceland's Tavern in Washington on the night of January 31, and set out next morning on foot for Wheeling, with slave Christian Sharp handcuffed and walking ahead of him.

A few days later the authorities found Carlyle's body, as well as Christian Sharp, who had hidden in the house of a free Negro in the area. He claimed that he had been set free by three men who jumped Carlyle and smashed his head in with a club. One of the men, said "Kit" Sharp, was a large, powerful Negro.

Now, there was just such a large powerful Negro in the area, a freedman named Tar Adams, who spent much of his time helping other blacks escape toward Canada. Nonetheless Christian Sharp was tried for the murder of his master, and although he was stoutly defended by the finest abolitionist lawyers in the county, he was convicted, sentenced, and finally hanged. The rope broke and he had to be hanged twice.

After so many years of quiet life, Washington was that same autumn disrupted again by the murder of a young woman named Rebecca McCrory, whose body was found one morning two hundred yards from her father's house in Fallowfield township, throat cut from ear to ear. Suspicion fell on a young man with whom she had been keeping company, one Edward Nixon (no known relation to our Nixons). He was tried and acquitted, and left the country hurriedly.

The excitement, the swelling population, the rising prices, were again pushing George Nixon westward, even though he was in his seventies. In the spring of 1830 George Nixon sold the remaining 120 acres of his farm to Robert Judson, and moved West along with his sons, Seeds, who was thirty-eight, and Francis, who was thirty-four, and their families. The lure of the West pulled them on.

8

The Nixon
Family Splits Up

George Nixon, lieutenant in the Delaware militia during the War of Independence, moved on to Clinton county, in southwestern Ohio, where he bought a sixty-three-acre farm in what is now Washington township. A clue to his choice of Clinton county may be found in the presence there of one William Nixon, who was accounted one of the earliest settlers, and may have been the son of George's brother James.

Early, in terms of Clinton county, meant the first two decades of the nineteenth century. The difference between George and William Nixon is that the latter came and cleared the land. Clinton county was heavily wooded, and so clearing meant starting with an ax, building a log house, scratching out a patch for corn, and then moving on to refinements. When the Nixons arrived in the county, men were still following this rule, but there had been improvements that hastened the development of the area. One of them was the cast-iron three-piece plow invented by Jeth-

row Wood in 1819 to replace the old moldboard which went
back to the days of Washington and Jefferson. Although
George Nixon was now nearly eighty years old, he and his
sons worked the land, planting the staple crop, which was
then corn, and some flax. By 1830 most of the wolves were
gone, and they could raise sheep. So the men ate coon and
mutton and dressed in linen shirts and homespun coats and
trousers, or deerskin, wearing woollen caps in the winter
and straw hats in the summer.

The farmers traded in the towns of Hillsboro and Wilmington and bought their salt at the Scioto saltworks.
There wasn't much money in sight in this Western country,
and most trading at the stores was done by barter, but a
backwoods family did not need much from stores. They
cooked at an open fireplace and ate at a slab table on plates
of pewter and earthenware. They drank milk from their
own cows, and sassafras tea, and the men drank whiskey
when they could get it or make it. They took their grain to
the mills of Israel Nordyke near Martinsville, or to others
like it on the east fork of Todd's Fork, or one of the other
small streams that watered the region. Just three years before George and his family arrived in the county Christopher Hiatt had built a carding machine, which was run by
oxen on a treadmill. Three years after his arrival, Amos
Holloway built the first steam mill, near Martinsville. Progress was coming to Ohio, too, but the farmers still cut their
grain with sickles and cradles, so it took the whole Nixon
family to run the sixty-three-acre farm. They plowed and
planted and tended the grain, then scythed it, brought it in,
and flailed it by hand. One road ran along the north side of
the county but there were few others when George Nixon
and his family came, yet the 1830s were a time of road-
building and growth, with brick buildings going up in the
villages to signify that civilization had come West to stay.

It was a backwoods community and there was no question about that: Christopher Hiatt was the first man to
bring a cookstove into the county. The first doctor to come

to the county, Dr. John E. Dalton, physician, inventor, and merchant, who dealt in general merchandise, brought the first case of boots of Eastern manufacture that were ever offered for sale in Martinsville.

The year that Dr. Dalton came to town was also the year that George Nixon began to receive his pension from the federal government for his service in the Revolution. In spite of the manner of his service during the war, he had applied for pension for four and a half months of service as an ensign and half a month as a private, and that is what he got, which amounted to a stipend of fifty dollars a year. George Nixon was then eighty-two years old, and still working the farm.

As they gained confidence and a foothold in the community the boys spread out a little. Seeds moved in 1838 to Cuba, in Washington township, and settled down there. Francis, the youngest son, was slower but he bought 130 acres of land near the Nixon farm in 1839.

But now land was opening even further West, and those who came back said it was wide, open land, fertile and capable of yielding huge crops without putting ax to tree. The westering fever seized old George anew, and he and his youngest son Francis sold off their farms in 1841 and headed West. They took the road from Martinsville to Cincinnati, one spring day in 1842, stopped off in Cincinnati long enough for old George to visit city hall, make affidavits before the mayor of that city that he was entitled to his pension as a Revolutionary War soldier, collect his twenty-five dollars and move on. Apparently they left town just in time, for on March 8 a suit was filed in Clinton county court charging that Francis had not held title to the farm he sold the year before. The authorities reported that he had left the county. Far more, he had left the state, for the boundless West, and no one knew how to find him.

The Nixons then went on to western Illinois, to what is now Colona township, in Henry county, near Moline. Eventually the authorities of the Ohio courts found them there, but it was too late: Francis had died in the spring of 1842 at the age of forty-six.

Old George and Francis's widow and the children lived on a farm on the banks of the Rock River. George Nixon was now ninety years old, and although he was spry enough to repair fences and ride herd on the stock, he did not buy another property. With the help of the elder children he looked after the farm until he died that year and was buried in Glennwood cemetery. Francis's widow soon moved away to another county, and the grave lay neglected for many years, until 1925, when two great-granddaughters from Freeport, Mrs. Emma Richardson and Miss Mabel Nixon, found it once again. The Henry county chapter of the Daughters of the American Revolution then erected a monument to the old man's memory, since he was the only bonafide Revolutionary hero to be buried in Henry county. At the dedication there was music and tribute, and a veteran of the Spanish American War gave an address: "The Life of Lieutenant George N. Nixon" while members of the Genesco and Cambridge posts of the American Legion stood at attention. The chairman of the Henry county board of supervisors made a little speech presenting the monument, and the great-granddaughters proudly unveiled it. A hundred people stood in the rain as Mrs. Harry Ainsworth of the Moline chapter of the DAR paid tribute to old George.

As for George Nixon, Jr., who would be the great-great-grandfather of the President of the United States, he did not share the ambitions of old George and his brothers.

Years before, George Nixon, Jr., had taken up residence on the west side of the Pennsylvania family farm south of the old York road and had begun raising the fourth generation of Nixons in the New World. His first child was William Wilson Nixon, born in 1806 on the farm. Three years later a daughter, Eleanor, was born, and then the children kept coming along: Sarah, Mary Ann, James, and finally George Nixon III, who was born in 1821.

The seventh child, Nancy, was born in 1826. Next year came tragedy, with the death of Hannah. George waited a respectable three years but married again, for in this Western country there was small room for a bachelor father with a large family. His second wife was Christine Pence of Canton township, and he was obviously courting her at the time that his father and brothers made the momentous decision to go West again, so he did not join or follow them.

Shortly after the marriage, George moved from the old house on the farm, with all its memories, to a new house in Smith township a few miles away. Now he began to dispose of his portions of the farm, selling a little plot in 1833, and holding only forty-two acres of the original.

The family was split up and kept in touch irregularly, for the distances were great and communications scanty. The children grew up. William, the eldest son, married Ann Lingenfelter in 1825 and went off to make his own way, and so did the others, one by one. George Nixon III, who would be the future President's great-grandfather stayed at home, helping his father. In 1843, his grandfather Wilson died, and he received five dollars in remembrance from the estate. That year he also married the daughter of a neighbor, Margaret Ann Trimmer. The wedding was conducted by the presiding Methodist elder of the Washington district, the Rev. Thomas Hudson, and it was held at the home of George's older sister Eleanor, who had married John Scothorn and gone to live in South Strabane township. George was twenty-two and Margaret was seventeen.

Washington was now a settled, prosperous community, growing so that it was necessary to tear down the old public buildings on the square and build new and larger quarters for the county and town offices. A college had been founded there early in the century, and was flourishing, lending an unusual tone of culture to the community.

There was now a serious breach in the community, on the issue of slavery. The abolitionists had formed the Washington county Anti-Slavery Society in 1834. Next year a

group of the town's most prominent citizens (and capital-
ists) gathered to condemn "any combination of citizens of
one State organized for the purpose of disturbing the civil
institutions of another state." In 1836 Chief Burgess John
Griffith called a meeting to devise ways and means to prevent the abolitionists from holding meetings and spreading
their doctrine. But it was a hopeless cause; the abolitionists
went right ahead with their work, and friend turned against
friend.

The Mexican War caused some stir in Washington
county, but it was not so popular that many but the young
bloods seeking adventure decided to go to the colors. In fact,
only five men from the whole county enlisted, and the re-
mainder of the young men stayed at home, like George
Nixon and his cousins.

As the Nixon children married, they scattered. George
Junior's daughter Nancy married Thomas Sinclair and
went to live in Vinton county in southern Ohio. Sometime
before 1850 George Junior followed his daughter and her
husband.

For a time he lived with them. George now won the
dubious honor of being involved in a criminal case. Apparently he and a neighbor named James B. Johnson became
involved in an argument over the ownership of some grain.
The argument was extended, and in the spring of 1850
George Nixon was charged with the theft of two dozen
sheaves of oats. In the charge brought by the state, he was
said to have used "force and arms" in taking the oats away
from Johnson. George went to court, was convicted and sentenced by Judge Brown to pay a fine of two dollars, to return the oats twofold, and to pay court costs of $7.09.

When the hullaballoo had died down, George bought
land of his own, and then suggested that George III come
out to this country of such promise.

Once again it was back to log cabin and open fireplace
for the Nixons, but also, once again, land was cheap and
there was opportunity. George III shared the problems that

had driven his father and his grandfather West in the first place: the large family and the rising costs of land. He had five children, Martha, David Palmer, Samuel Brady, Margaret Lavina, and Sarah Elizabeth, the last born in 1851. The third child, Samuel Brady Nixon, was to be the grandfather of Richard Milhous Nixon.

To the Nixons, Ohio was a repetition of Delaware and Pennsylvania, hard work on the farm, so hard that a man could not really give his attention to much else.

Four more children were born to George III and his wife. In 1854 George Junior transferred fifty acres of land to George III in Richland township.

Richland township was organized a quarter of a century before the Nixons arrived and after about a dozen years had begun to boast of mills and furnaces where iron was made, and new church buildings. The Methodists—of which the Nixons were now members—built a church in 1848 near Allensville, the village that was the center of the township, located on the big road that would one day become U.S. Highway 50. The Nixons lived near the boundary of Elk township, in the north. In the west lived people who had come from the Carolinas and other Southern states, and during these years tension ran high in the area because of the issues of race and slavery, so high that both Richland and Harrison townships took the unusual step of raising local militia companies of about one hundred men each, to maintain order.

9

A Nixon in
the Civil War

War came in the early months of 1861 with a finality that
was shocking to the people of Ohio, and more worrisome
still was the disastrous rout suffered by General Irvin
McDowell at the first Battle of Bull Run.

In the town of Chillicothe near the Nixon farms these
sentiments were expressed far more regularly and openly
than in the farming community, and the city men decided
to do something about it: to create a new regiment of volunteers to meet President Lincoln's call to arms.

There existed in Chillicothe an organization of young
gentlemen who amused themselves by dressing up in uniforms and practicing military drills. They were known as
the Chillicothe Greys, and their captain was Orland Smith.
He was the logical man, so he was elected colonel of the new
regiment, and Jacob Hyer, Esquire, was elected lieutenant
colonel. They undertook to organize a military company to
help save the Union.

The work began in September. By October, the regiment existed on paper, and the officers had commissions approved by the state government, on condition that the enlisted men could be found to man the regiment.

Recruiting stations were opened in Ross, Highland, Pickaway, Jackson, Pike, Athens, and Washington counties for a new regiment which would be known as the 73rd Ohio Volunteer Infantry.

The people of Ohio, like those elsewhere, were very gloomy about the prospects of the war. They had believed in the spring that the rebellion would be crushed in sixty days, but the sixty days had come and gone, and so had one hundred and twenty days, and the rebels seemed to be stronger than ever, while the Union was disorganized. And in southern Ohio, there were many who sympathized secretly, and some not so secretly, with the aims of the Confederacy, and read of the growing acceptance of the split by Europeans with every indication of pleasure.

Recruiters came to Vinton county with newspaper advertisements, fliers, and martial pep talks. And some one of them so appealed to the third George Nixon that he decided to go to war. He was forty years old, he had a wife and nine children, but patriotic zeal had caught him up, so he left Margaret and the children in the care of his father, and enlisted at the Pike county recruiting center in Waverly.

George enlisted on November 9, but by that time Company A was full and he had to wait until November 20 when Company B was organized at Camp Logan, near Chillicothe. In the meantime he went to camp and began learning how to drill.

There was very little time for this citizen's army to develop. On November 20 Company B came into existence; forty days later the regiment was declared organized and in the service of the United States government. And on January 24, 1862, after less than three months' training, the 73rd Ohio was ordered to General William S. Rosecrans, head of the Department of West Virginia, and to be ready to go into action.

Charles Shepherd was the apt name of the first sergeant of Company B, and on the morning of the 24th he herded his boys together and loaded them on cars of the Marietta and Cincinnati Railroad. They transferred to the Baltimore and Ohio and eventually came to Grafton, West Virginia, and camped at Fetterman, which had been turned into a military enclave. Here the raw 73rd Ohio joined three other regiments of recruits, the 55th, 75th, and 82nd. On February 3 the regiment moved to New Creek on the north branch of the Potomac to serve under General Lander, and within a matter of hours was sent into the field, to attack a Confederate force at Romney, thirty miles away. Colonel Dunning, of the Fifth Ohio was commander of the post, and he led the men in their trek across the mountains, through roads covered with snow and ice in the morning, roads that turned to mud in the warmth of the middle of the day, and then began to freeze again as the gray shadows of evening moved in. The regiment was green but eager, and marched willingly with a sense of excitement into this adventure—but it was no adventure at all. When the force reached the south branch of the river, it was swollen and full of ice, and besides, scouts reported, the enemy had moved. So on the third day, tired and dirty but hardened, Private George Nixon and his comrades returned to New Creek.

The baptism of fire came a little over a week later. On February 12, the 73rd Ohio was part of a force of eighteen hundred men sent to drive the enemy out of Moorfield, a town further up the south branch of the Potomac. The men marched all that day, camped, and marched again on the thirteenth. Near midnight they came to the ferry four miles below Moorfield, but discovered there that the "rebs" had burned the ferryboat. Colonel Dunning stopped the column and gave orders to bivouac for the night. George and his companions foraged along the riverbank and found wood dry enough to burn and began building fires to shield them against the bitter cold. Suddenly the still of night was broken by the rattle of musket fire, a scant three hundred yards away on the left. Two men were wounded, but George and the rest seized their guns and made ready for action.

The movement began at several places, under fire from the rebels on the other bank, until three battalions crossed. The rebels saw that they were outnumbered and would soon be outflanked, and fled into the town. The Union force was two or three times the size of the Confederate, and it was not long before Colonel Harness beat a retreat.

Then, Colonel Dunning decided not to hold the town, and recrossed the river and started back to New Creek. The futility of the maneuver was matched by its evil effects on the men of the 73rd Ohio. Less than half trained, not yet hardened, the men had made two long forced marches in the frost of midwinter within two weeks, and the draining of their strength caused them to come down with colds and influenza and even pneumonia. By the time they reached the camp, half the men were sick. Two days later, as if the high command could not make up its mind, the regiment was ordered back to General Rosecranz and entrained for Clarksburg. Perhaps the generals realized what they had done, sending green troops into such a situation. The damage was there, however. In two weeks three hundred men of the regiment were sick in the hospital at Clarksburg, a man dying every day of pneumonia.

George Nixon was lucky in that he had spent his whole life in the rough and hardy ambience of a backwoods farmer, for he survived this foolish ordeal in the beginning.

The shock had been so great that men lingered on sick for a month. Even when the regiment moved to Weston, twenty-five miles up the Elk River, some men were still coughing and wheezing. Adjutant Frederick C. Smith was the first officer to die, in the hospital there, just as the regiment moved out to join General Milroy on a real expedition against the rebels.

By the first of May the 73rd had straggled into Monterey, 120 miles from Weston, by way of Buchanan and Beverly, and joined Milroy's army of some four thousand men. It was a badly run army, which succeeded almost immediately in losing a foraging party which was surprised by Confederate cavalry near Williamsville. The general decided to go after the rebels (having very little idea of their strength) and began committing his troops. He sent out a small punitive force and moved the whole army to McDowell, at the foot of the Bull Pasture mountains. Then he moved out two more regiments across the Shenandoahs, with all their equipment and baggage. On the morning of May 7, the enemy attacked the advance regiments and drove them back to McDowell, capturing most of their supplies and equipment. It was another of those retreats that was almost a rout, and the 73rd Ohio was rushed forward in support.

Another forced march. Colonel Smith led the 73rd toward the mountains. Four miles out they met the retreating column on a narrow mountain road, and the confusion was almost disastrous. Here, heading toward the enemy was the 73rd with Hindman's battery, and charging through them, willy-nilly, came the exhausted, frightened troops who had just been beaten in battle. It was an hour before the colonel could make order of his regiment, turn his guns around and begin an orderly retreat, covering the shattered force that had passed him by. As the men moved back down toward McDowell, the enemy came up, and three miles away the rebel column wound down the Shenandoah mountains. Colonel Smith stopped one battery on the side of a narrow valley, and halted the enemy movement, while the infantry marched back to McDowell, and George Nixon and the other exhausted men threw themselves down to rest.

The trouble with the army, aside from its greenness, was the incapability of its generals. General Milroy still did not have the slightest idea of the strength of his enemy. George and his comrades of the 73rd were lucky enough to be skirmishers, for soon four other regiments were moved through, across the river, and up the slope. They marched through the woods, on the right of the pass, for nearly a mile before they came to open fields that moved up to the summit of the mountain, where the Confederates awaited them.

Just before dusk the attackers emerged bravely from the woods and across the fields against the enemy. They charged, and charged again, but each time they thought they might gain the summit, the Confederates brought up reinforcements and repelled the advance.

Only now did General Milroy learn what he was up against, and General Schenck now took over. To prevent total disaster, he determined to move out that night and retreat to Franklin, leaving George and his comrades of the 73rd to hold the skirmish lines as a rear guard. Very quietly, during the night, the troops moved back on Franklin, the skirmishers replenishing the fires and making enough noise to assure the Confederates that the camp remained. Ten of George's comrades were out on picket duty, and when they could not be found, were deserted to fall into the hands of the Confederates, for just before dawn broke, the rear guards were called back to join the retreat.

The enemy followed, and when the Union force stopped twelve miles out on the road to Franklin for rest and a meal, Confederate cavalry attacked and captured a part of the 73rd rear guard. But George Nixon got away, and followed Schenck to Franklin.

The cloudy situation continued. Milroy's rash attack had ended with the Union army burning much of its supply train rather than have it fall into the hands of the Confederates, and food was short in Franklin. Then, on May 13, General John C. Frémont arrived to take command, having been sent ahead of his army of ten thousand men to retrieve the dangerous situation. Next day the ten thousand men marched into camp, bands playing and flags flying, and on the other side of town the Confederates watched the regulars of the Army of the Potomac come to camp, and withdrew toward the valley of the Shenandoah.

Frémont, too, was short of rations. He had plenty of dried beef for the camp, but not much else, and soon George and the other men of the 73rd were selling their bread; then crackers began to go for a half dollar apiece. There was no grain—or so little that the men began to steal from the horses—and nothing to eat but beef, beef, beef. They would not starve, but they went hungry, and stayed that way for another ten days until supplies arrived from New Creek.

Until now, George Nixon had very little reason to be proud of his service or his army. His raw regiment had been thrown into the hands of bumblers. But now the charismatic Frémont, with his leonine head and his commanding figure, was in charge. He announced to the troops that they belonged to the Army of the Mountains, and he placed the 73rd Ohio in General Schenck's brigade. The men cheered and vowed to fight like soldiers.

On May 25, the new army moved out, taking the wounded and the sick to the hospital at Petersburg, on the south branch of the Potomac, and then moving down the valley to Moorfield. George and his comrades had been there just three months before, raw recruits led into battle at the wrong time by the wrong men for the wrong reasons, but now they were back, having come full circle, and they were veterans. They sat around their campfires at night and swapped tales. They also gave a thought to those who were gone, from B Company—Private John H. Double, Private George Haynes, Private David F. Lee, Private David Mitten, Private Isaiah McCandless, Private Joseph T. Shade. These men were dead, but replacements were coming in, eighteen of them, and to them George and his friends were now regarded with wide eyes as seasoned veterans of the war.

10

The Seventy-Third
Ohio in Action

The morale of Private George Nixon and the other men of
the 73rd Ohio Volunteers had never been higher. It was
spring. The Army of the Mountains marched on May 28,
headed for the Shenandoah Valley. The going was hard,
but moving through the green woods in the sunshine it
seemed easier to climb the mountains, and they were going
on a mission against the Confederates, and to rescue a force
in danger.

The force was that of General Banks, who had been attacked by Stonewall Jackson at Strasburg, and been driven
back disastrously through Winchester to Harper's Ferry and
Maryland Heights.

Stonewall Jackson made a stand at Cross Keys, where
on June 8 Frémont's army engaged him. George and his
companions of the 73rd Ohio's Company B were put in support of a battery of artillery and defended it stoutly, with
the men of another company. The Confederates attacked

several times, but George and the others stood firm in defense. The battery was not taken.

The struggle lasted until nightfall, when the Confederates withdrew, and the men of Company B could count their casualties. Half a dozen men were wounded. Private William Labar was killed, and so were several men from other companies of the regiment. That night, George slept beside the battery, gun at his side, ready to repel attack, and ready to start fighting again in the morning. But the next morning, the Confederates were found to have slipped away to Port Republic, where they did serious damage to General Shields' forces, which had come up to turn their flank. Stonewall Jackson made a piece of his reputation that day, turning defeat into a sort of victory, slipping back across the river through one of the gaps of the Blue Ridge, and moving toward Charlottesville—escaping the two Union armies that seemed to have him trapped. Frémont decided not to follow so deep into Confederate territory, his supply lines so questionable. So the battle ended, the first real action for the 73rd Ohio Volunteers.

On June 10 they marched again. The 73rd Ohio and its fellow Ohio regiments were worn out from their stay in the line. George Nixon had not slept in a tent or any shelter more secure than a shed or haystack for six weeks. He had eaten and drunk and washed in the open, when and where he could, and shaved very seldom. He and his fellows were dirty and exhausted. Frémont was sensitive enough to recognize this state of affairs, and after a few days at Strasburg moved back to camp at Middletown, for rest and reorganization.

The Army of the Mountains was disbanded, to become the first corps of the Army of Virginia, under General Schenck, with Colonel N.C. McLean as head of the brigade in which the 73rd Ohio was assigned. It was an Ohio brigade altogether, four regiments of neighbors one might say, going to fight for their Union. Frémont left the army—George did not know it but the matter was political. Lincoln had placed Frémont under General Pope, and Frémont, who had just been demoted in another political fight from Commander of the West to take the Army of the Mountains, decided he had suffered enough from the politicians.

The political maneuvering in the armies of the West brought a welcome respite for Nixon's brigade, which moved to Sperryville, on the eastern side of the Blue Ridge, and went into camp for a month. This was lush country, and the troops picked blackberries and cherries and stuffed themselves with all the fresh foods they had missed for so long. Discipline was relaxed, they hiked up onto the ridge and sat in the sun, singing, or listening to the bees buzzing around them. They lolled in real tents, and washed in warm water. It was luxurious.

The holiday atmosphere was broken only once. The 73rd Ohio was sent out on a reconnaissance and foraging mission toward Madison Court House, accompanied by a section of artillery and cavalry. The regiment marched sixteen miles in one day, then stopped, and the cavalry went on up the road to Madison Court House, to learn that there were no Confederate troops in the area, except for a few militia. Private Nixon and the others were put to work harvesting corn, and they filled a train of wagons with the ears while they waited for the cavalry, then next day marched triumphantly back to camp.

Morale in the 73rd was high, until the regiment learned of the fighting in the Peninsula campaign, where McClellan was opposing Lee. Then came the six days of fierce battle that began at Mechanicsville, and included the Union withdrawal across the Chickahominy, which ended with the stinging defeat at the battle at Malvern Hill. The troops had hoped that McClellan was marching to Richmond this time. They did not know that, while McClellan had fallen back, the Union armies had inflicted twice as many casualties as they had themselves sustained; they knew that McClellan had not done what they hoped, and that the chances of being home for Christmas were not so good.

Toward mid-month General Halleck took command of the army. He was planning a master stroke: to bring three armies to bear on Richmond, capture the capital of the Confederacy, and bring a swift end to the war. But the Confederates began to move, and in particular, the 73rd's old foe, Stonewall Jackson, was on the prowl. For the 73rd Ohio, the pleasant big white tents were abandoned and the men marched again, all night long on August 8. At dawn the forced march stopped for an hour of rest and a meal, but the urgency was great and they marched again after breakfast until they reached Culpepper at noon.

As they approached the place they could hear the sounds of cannon and musketry, which came from Cedar Mountain, where Jackson had attacked General Banks' army. George and his comrades were told to get a little rest, and they did, as much as possible while hearing the sounds of battle and watching the puffs of smoke from the batteries in the distance.

At sunset the 73rd was ordered to march to Cedar Mountain (where Banks had just suffered a serious defeat) and moved forward, flags flying. Here is the eyewitness account of one of George Nixon's comrades:

"We immediately begin to observe the evidences of a sanguinary battle. There are ambulances loaded with wounded, some of whom are crying out as if in excruciating pain. There are dozens of slightly wounded, walking back to Culpepper. There are some on horseback and some in wagons; and all tell of a bitter and bloody contest at the front. We move on four miles, and then turn aside into a field, and rest on our arms. Night has seemingly brought to an end the fiercer part of the conflict, but there are occasional outbursts of musketry and cannon, which tell that the two armies are still grappling in the terrible embrace of battle, probably to be renewed with fiercer and bloodier fight on the morrow.

"A little after midnight our brigade is roused up and we proceed to the front. In the stillness of night, we pass groups of stragglers and camp followers, and parks of ambulances and artillery, and reserves of cavalry and infantry; and two miles from our bivouac, we file into an open field, with only pickets in our front. We lay down to await the coming daylight.

"Just at dawn, a picket-post, within a hundred paces of us, opened with a volley on a squad of rebel cavalry that had stolen up very near to us. The whole brigade spring to their feet, and were in a moment ready for action. But the cavalry scampered away; and after standing to arms awhile, we were formed in the main line of battle and awaited what the day might bring. . . ."

One can see him there, crouched, waiting—the short brown-haired Private George Nixon, his lean arms gripping his gun, blue tunic covered with the dust of the road, adjusting his cap nervously and peering around.

But nothing happened.

Next day the 73rd had an unpleasant task, cleaning up after General Banks, who had been driven back a mile, so rapidly that he had left his dead and wounded in the hands of the enemy. Officers went out with a flag of truce, and arranged for the burial of the dead. The soldiers came then, with their entrenching tools, and the day was spent digging and filling, as George Nixon and his companions sweated at their melancholy task.

The soldiers of the 73rd Ohio were learning a mighty respect for Stonewall Jackson. On August 12, they moved forward with the rest of their corps to the Rapidan River. They stayed here a week, waiting in the woods.

Then it was move again, for the rebels were on the other bank of the river, and the Union forces had to fall back or run the danger of being cut off. The 73rd remained with the rear-guard artillery, which marched and fought and fought and marched slowly, from the ford to the hills above White Sulphur Springs, to Waterloo, and finally to Warrenton.

11

Pvt. George Nixon
and the Narrow Escape

At the end of August, George Nixon and his fellow soldiers were caught up in the two days of warfare called the Second Battle of Bull Run, which brought disaster to the Union forces and much suffering to the brave men of the 73rd Ohio Volunteer Infantry.

The first day was inconclusive. The 73rd was moved to the left flank as the battle progressed, and on the morning of the second day, the men of the regiment found themselves on a hill, with much of the army on the plain below them.

In the afternoon the unit was ordered to a new position, forming on a bald hill on the left of the road, half a mile from Groveton, the line nearly perpendicular to the road, and extending forward some eight hundred yards. The whole brigade was on the left flank, holding a second line of battle, with the 73rd Ohio on the very outside flank, with an open field on the side of the men.

During the afternoon, General Pope came to the conclusion that there would be no work for the 73rd to do that day. He and his staff looked over the field, saw the apparently lackadaisical fighting of the Confederates, watched their own right flank move forward, and decided that they had already won the day. He so telegraphed President Lincoln in Washington.

Hardly were the telegraph wires cooled, and the sun lowering toward the horizon, when the battle began to pick up tempo. Around four o'clock the sound of small arms increased from a popping to a steady crackle, and the artillery shells went out with noise that ceased to be individual, but became a dull continuous roar.

From the center, the Confederates moved in a long gray line through the first line of battle, sweeping away the Union soldiers and coming on to the turnpike below, and across it, and into the woods on either side.

"They came on rapidly," wrote a soldier of the 73rd, "firing, shouting, and cheering; and so terrible was their sweep that all opposition seemed to melt away before them. In the center, our troops became confused, and seemed, in their retreat, to be huddling together, and crowding into and along the pike in some disorder. . . ."

The Confederates came on, through that first battle line, and charged a battery three hundred yards ahead of the 73rd Ohio. From the right came a volley of fire, as another Ohio regiment opened up. The 73rd was still silent.

The burst of fire from the right drove the rebels flat behind a hill, where they stopped to re-form.

On the left front of the 73rd two hundred yards out, was a wood lot. From it, a deep ravine led down to the right some three hundred yards. Now, skirmishers saw, the Confederates began moving in file up this ravine and into the woods. The troops on the right of the 73rd could see the enemy, and fired into them, but the woods masked much behind. From their vantage point, the men of the 73rd counted the battle flags that moved into the woods—one, two, three of them. So it was to be a whole brigade of rebels against the single Ohio regiment.

Suddenly, off on the left, George and his comrades saw a column of men half a mile away, marching steadily toward them. An officer of the regiment rushed to brigade headquarters to report. "Don't worry," he was told. "They are ours, coming up for support."

The attention of the men of the 73rd was now drawn to the front, for the rebels were coming out of the woods, yelling. The order was given, and Private George Nixon and the others fired, reloaded, and fired again. Men in gray began to stagger and fall, and the whooping stopped as they retreated into the woods, where they sought cover, and began firing back at the regiment.

Now it was the 73rd's turn to cheer, and the men did as they stood up, aimed, and fired again. The Confederates were stopped, seemed to be wavering.

But now a new threat presented itself. On their left, the stars and bars of the Confederate flag were now so close that there was no mistaking them, and even the officers of the brigade command could no longer fool themselves.

The realization that the 73rd Ohio was being flanked came just as the rebels put their artillery into play in the woods out to the left, and began centering on the 73rd's position. Shot and shell came plowing down the long line of the regiment, bringing wounds and death to the soldiers.

From the left the flanking column spread out, and began moving toward the rear of the regiment to cut it off completely. The Confederates in the front now came on again, and the cross fire was literally murderous. Pvt. George Nixon and the others stood, but their officers saw the futility of it. They were taking fire from three sides, and the order came to fall back on the right. Out on the extreme left, twenty men of the regiment ducked behind a stone fence. They seemed to have gained a vantage point, but in a few moments they were surrounded by men in gray, and were prisoners. For Pvt. Nixon there were three hundred yards to cover, firing, crawling, falling back, running, dodging, and firing again. He made it, so did many others, but many did not, and the field behind was left dotted with still blue forms.

It was many long minutes before George Nixon found the safety of the woods to the right, where the other Ohio regiments had seen their plight and formed a line of battle to fight off the Confederates coming in on the flank. George and his fellows struggled through the line, protected now by rifle fire, and the sergeants began re-forming the company. They searched for First Sergeant Shepherd, but without success—his was one of those blue forms lying so still in the grassy knoll behind them.

When the officers gave orders to re-form the company, George and eighty others drew together and made ready for new action. It was ten o'clock at night before George crossed Bull Run and then Cub Run. The 73rd bivouacked not far from there, and the surviving officers and sergeants counted up the dead and reassigned the living.

The regiment had gone into battle with 312 guns but in that withering flank attack had lost more than half its strength; 144 men had been killed or wounded, and 20 had been taken prisoner. Captain Burkett was dead, and so was Lieutenant Trimble. And in all only 148 men were left for duty. Of Company B, First Sergeant Shepherd was gone, and so were Sergeant Ben Morrison and Corporal Jim Smith. The regiment and the company knew they and their army had suffered disaster.

Perhaps luckily for the disorganized Union army, the morning of Sunday August 30 dawned dismal and rainy; hardly the weather to instill confidence in anyone.

George and the other men of Company B huddled around their campfires day and night, resting from the hor-

rors of battle, and wondering about the fate of their unfortunate army.

The 73rd Ohio marched again on the night of August
31. George rolled his blanket, tucked it around his knapsack, shouldered his gun, and responded to the call of his
sergeant. The company had to wait to slip into line, for the
road to Fairfax was jammed with soldiers, ambulances, and
trains of wagons whose iron-bound wheels stirred the mud
of the road into froth, and where there had been potholes,
the soldiers sank in up to their knees.

They marched, the rain pelting their faces, and running down their collars. The night was black, without the
hint of star or moon; it was the darkest night of the war in
every way, the shadows of defeat and futility hanging in the
air.

Now came the new changes that signified to the enlisted men just how disastrous the defeat at Bull Run had
been. General Pope was out, and General McClellan was
in. The Army of Virginia had been hurt so that it was now
merged into the Army of the Potomac. And as for them, the
men of the 73rd, they and the rest of the corps were again to
be rear guards.

The war swirled around them—South Mountain,
Crampton's Gap, Harper's Ferry, Antietam—and a strate-
gic victory at last for the Union, as Lee was forced to abandon his invasion of the North and fall back into Virginia.
McClellan was slow, as usual, to move south, but late in
October he came, recrossed the Potomac, and moved down
the base of the Blue Ridge, pushing Lee out of Winchester
and south deep into Virginia.

Reorganization again—the 73rd Ohio was transferred
from McLean's Brigade to a new one. Hereafter it would be
the 73rd Ohio Volunteer Infantry, Second Brigade, Second
Division, Sigel's Corps. The new associates of this weathered
regiment would be the 134th New York, the 136th New
York, and the 33rd Massachusetts. Except for George and a

few other veterans, it was an entirely green organization; even the 73rd Ohio drew 120 recruits. But at least the command would be right: Colonel Smith of the 73rd was promoted to take charge of the Brigade, and Lt. Col. Long became regimental commander.

12

Pvt. George Nixon's War Ends

Pvt. George Nixon had served his country for nearly a year. He was still a private, for there were few promotions within the 73rd Ohio, but by this time the experienced men were more interested in survival than in promotion. There was no longer much optimism within the regiment that they would be home soon. Indeed, spirits fell every day as the generals bumbled and delayed.

The master politician, Lincoln, appointed General Burnside now to take command, and Burnside moved Sigel's corps back to Fairfax, where the men sat. Morale had never been lower.

For a time the men consoled themselves that at least they were going into winter quarters. The rumor was out that they would be held in reserve that long, building a new camp. They stayed at Germantown at first, near Fairfax Court House, but then were moved to Fairfax station four miles away to build a road as well as the camp. Then came days of pick and shovel work, and when that was finished, the supplies came in for construction of a permanent installation. The buildings were up, and the men talked about moving into winter quarters and settling down. Then came the rumor that a new campaign was about to start.

On December 12 winter camp was forgotten—the men were on the march to Fredericksburg. Hope rose again as the soldiers of the 73rd Ohio moved out, waited to take their place in line as the column marched past the station, and moved on.

The men of the 73rd expected to go into the battle of Fredericksburg. They could hear the firing of artillery across the Rappahannock, and they waited for orders. They waited all one day, and at evening the orders came, so they marched, at dusk (until one o'clock in the morning), but the column moved only two miles. Then the word began to come—the battle had gone so badly that the Union forces were stunned. The corps was turned aside on the Fredericksburg road, and at one o'clock the men lay down, resting but ready to move on a moment's notice.

That night the battle ended. Burnside had a huge army at his disposal, more than a hundred thousand men. But he had used them so badly that he lost 10 percent in killed and wounded, and made no dent on the enemy. During the night and the next day, the men of the 73rd learned some of the details from other soldiers, and their morale sunk to a new nadir. "The brave old Army of the Potomac seems doomed to failure," said one.

The men scarcely paid attention when there were rumors that President Lincoln would now cashier Burnside. Generals came and went in this army of the Union with dreary regularity; only the war and the stream of men went on forever.

Once again the 73rd Ohio went into a period of inactivity, mostly on picket duty along the river. Toward the end of the month, the regiment was sent to build a new camp. The men turned to and put up the cabins quickly, and some of the recruits talked about how pleasant it would be to spend the rest of the winter in the park of evergreens. George and the veterans knew: it was the inexorable law of warfare that once the regiment had found a pleasant spot, and officers and men were tucking themselves in for a comfortable time of it—that was the day the marching orders came.

So it was with the 73rd. The last cabin was built, the last door hung, and the men had spent two nights luxuriating in their new quarters, when the orders came to rejoin the corps at Stafford Court House.

It was the old story: Burnside had been relieved, and now General Hooker was going to show what he could do. The first thing, of course, was to reorganize everything whether it needed it or not, and thus the 73rd was moved out of its winter quarters, to a position halfway between Stafford Court House and Brooks Station—where the men went to work again building cabins. This time they did get to stay a while, for Hooker spent three months reorganizing—changing equipment, examining and writing off inferior guns, checking ammunition, equipping the men with new shoes.

One thing that new clothes and new shoes did was raise the morale of the army. President Lincoln came to visit in April, and the troops were called out for review. It took three days, with the cavalry and the flying artillery going first, the infantry on the next two days, with George's regiment coming very near the end, passing along the plateau above Falmouth station before the President and the assembled generals. The bands played and the men marched, and indeed it was an impressive spectacle. Lincoln went back to Washington believing the army morale had been restored, and to an extent it had been.

The Confederates had spent the winter holding their strong position at Fredericksburg Heights, and in April General Hooker decided to attack.

The 73rd missed the main battle of Chancellorsville.

Afterward, General Hooker ordered the army to pull out and retire across the Rappahannock. The men of the 73rd could not understand why: a few thousand had been killed and wounded, (eleven thousand, to be exact) but there were more than a hundred thousand men left to fight, and two thirds of the army was untouched, uncommitted to battle. But generals do not consult privates, and back they went, to their old camp. At least the next month was spent in the cabins of the pine hills of Stafford while Hooker reorganized again. The 134th New York was transferred out of the brigade, and the old 55th Ohio came back. George and his comrades had many friends in that regiment, which had fought with them early in the war, in what they remembered now as the Old Ohio Brigade, when General McLean had it. The men of the 73rd were pleased, for they expected to do great things in the battles yet to come.

Early in June 1863, the men of the 73rd Ohio heard rumors that the Confederates were again going on the move, to cross the Rappahannock and come North. Rumor gave way to fact: Lee was moving up the Shenandoah Valley and there was every indication that he was going to attack deep into Northern territory. So General Hooker again put the army in motion.

The men of the 73rd had their orders: pack knapsack, blankets, sixty rounds of ammunition and three days' rations, and be ready to move out on an hour's notice.

George and the other soldiers of the 11th Corps got their marching orders on the morning of June 12, and they moved out singing. Wonders for their morale had been done by rest and reorganization.

On July 1, the force headed into Pennsylvania. George and his comrades had just crossed the Pennsylvania line when they heard the firing of cannon ahead, and they were moved forward at double time toward Gettysburg. Just before noon they reached Cemetery Hill.

From the hill, George could see the rebel line advancing, while the Union forces were slowly falling back on the town of Gettysburg. And just then came another of those bits of information, passed along the line, that did not help morale a whit. Hooker was relieved and General Meade had been appointed to command the Army of the Potomac. He would take command as soon as he arrived.

George's unit was the Second Brigade of the Second Division of 11th Corps, with General Adolph von Steinwehr in command of the division, and Colonel Smith, once of the 73rd, in command of the brigade. Now the First and Third divisions of the corps were sent to the north of the town, while George Nixon and the other men of the Second Division were held on Cemetery Ridge in reserve.

The Confederates attacked. At about two-thirty in the afternoon, Confederate General Jubal Early sent three brigades against the Union right, General A. P. Hill attacked from the left, and General Heth's division attacked in the weak spot in the center of the Union line.

General Steinwehr's Second Division was ordered into line on the right of the town, across and parallel to the Baltimore Turnpike. George Nixon and the others knocked down the cemetery fences, and took their position to hold the hill in case of any further difficulties. They remained there until about four o'clock, and here they covered the retreat of the other two divisions of the 11th Corps, which came staggering back after being slashed by the Confederates.

The 73rd Ohio was moved to the front of the batteries on the left of the turnpike, and covered the retreat of the First Division. By the end of the afternoon the line of battle ran along the Taneytown road facing north, and along the Baltimore Turnpike facing east, the lines meeting at a right angle at the edge of the town, enclosing Cemetery Hill, where the artillery batteries were massed. It was a critical moment. Had the rebels chosen late in the afternoon to throw their might against the ridge, they would doubtless have taken it. But they did not, and the opportunity passed as the faltering Union forces closed up around the hill.

In its position in front of the batteries the 73rd was extremely vulnerable, and men began to fall, wounded. Toward evening, as the rebels gathered in the town, their sharpshooters found cover, and the harrying of the men began. To cover the final Union withdrawal from the village, the 73rd Ohio was sent again across the turnpike, a few yards away from the part of the village nearest the hill, and here the sharpshooters got after them, wounding two more men. George and his fellow soldiers hugged the ground and every bit of cover available to them, but held their positions, until relieved at ten o'clock that night. Then, exhausted, they threw themselves down on the grass among the gravestones and slept, knowing that the next day would bring a return of battle.

That night as Private Nixon slept on the cool grass of the cemetery, General Meade closed his headquarters at Taneytown and moved up to Gettysburg. He had decided to make this a decisive battle, even though it had not gone well in the beginning. Meade and his staff reached Cemetery Hill about one o'clock in the morning and began inspecting positions. The general gave some orders—and at three A.M. the officers and sergeants began quietly awakening the men of the 73rd Ohio. The word was passed to get ready to move.

The heavy fighting missed the 73rd Ohio that day; the men were harried more by cannon fire than by attack or by snipers, and even darkness did not bring the end one might have expected. At about nine o'clock the sound of cannon began to subside, and the men of the 73rd could look around them.

They wrapped themselves in blankets, placed their guns carefully on the grass, and lay down to try to sleep around ten o'clock. The night was still except for the horrible cries of the wounded of both sides who lay in the no man's land between the armies.

The groaning and wailing were suddenly drowned out by renewed firing, and the men of the 73rd leaped to their feet, throwing aside blankets and grabbing up their guns. The noise was coming from the point of the hill in front of the batteries, and Company B of the 73rd Infantry moved out with the rest of the regiment.

Confederate General Jubal Early's troops were moving to capture Cemetery Hill and the sixteen guns placed there. They came on, ran into General von Gilsa's First Division, and those troops turned around and ran. The rebels charged up the hill and very nearly took it, before the artillerymen could rouse themselves and begin to fight back.

Quiet again descended, again punctured all through the night with the distressing sounds of the wounded. The third day of battle dawned on July 3. With morning the fight began to move toward the 73rd Ohio's position.

As the day wore on, the sharpshooters in town became so troublesome that a six-pound gun was brought up along the Taneytown road to shell the houses where they hid.

Toward noon, a strange silence descended upon the whole field, as though the generals were pausing for reflection. Indeed, Union Generals Meade, Hancock, Gibbon, Newton, and Pleasanton managed to make a simple luncheon, and then sat down on boxes and a fallen log on the ridge to smoke a postprandial cigar.

Just then the roof of the world seemed to cave in. It was 1:07 P.M.

The rebel guns opened up, and the Union guns replied; soon more than two hundred fieldpieces were barking their messages of death. The artillery duel continued for two hours, so intense that General Meade was forced to move his headquarters away from the cemetery area.

Thirteen thousand men in gray began to march, in three lines, and forty-one regimental flags fluttered in the breeze, and they came on toward the Union positions, in what everyone knew was to be the decisive action of the engagement. Behind the fences on the road below Cemetery Hill, along the raised ground known as Cemetery Ridge,

George Nixon crouched, as thousands of other Union soldiers crouched or lay or knelt behind the best cover they
could find. They waited.

General Hunt's artillery waited, too, until the line of
skirmishers reached a point just above the Emmittsburg
road. Then he gave the signal, and two hundred Union
cannon began to blaze, tearing big holes in the Confederate
lines. The Confederate artillery fired a few shots, but it became apparent that the rebel soldiers had reached a point
where their own artillery could not fire without running the
danger of killing them. So the Confederate guns stopped
firing. Here is the eyewitness report of one officer of George
Nixon's regiment:

"Here were the three chosen divisions of their army,
marshaled by their best officers; and we shall see whether
Northmen can stand before them.

"Across the sloping ground in front of Hancock and
Sickles, they came on with flying colors and well dressed
ranks. The scene is like a pageant rather than a battle. Our
artillery opens up on them and shot and shell make occasional rents in their line; but they close ranks splendidly,
and move on like veterans, as they are. We have a single
line of infantry in front of our guns—which line now opens
fire upon the foe. Still they come forward, cheering and
hopeful—aye, confident of victory. At the Emmittsburg
road, where our line has the protection of a stone fence,
there is a bloody contest. But the enemy's second line comes
forward, and our infantry are driven back. Our cannoniers
hold their fire, they must not sweep away their own men.
On, on come the exultant foe; one of our advanced batteries
is already in their hands. Our retreating infantry gains the
crest of the hill, and our batteries open with canister. At
every discharge, there were gaps in that line of gray. The
ground was covered with their dead and wounded. Their
line wavered for a moment. Their third line did not come
promptly to their support; then our men went in with the

bayonet and a shout; and the enemy broke and went back in disorder. [General] Hancock threw forward his right on the double-quick, plied the Bayonet and captured several thousand prisoners; while the bleeding remnants of those proud divisions went flying back all over the field—our artillery playing upon them all the time—till they reached the cover of the woods."

The gray line was broken, leaving more than seven thousand of the thirteen thousand men dead or wounded on that field. The men in blue suddenly seemed to realize that they had won a great victory, the first in the story of the Army of the Potomac, and they rose along Cemetery Ridge to give cheer after cheer.

The field was quiet after that. General Meade rode out along the line to decide what action he would take next, and the officers of the regiments began checking the condition of their battalions and their companies. First Sergeant Joseph Reid moved among the squads of Company B, asking questions. Sergeant Johnson Pryor was dead, Sergeant Thomas Rice was mortally wounded. Corporal William Haines was dead, and so was Corporal Samuel Turner. Private William Call was wounded and so was Private William McLuens. One by one the men were accounted for.

They found George Nixon on the field. He had been struck in the abdomen by a bullet, one of the dreaded Minié balls. He lay there on the grass, wounded and groaning, until a young drummer boy from the regiment volunteered to crawl out, and dragged him back to the safety of the line. And now, the battle done, he was moved back behind the line to the regimental aid station, his comrades carrying him gently on a stretcher. The regimental station, which was largely a first-aid unit, could do nothing for such a serious wound. He must go to divisional hospital. They carried him down to the tents on Rock Creek, east of the ridge. There the surgeons moved among the men, sorting out the ones who might be saved, and setting aside the hopeless cases. They came to Private George Nixon and examined him. Minié ball in the abdomen. Prognosis: hopeless.

Gently he was moved, along with other men who had head and abdominal wounds, into a special section of the hospital. These men did not know it, but the decision had been made by the doctors that no treatment would be wasted on them.

Pvt. George Nixon was consigned to die. He was not the only one by far; the 73rd Ohio went into the battle with only 300 men; at the end it had lost 144 in killed and wounded, and many of those wounded, like George Nixon, lingered a few days in the hospitals, and then died.

Pvt. George Nixon was buried then on the field at Gettysburg, in the cemetery he had defended so stoutly for three days. And not long after, President Abraham Lincoln came to Gettysburg and observed the scene of the carnage. The President dedicated the cemetery to the dead and to the future of the nation. He stood near the spot where a simple headstone would be raised, reading: George Nixon, Co.B. Regt.73.

13

The Nixons
Produce a "Labor Skate"

When George Nixon III had gone to war, he had left his wife and nine children in the care of his father. Old George Junior was sixty-seven years old then, but the Nixons were a hardy family, and like his father he was able to work the farm and manage the family affairs. A month after George III enlisted, his father sold some property in Prattsville, and that must have satisfied the family need for cash, for no other land was sold during the war.

Margaret Nixon stayed at home, taking care of the children as her husband soldiered for his country. The oldest was Martha, who was seventeen when her father went away to war. She married John Vansky the next year, and they named their first child George in honor of her father.

Before her husband died, Margaret had lost one of the fold. David Palmer, seventeen, and Samuel Brady, sixteen, were the "men in the family" on whom she and Old George had to rely for help in running the farm. Margaret Lavina was fourteen, and Sarah Elizabeth was twelve; William Francis was nine, Boston was seven, Hiram was five, and Elihu was only three.

As if one tragedy in a year was not enough for a family, the Nixons were visited again that summer of 1863 by death: little William Francis died on August 12. Margaret survived her husband by only twenty months. She died in the spring of 1865. But the eight remaining children lived on, most of them to a considerable age, and they scattered across the continent, some moving West, as far as Oregon, others moving back eastward, and some staying on to live out their lives in Vinton county.

For a time Old George made the farm prosper, but of course during the war years the urgencies of the nation created a demand for any and every bit of produce. In 1869 George bought another thirty-nine acres of land in Richland township from William Hoffhines. Again the problem of providing for the young ate into the slender family fortunes: David Palmer Nixon married Rachel Clark in 1871 and George arranged for him to have that thirty-nine acres. George also apparently ran into difficulties, for there was a sheriff's sale of 38¾ acres of land in the spring of 1871, and the next spring George sold another forty acres to R. T. McClinticke—and that was the end of his land dealings.

During these years other members of the Nixon family had settled in Vinton county. One was George Junior's nephew John, who had land in Elk township and Richland township. Another was George's son William, and still another his brother Seeds, who came here from Clinton county at about the time that Old George the Revolutionary soldier headed west for Illinois.

So the children of George Nixon III grew up among family, even Elihu, the youngest of them. And among those who elected to make their lives in the county was Samuel Brady Nixon, who was to be the grandfather of a President of the United States.

Samuel Brady Nixon was born on October 9, 1847, in Washington county, Pennsylvania. He acquired his name from an old Indian fighter of western Pennsylvania who was more famous in that part of the country than Daniel Boone. This legendary character had hated Indians ever since his father was killed by them at Wolf Run in Lycoming county. "Captain Sam," as he was known, was said to have fought with the Revolutionary forces at Long Island, White Plains, Trenton, Princeton, and Brandywine. He may even have been a friend of old George Nixon, Sr., from the days of their military careers. But Samuel Brady had spent his adult years in a one-man vendetta against the Indians of Pennsylvania and Ohio, had been twice captured and sentenced by Indians to burning at the stake, and had twice escaped, once by running a gauntlet and disappearing in the woods, and the second time by seizing a papoose and throwing it in the flames intended for himself, then running off in the confusion. That time, they said he had run a hundred miles, naked, from Kent on the Cuyahoga River to Fort McIntosh. He died at the age of thirty-seven, and Lake Brady and countless children were named for him.

Samuel Brady Nixon married Sarah Ann Wadsworth, a teacher at Bethel who was the daughter of a neighborhood storekeeper, in 1873, and the next year bought forty acres of land for farming in Richland township. As a farmer he did not prosper. He turned to schoolteaching, and delivered mail for a number of years.

Samuel and Sarah had five children, the third of whom was Francis Anthony Nixon, who would become the father of Richard Milhous Nixon. This boy was known in the family as Frank, by his elder sister Irene and his elder brother Walter, by little sister Carrie and little brother Ernest.

Ohio was ceasing to be frontier country in those days, five years after the end of the Civil War. The population of the state had jumped from less than two million in 1850 to 2.6 million in 1870, and people were turning to the towns as much as to the farms. The pressure was on the land again, and the size of farms was going down. But a man could still make a living raising corn, wheat, oats, barley, rye or even buckwheat. And of course, sheep.

Samuel Nixon might have succeeded as a farmer had he not been so much in love with his wife. She fell ill with tuberculosis in the 1880s and her husband decided to devote his every effort to improvement of her health. The doctors recommended mountains and the warmer climate of the South, so Samuel sold off the stock and the family farm and their furniture. They took with them the five children, the family Bible, for they were devout Methodists, their clothing, and a canary in a cage, for the canary was the pride of Sally Nixon's sad life.

They took the train to Ronceverte, Virginia, a little town where they hoped to settle down and find Sally's health. The children were fascinated by the town; village though it was, it was the largest place they had seen. Little Carrie saw a China doll. There was so little money that the family was living outside the village in a rude cabin, but Sally Wadsworth Nixon could not resist the yearning in her daughter's eyes, and she sold the canary in its cage so the little girl might have her doll.

The treatment for tuberculosis was rest, and milk and raw eggs, and long walks in the countryside (which probably exhausted the patient). Sally Nixon was meticulous in meeting the schedules, and went walking with her children until she actually was exhausted. No one told her she was killing herself more quickly.

If she improved at Ronceverte, it was not readily apparent, and Samuel Brady Nixon took her and the family further south, to the Carolinas and Georgia. They traveled by wagon now, and he worked when he could to support the family and eke out their slender supply of money. But Sally Nixon grew no better, but worse, and she knew it. She asked to be taken home to Mount Pleasant, and Samuel turned the family back to Ohio, and the house of his father-in-law. There Sally Nixon died. She was buried in Ebenezer Meth-

odist Cemetery in Mount Pleasant and the children were
sent around to the families of various relatives until Samuel
could get a new start in life. He settled in a little log cabin
at the foot of Ebenezer hill. He was nearly dead broke. In
fact, one of the children recalled that he had only five dollars left in cash. He gave that to the man who brought his
belongings to the log house.

"Root, hog, or die," he said, and that backwoods statement epitomized the spirit of these Nixons. Down they
might be, but never out, nor was that so much different
from the condition of their fellow farmers here in Vinton
county. It was not rich country, men worked by the sweat of
their brows, and tried to amass a little capital to buy more
land or more stock. There was seldom much thought of getting rich, except by the merchants and sharpies of McArthur and the other towns. The farmer was content to live on
the land, raise his family and work out his life.

Samuel Brady went back to schoolteaching and mail
carrying. He also worked sometimes in a pottery factory
nearby. They made fruit jars, milk crocks, jugs and pitchers,
and then peddled them by wagon across the countryside.

After a time his son Walter went to work in the pottery
factory, too. All the children came back and worked hard at
tending the animals on the farm, raising crops, keeping
house, and earning cash to pay taxes and buy the staples
from the stores. They helped shear in the spring, and Walter sometimes drove a wool wagon to market in Chillicothe.

Samuel Brady Nixon married again, this time Luth-
eria Wyman, and they had one more son, Hugh. Samuel
soon had fifty-three acres of land and he farmed it, and continued to live in Vinton county in a farmhouse just south of
Hue on Elk Ridge. The children grew up on the farm. Walter worked. Frank walked to Ebenezer school, several miles
away. His younger brother Ernest, raised in the same background, did seek education, and did prove the workability
of the American system that said a man could raise himself
by his bootstraps, for Ernest Nixon went on to college, and

became a professor at what is now Pennsylvania State College.

But Frank was impatient with the educational process, and he had another problem. He had been just ready to start school when his mother became ill and Samuel Brady Nixon had decided to take her to the mountain country. Frank, then, had missed formal schooling for the first few years. Since father and mother had both taught school, they now taught their children, but by the time they returned to Ohio, so much had happened in Frank's young life that he was out of place. He started school in the one-room schoolhouse, but he was too old for his grade level (he was fourteen years old and in fourth grade) and there was the problem of supporting the family. He volunteered to leave school and go to work to help support the family, and from that time on basically supported himself.

For a time Frank worked for his father, driving ox teams to haul logs to the sawmill near their house. Then he went to work as a hand for a farmer named Finney, at first for twenty-five cents a day and board, which he recalled as consisting of large quantities of bread and milk. Later he was paid thirteen dollars a month, and given the right to pasture a calf on the farmer's place.

He worked all that first summer, sold his young steer, and spent the money on clothes. He was a lively young man.

Although his father was a Democrat, Frank Nixon saw the hardships of the farmers around Vinton county, and heard the talk that it was all the fault of President Cleveland and his hard-money policy. The argument made a lot of sense to him, too. In the fall of 1896, then, when he heard that Governor William McKinley was coming to Swan township, he was interested. By this time Frank had earned enough money to buy a horse, a four-year-old sorrel, and he was very proud of this horse. McKinley was to be escorted by Republicans of Swan township on horseback over the last ten miles of his journey into the county seat of McAr-

thur. In other words, it was to be a parade; and for Frank
Nixon it was a chance to see the Republican candidate, and
a chance to show off his fine horse.

Frank saddled up his sorrel, trimmed reins and saddle
in gold cloth and ribbon, and joined the parade. The parade marshal came riding along the line and saw the capar-
isoned horse. Just what he wanted. "Come along, son," he
said to Frank, and took him up to the front of the line.

Frank galloped up after the marshal and found himself
riding beside McKinley's carriage. When the parade
reached McArthur, the governor got out of the carriage and
walked over to Frank and his horse. He patted the sorrel on
the neck and spoke.

"Mighty fine horse you have there, son. Finest I ever
saw."

Frank was a country boy and not used to the city ways
of politicians, so he was overcome. He thanked the governor. As McKinley turned to others, he spoke over his shoul-
der, "How are you going to vote, son?"

Frank was not going to vote for anybody; he was just
eighteen years old. But of course wild horses would not have
dragged that admission from him that day. He raised his
courage and shouted back.

"Republican, of course."

And when the time came, he did cast his first vote for
McKinley and voted Republican ever after.

The parade over, Frank went back to the farm and the
slogging work, but his heart was no longer in it. Not every
eighteen-year-old becomes the confidant of governors.
Frank had learned the power of initiative and he had no
fear of getting along in the world, so he decided to go out
and brave that world. He was fiercely independent, even
pugnacious:

"I never missed a day's work in my life because I
couldn't get a job," he said.

He went to Union Furnace and got a job in the brick
works there. He came back to the farm, and went into busi-

ness for himself raising potatoes for a while. He covered
the potatoes with straw, which kept the moisture in and the
bugs and weeds out. "All you had to do was wait until the crop
was full grown," he said later. "Then you'd pull off the straw,
pack the potatoes in a wagon, and cart them off to town, where
they would bring a dollar a bushel."

His friends began calling him The Potato King, but he
was not satisfied with potato farming, even though he had
found it profitable. He took the money and decided that he
would, indeed, see the world, so he headed west for Colorado. For a time he worked on a sheep ranch there. Later
he worked for an electric company, and the infant telephone company of the Rocky Mountains, helping install
the old crank wall telephones.

He came home again for a visit and then decided to
seek his fortune in Columbus, where there seemed to be opportunity for a young man with courage and vitality. For
Columbus was a city with more than nine hundred factories, making everything from carriages to watches. An ambitious young man might earn as much as five hundred dollars a year working in the foundries or other factories, and a
skilled worker could get three dollars a day, in the Carnegie
Steel Company's works or the Columbus Buggy Company.

Frank Nixon found a home of sorts in the city at 398
East Walnut Street, and set out to look for work. His first
job was as a laborer, and then he got a job in a similar ca-
pacity with the Columbus Railway and Light Company,
which had the franchise to run streetcars in the city.

Industrial development was coming rapidly at this
time, and bringing with it some rough edges. Cities were
beset with strikes, and workers were unionizing or seeking
the protection of civil service. Columbus had suffered one
serious street railway strike about ten years earlier, and at
the moment management and labor had an uneasy truce.

In 1901, a new electric railway company promised
service to connect Columbus with the northwestern counties
of Defiance, Henry, Hardin, Union, and Marion. There *was*

a future in street railroading, that much was certain. The Columbus company secured a new franchise, promising lower fares and "owl" cars, which ran at night. A passenger could buy seven tickets for a quarter.

The life of a streetcar man had its exciting moments, too. That spring Conductor D. Burnham was involved in an incident on one of the cars. Three burly men got on Burnham's car at High Street. For some reason or other they began abusing the conductor, and made so much noise that by the time the car had reached Third Street he told them that if they did not quiet down he would put them off the car at Fourth Street.

One of the men jumped up, shook his fist in the conductor's face and called him rude names. Conductor Burnham pulled the bell cord and started to put the men off the car. The men jumped him, and in a moment the car was filled with men struggling and women and children shouting, crying, and screaming. Somehow three windows got broken.

A city fireman jumped up and went to Burnham's assistance, pulling off one of the men and shoving him out of the car. Burnham then landed a "right and a left" on the other two, and one named Radepouch ended up with a badly cut head. Radepouch got off the car and went into Meggenhofen's drugstore at Long and Fourth where clerk Goble dressed his wounds. Conductor Burnham threw the other man off the car, which had emptied in the panic, and then he and the motorman went their way.

Radepouch complained bitterly to the clerk, and went to the police station and swore out a warrant for the arrest of Conductor Burnham on a charge of assault and battery. But when the newspapers printed the story, with the definite implication that the three men were not only assailants of the conductor but were *gamblers*—that was the end of the affair.

Yes, Columbus was a busy, exciting place. Frank Nixon was interested in politics, although in no sense was he a politician or worker for his Republican party. But he could be satisfied in the spring elections in Columbus, Cleveland, and Toledo to see that the GOP held its own and the voters gave no satisfaction to the Democrats that year. A big issue was still free silver—cheap money—and as a loyal Republican Frank Nixon had to oppose it, although some of his radical friends in the labor movement took quite an opposite point of view.

Labor was struggling to keep its head above water these days. The carpenters' union had negotiated a contract for thirty-five cents an hour, but some builders took exception to these high wages, so the carpenters had to get together again and pledge public support to the men who kept the contracts.

Life was hard but not all hard. There were parties and picnics in the summer, with baseball games and pie-eating contests and sack races, chases after greased pigs and beautiful baby contests (six months to two years), with prizes for the prettiest baby and the fattest baby. There were swimming races in the parks and bowling contests and boxing matches, and smokers at the beer halls, where a man could relax over a cigar.

On the Fourth of July there was a huge parade. Frank Nixon may not have known that his great-great-grandfather had fought in the Revolutionary War, but that didn't matter. Flags were everywhere, and the streets resounded to the racket of firecrackers, torpedoes, and even pistols. In the suburbs small boys placed a mixture of sulphur and saltpeter on the streetcar tracks to explode; if it did, life and limb were endangered, if it did not, it still made a mess. There were band concerts in nearly every park in the city, picnics too, orations, and a half-dozen baseball games. Frank's celebration was an end in itself, rather than a tribute to the past. But this was not at all unusual in Ohio—the "West"— which had been but an extension of a colonial dream in the days when old Ensign George Nixon was fighting for the independence of Delaware from the British. People who had drifted West had broken the family ties, by and large, and most of them were very dim about their heritage. Indeed, it made no difference in a land where immigration was increasing every year, and the concerns were for the world of NOW and the future, not for the pretenses of the past. Frank Nixon's future lay before him, bounded by his desires, ambitions, and his luck, for that is the way the country was growing and going.

He had chosen the street railway business, and that summer of 1901 the future looked bright. The Interurban that had been promised came into being that year, with modern cars painted a royal blue. There was excitement in the opening, for the coming of the loop line promised new business to Columbus. Farmers could now send their produce "fresh and dew-covered" from orchards and fields to the city markets. Passengers could ride from Cleveland and Toledo to Columbus and Cincinnati on the new line, which meant new customers for the stores. Families could now escape the heat and dust of the cities in the evenings and take a ride into the country in these marvelous new cars with their air brakes and reversible seats.

Columbus was justly proud of this street railway system, for it was about the best in the country, and had the lowest fares. There was a public feeling about such franchise, too, which seems somehow to have been lost in a more modern America—that the company existed for the benefit of the public. When the franchise was granted, the company promised the seven tickets for a quarter but also that when the gross annual receipts of the company should reach the sum of $1,750,000, tickets must go to eight for a quarter.

As far as employers were concerned, the street railway company was regarded as enlightened. The men worked nine hours a day (six days a week) and if they worked overtime they were paid extra. The company had started a profit-sharing plan, paid on total wages at the same percentage that profits were paid out to stockholders on their stock, and any man who had worked for the company for six months was eligible. Then, of course, there was the union, which had its beneficial association. The men paid dues and the dues went for weekly payments to the sick and the relief of widows and orphans. If a man rose so high as to become a motorman or conductor, when he had been with the company for five years he got a free uniform every year, and when he had been there ten years he got two uniforms a year. At Christmas married employees got a turkey from the company, and Frank Nixon and the other single men received a silver dollar. All this was in addition to the annual picnic and the union picnic, and endless get-togethers of the single men to go to the baseball games or the fights or the pool hall.

Frank Nixon received one serious shock that year, and it was a rather personal one for him, when President McKinley was shot by an assassin at Buffalo and died a few days later. All Ohio mourned, for McKinley was a favorite son of the Buckeye State, but not many had met him, as had Frank Nixon. Not many men in Columbus could say that the President had talked "horses" with them, as Frank could.

But life went on. Frank moved to 60 East Elm Street and stayed there a year. In 1903 he moved again to 308 Hubbard Alley, where he lived for three years, and then, in 1906, he moved to 502 South High Street.

That was the year he was promoted to motorman, and put on the dark double-breasted suit with its gray piping and brass buttons, and the big chain on which he carried his watch so he could keep the car on schedule. His cousin Bert joined Frank in Columbus at about this time, and Frank helped him get a job as a conductor on the street railway. But then, the winter of 1906 brought an incident that soured Frank Nixon on the street railway company and on Columbus. It was a matter of common complaint among the motormen that they were not given the consideration a man should have. They ran the cars from the open vestibules in front and back, and while the cars themselves were heated by stoves, the vestibules were not. On cold and windy nights the life of the motorman was miserable. One such bitter night Frank Nixon's feet froze, and his love for the company and Columbus suffered a severe reverse.

The system was not that satisfactory, either. As a motorman, Frank was paid twenty cents an hour—$1.80 a day if he worked nine hours, and he often worked much longer. As a motorman his position was slightly better than if he had been a conductor as was his cousin Bert, because the company was forever snooping on conductors, suspecting them of dishonesty in handling the receipts. The union in the streetcar company was the Amalgamated Association of Street and Electric Railway Employees, founded by William D. Mahon, a Columbus man, but it was very weak here because the company was regarded as "paternalistic," with its turkeys and silver dollars for Christmas and, besides, many men who took jobs with the railways regarded the work as temporary, until they could move up in the world.

There had been strikes in 1890 and 1892 but they had been defeated. The union was so ineffective that there was no point turning that way to seek a change in the conditions of the motormen.

Still, Frank made an attempt. He got together with the motormen and persuaded enough of them to back him so that a complaint could be made. The company did nothing.

Frank decided to try the political tack. Ohio was gearing up for a political campaign, and with the workingman population the affairs of the workers on the street railway would be of more than moderate interest. Accompanied by another motorman named Miller, Frank went to see a Mr. Brant, a young Columbus lawyer who was running for the state Senate. Frank had a proposition.

"If you'll help us get legislation against open vestibules," he said, "we motormen will help you get elected to the state Senate."

Brant agreed to the deal. Frank went to his motormen

and organized them and the conductors to work for their candidate, and he *was* elected. Then, Senator Brant introduced a bill to improve the working conditions of Ohio streetcar motormen and conductors. Primary in the bill was a provision for vestibule doors and heating for the whole streetcar, and not just part of it. General Manager Edward K. Stewart of the Columbus Railway and Light Company led the fight against the bill, and complained that it would increase costs so greatly that the company could not reduce fares, might even lose money. But the bill passed, and went through the House of Representatives as well. It soon became a law.

Without an effective union in Columbus, the leaders of the drive to force the company into changes had very little protection against the management. No workingman really dared stand up openly against the company in those days; it would be another three years before the men were organized enough to strike effectively. In 1907, if a number of men got together and asked for a raise—they were fired out of hand. General Manager Stewart was a very determined man, and "labor skates" were not going to take him over if he had anything to say about it.

Frank Nixon saw that he had no future with the company. So he decided to leave Columbus and go West to find new opportunity in his life. He had already broken with Vinton county. Back home they didn't expect Frank to return; they knew he had always talked a lot about seeing the world. So it was no surprise to the Nixon household at Hue when he announced that he was going to California. A friend from the line named Alfred Caldwell decided he would go too. So they packed their bags, and took the train for the West, bearing letters of recommendation from friends, but not one from Manager Edward K. Stewart.

In California, Frank Nixon found a job with the Los Angeles street railway, which had just started a line that ran south to Long Beach and inland to Whittier. It was a long run, and some cars were housed in Los Angeles and others in Whittier. Since the day began at Whittier, Frank Nixon lived there. And it was soon after he arrived in California that he met a young woman named Hannah Milhous.

14

The Proud Old
Name of Milhous

Hannah Milhous, who was to become the mother of a President of the United States, came from a proud line whose antecedents stretched so far back that many members of the Milhous clan in California felt that Hannah married beneath her when she accepted Francis Anthony Nixon as her husband. If the name Milhous was not a generally known name in America until the coming to prominence of Richard Milhous Nixon that is because the earlier generations of Quaker Milhouses chose to remain aloof from the mainstream of American society. In Quaker literature and Quaker records the name of Milhous is very well known indeed, as it is in the archives of the once-Quaker state of Pennsylvania.

Milhous. Milhaus. Millhouse. Mulhausen. A family genealogist has satisfied himself that the family can be traced back for centuries, and derives from Alsace Lorraine originally; that Milhous connections were responsible for founding Muhlhausen and Mulheim in Germany, but that the American branch of the family came from a line of Protestants who arrived in England in the fourteenth century and became prominent in the Quaker movement. They moved to Northern Ireland, to Antrim and Armagh. In the seventeenth century Thomas Milhausen and his wife Elizabeth lived at Carrickfergus. John Milhouse, his son, and the widow Elizabeth moved to Timahoe in Kildare county, but they did not stay there long nor leave much record. In 1729 Thomas Milhous, the son of John, came to America with his wife, the former Sarah Miller, and their children John, who was seven years old, and baby James, who was two. They settled in New Garden, in Chester county, Pennsylvania, and on December 28 attended the monthly meeting of the Society of Friends, where they produced certificates from the Meeting of Dublin, Ireland, showing that in the spring they had been members of the meeting there and were entitled to transfer where they would as good, practicing Quakers. The certificates were accepted, and the Milhouses settled down to a productive and deeply religious life in the new land.

The place to which they came was new enough, having been settled by Irish Quakers in 1711, who bought their land from William Penn, Jr. The settlers called the place New Garden after the New Garden Meeting in County Carlow, Ireland, and created a township of the same name. They bought land at a dollar an acre, and some of them had holdings in the thousands, but these were soon reduced, by sales to others, to manageable family farms of two hundred acres or so. Thomas Milhous bought around two hundred acres in a rectangular plot, not far from New Castle county—in fact about ten miles from the place where James Nixon settled in Brandywine Hundred, although of course these families lived in separate colonies and never met.

With the help of other Quakers, Thomas Milhous built his log cabin to house the furnishings the family had brought from Ireland, bought animals and feed and seed, and began to farm in the manner of his neighbors. The Friends were notable, even here, for their conservatism of dress. The early settlers, including the Quakers, had dressed in coarse cloth and deerskin; leather breeches and a long collarless coat that reached to the knees, waistcoat, neck cloth, woollen stockings, low buckle shoes, and a beaver hat. The women wore linsey and worsted and hoop skirts. But by the time the Milhouses arrived a reaction to the worldliness of Philadelphia had set in among the Quakers, and the meetings warned their members against:

"That immodest fashion of hooped petticoats or the imitation of them, either by something put into their petticoats to make them set full or wearing more than is necessary, or any imitation whatsoever, which we take to be but a branch springing from the same corrupt root of pride. And also that none of our friends accustom themselves to wear gowns with superfluous folds behind but plain and decent; nor without aprons; nor to wear superfluous gathers or plaits in their caps or pinners; nor to wear their heads dressed high behind; neither to cut or lay their hair on their foreheads or temples. . . . Also that friends avoid the unnecessary use of fans in meetings, lest it divert the mind from more inward and spiritual exercise which all ought to be concerned in. . . ."

And as for the men, they were abjured to lay aside the expensive and showy wigs that had been the fashion (even William Penn wore them regularly) and to devote themselves to things of the spirit.

The women spun and knitted, cooked, canned, washed, sewed, did the dairying and made candles. The men made harnesses and shoes and simple metal implements and worked the farm. They carried their produce to market at New Castle and Chester and sometimes at Philadelphia, where they traded for hats, linen, knives, scissors, and even for ribbons and lace for the women.

Life was not all prayer and solitary labor. The Friends got together at harvest time, or for a wedding or a funeral, or to help one another to raise a new house or barn. But the mainstay of their life was their association with the Society of Friends, which transcended the normal bonds of church. The Friends obeyed the laws of the colony, but they felt more bound by the laws of their own society, and the strongest force in their lives was the "meeting."

The meetings were held on First Day and on Fifth Day, and after a few years of settlement in New Garden, when the men had been able to establish themselves on the farms, they built a meeting house, and at the appointed hour the Friends assembled there, coming afoot or on horseback. There was no steeple, nor any bell. They walked into the plain room and sat down on the hard, unpainted benches, the men on one side and the women on the other side of the house. First would come a few minutes of silent prayer in which the devout Friends would "seek the soul's communion with the Eternal Mind." Then some person would arise, face the meeting, and deliver a spiritual message. It might be a traveler from another meeting. It might be a local person. The vocation of minister was bestowed on those members of the meeting who indicated an aptitude for it, a lack of worldliness that was observable, a feeling for humanity and God that transcended that of their fellows.

The Quakers were not superhuman, and occasionally a tired farmer would fall asleep in the meeting. And then some ardent person, like old John Salkeld of Chester, might take action, as Old John did one day when he spotted several of his neighbors drowsing through the message.

He jumped to his feet.

"Fire! Fire!" he shouted, and immediately the sleepy ones awakened.

"Where? Where?" they demanded.

"In Hell," responded Old John sternly, "to burn up the drowsy and unconcerned."

The prayers continued, until the meeting came to an end, which was signified by two Friends in the gallery solemnly shaking hands. This handshake was passed down, seat by seat, through the house, and the Friends began to wend their way out of the meeting house. Outside they would stop and chat, and strangers would be invited here and there to come home to dinner.

There were other kinds of meetings to transact business, but these were preceded by meetings for worship. At the end of the worship, shutters would be drawn down from the ceiling, screening the men from the women, and the men would conduct the masculine business of the meeting, while the women tended to women's affairs.

There was a quarterly meeting, which involved the meetings of the entire district, and this rotated from one meeting place to another, so it meant quarterly meeting time was also a time of family visiting and much cooking and baking. The yearly meeting was held in Philadelphia, and lasted a week, which also meant a trip to the city, and opportunity to see and buy things that could not be gotten locally.

But the important working body of the society, in a social sense, was the monthly meeting, where disputes were settled, delinquents were "reformed" if that seemed possible, or punished, or worst of all "disowned." Applicants for membership were tested by the monthly meeting, and received into the meeting. Children's education was examined here. The certificates of good standing, such as those that Thomas and Sarah Milhous brought from Ireland, were granted at these meetings so that members could move on and enjoy their religion elsewhere.

The meeting almost always had a place for the disciplining of the young, who tended to fall away from the straight and narrow path of righteousness.

"As many paces as the Person takes in the Dance, so many paces of Steps they take towards Hell," declared the elders, and when young people were discovered to have danced, there was no end of commotion. So, too, cards were declared to be "engines of Satan," and the card players were punished, as were Nehemiah Hutton and Joseph Hadley, who were discovered in the act by the elders of the New Garden Meeting. At one spring monthly meeting, the charge was brought:

"New Garden Preparative Meeting has Acquainted this Meeting ye Nehemiah Hutton has been found In Company keeping & playing Cards which has brought reproach upon truth & friends, & this Meeting has put him upon to Draw up Something for ye Clearing of truth Against ye Next Monthly Meeting which he Acknowledges and is willing to do.

"Joseph Hadley being Also in Company with Nehemiah Hutton and had ye Cards in his hand which he is Sorry for yet he Condemn the Same So far as he is Guilty."

Two months later the miscreants appeared before the meeting.

"Nehemiah Hutton has given in a paper Condemning himself for his playing at Cards which paper this meeting receives & orders him to read ye signed Paper in ye place where he was playing & in ye Presents of Benjamin ffred & William Halliday & that they give an account to ye next Monthly Meeting & that he is desired to forbear coming to meetings of business until friends be better Satisfied with him as to his conversation and Sincerity to truth. . . ."

The same punishment was meted out to Joseph Hadley. The elders were not satisfied with their protestation of reformation, and had decided to hold over their heads the threat of expulsion. To a sincere Friend this expulsion was a kind of death on earth, an excommunication—and it produced among the faithful adherence to the precepts of the society.

The abjuration of worldliness, however, did not extend to liquor in those times, for liquor was definitely a part of frontier life, and was used freely. Only later did the Quakers embrace the general cause of abstinence to include temperance. But the New Garden Meeting, like others, advocated temperance in the use of alcohol at all times, and took offending drinkers sternly to task.

Poor Nehemiah Hutton was an offender in this category too, and the meeting so recorded:

"Whereas Joseph & Nehemiah Hutton being both overtaken in Drink in ye county of New Castle & have condemned ye Same Under their hands which papers were read here to ye Satisfaction of this Meeting. . . ."

So the Huttons were let off.

But if the habit persisted, the meeting was harsher, as with poor Mary B——ly. In the summer of 1736 the New Garden Meeting announced that she "has been Addicted to Drunkenness for some years past & has been visited and Admonished against it Divers times yet does not Desist from it." A month later poor Mary was disowned by the Meeting.

The justice was swift and harsh, as it had to be to preserve order. One day in 1729 Roger Keirk was "rasseling for a wager" and was brought before the meeting for unbecoming conduct. He did not seem to be truly repentant but "Rather a cavelling Contentious Spirit" and the meeting disowned him, although his father was a respected member. And when two members engaged in a fight, and one seemed truly repentant but the other did not, the repentant one was punished by deprivation of his privilege to sit in business meetings, but the other was disowned.

Thomas Milhous and his wife were conscientious members of the New Garden Meeting and had no troubles with the others. They tended their affairs and raised the family. Son Thomas was born in 1731, son Robert in 1733, daughter Sarah in 1736 and son William in 1738.

In 1744 Thomas Milhous moved to Pikeland township, still in Chester county. This township had been granted to Joseph Pike, a wealthy Quaker merchant of Cork, by William Penn in 1705. It consisted of ten thousand acres of land, lying north of the Great Valley, and it was held together until Pike died, when his son Richard began to divide and sell land. Thomas Milhous found opportunity here, and was one of the earliest purchasers, along with

Samuel Lightfoot, Michael Lightfoot, and Timothy Kirk. So it was here that most of the family grew up.

William Milhous, who was to be the great-great-great-grandfather of Richard Milhous Nixon, was married to Hannah Baldwin, a Chester county girl who was related to the Lightfoot family, in a Quaker ceremony.

To the Friends, marriage was a sacred institution, but it was also governed by the human beings of the meeting. To be married within the church, the couple must appear at two monthly meetings to "pass meeting" and get consent. A committee was appointed to make a searching inquiry into their behavior and "entanglements," and if they were cleared all was well. The men's meeting investigated the men, and the women's meeting investigated the women. At the second meeting the committees reported, and the meeting gave or withheld its consent. And it might withhold consent, if one had been dallying with another man or woman, or even if the young man had not secured the consent of the father of the girl before he began to court her. Such problems might be resolved, but they were resolved within the discipline of the meeting, or the offenders were disowned. A Quaker who married outside the Society, in a church or by a priest, was disowned, and Old Swede's church over in Delaware, where George Nixon was married, was also a favorite place for runaway Quaker youths to come and be married in the sight of man if not the sight of their parents' God.

The Quaker marriage was very simple. On the appointed day, in simple clothes, Hannah Baldwin rode to the meeting house on a pillion behind her father. They entered the place without ceremony, there she met William Milhous and they stood up together. It was October 22, 1767.

William took Hannah by the hand.

"Friends," he said, "in ye fear of ye Lord and before this assembly I take this my friend Hannah Baldwin to be my wife promising with ye Lord's assistance to be unto her a loving and faithful husband until death separate us."

The couple then signed the marriage certificate, and Hannah assumed the name of her husband. All the members of the meeting signed the certificate, and the newly married couple went out of the meeting, where someone had transferred the pillion from Hannah's father's horse to that of William. They rode off together to their new home, while the members of the meeting gathered at the Baldwin house for a celebration that was bountiful, but not too bountiful, because even an elder could be called to account by the meeting for making "unnecessary provision."

15

The Milhouses
and What Is Right

There were troubles along the Maryland-Pennsylvania border in the 1730s, over lands and rights of citizens of the two colonies, and only the restraint of the Friends on the Pennsylvania side prevented the outbreak of serious violence. They were always against violence as a method of settling dispute, these Quakers, and if their acquaintances on the other side of the border could not understand them, at least they grew to respect the Friends for having the courage of their convictions.

In 1739 England declared war against Spain, and recruiters came to Chester county to raise a force for an expedition against the West Indies. It was not a very successful effort. Five years later war was declared against France (French and Indian wars) and again the good Quakers refused to participate. But in 1753, when the French invaded western Pennsylvania, many Quakers sympathized with the cause, although the most strict of them would not allow themselves to support the war in any way. In Philadelphia there were difficulties between the governor and the Quakers of the Assembly. The result was that no persons in Pennsylvania could be forced to take up arms against their consciences, and some of the meetings did disown members who took up arms. They were particularly angry when the governor issued a proclamation offering a premium for scalps of the Delaware Indian enemies who were fighting with the French. And the Quaker effort was devoted to making peace with the Indians as quickly as possible.

William's father, Thomas Milhous, was then a member of the Goshen Meeting, having transferred from New Garden when he moved to the new farm. In 1757 that meeting disowned Francis Meehan "for that he voluntarily inlisted himself as a soldier in military service & intends to continue there." Two years later the meeting was carrying on a vigorous but not totally successful campaign to prevent its members from furnishing anything to the troops, or furthering the military effort. ("There is a degree of Love and Unity subsisting among us tho' unity hath suffered some interruption on account of the occasion of furnishing Waggons and Horses. . . .") These wagons were for Brig. Gen. John Forbes' expedition west against Fort Duquesne (Pittsburgh).

William and Hannah Milhous were also members of the Goshen Meeting, as were her parents, the Baldwins. Like all Quakers they were troubled when men were speaking out loudly and bitterly against the King and the British government at home. Most particularly, however, these Quakers were concerned with the salvation of their own souls, and their own deportment in these times of trial. One day early in 1772 after the meeting at the meeting house Hannah Milhous and her father talked about a recent altercation with some other person. The conversation was not completely satisfactory to Joshua Baldwin, and when he returned home he sat down and wrote his daughter a letter.

"Dear Child

The answer thou gave me at the Meeting House today somewhat troubled me and occasioned me to think something of the effect of a truly Christian Spirit and disposition of mind viz: Suppose my relation or friend manifests coolness or disregard toward me, let it be with cause or without, ought I not to go to him or her in meekness and good will, and by frequently so doing and giving no occasion of offense, is it not the likeliest way to provoke one another to love and good works and exercise patience toward such as the adversary may have got some advantage over. Or will not doing evil for evil strengthen Satan's Kingdom in our hearts till at last perhaps open difference and contention get in and maybe hatred which wholly banishes Heavenly mindedness. Remember Christians must and will love their enemies. Now it may be so that we do not at all times feel our minds disposed as above pointed out, but instead thereof coolness and a disposition for shyness may attend our minds, and we cannot help ourselves, even if we have some desires to be otherwise we cannot cause our selves to be so—Well what must we do then, poor helpless creatures, Why it is our duty to remember that help is laid up on one that is mighty to save and able to deliver from all the snares and temptations of the adversary, both inwardly and outwardly and be sure not join in with any bad disposition that may present to our minds. And watch unto prayer continually, and desire to be delivered from every evil spirit or inclination. If we keep to humility and meekness we shall be truly incapable of our own weaknesses, and that we are daily liable to many. Therefore we shall not be apt to take offense at any that may not conduct wisely toward us, neither willingly give offense to any but rather manifest forebearance and patience towards such with desires that they may have a true sight of their condition and state."

As good Quakers, the Milhouses joined their neighbors in resisting violence and war, and Thomas continued in the faith until he died in 1770. Young sons Robert and William and his widow each shared a third of his estate. But by that time, his elder sons James, John and Thomas were all well established and living on places of their own in Chester county. Thomas was an elder of the New Garden monthly meeting. John was active in the Western quarterly meeting.

Although the Milhouses were particularly aware, as were all Pennsylvanians, of the difficulties of the colonies with the home government in Britain, the War of the Revolution came as a frightful and unwelcome shock to the Quakers. When asked to support the war, here is a view they gave one outsider:

WHAT THEN IS WAR?

"War is a game of hazard, at which kings and rulers and their courtiers play, leaving, we, the people, to pay the forfeits which they incur without treasure and our lives.

"Already the educational and financial resources of the nation are profusely lavished upon the gamesters to fit them for war; already the richest emoluments, the highest honors which it can bestow, are given to the warriors; already the Western domain is made a camping ground for the new recruits, and Indians the targets for them to practice on; already the candidates for almost any office, civil or military, from a constable to the President, are fain to rest the claim upon their military record. Such appears to be war in the popular estimation.

"But from whence come wars and fightings? Come they not even of your lusts, the lust for power, the lust for conquest and plunder, the lust for fame, the lust for revenge? Divest war of its meretricious tapestry, its emoluments, its honors, and the halo of false glory which has been thrown as a pall over its atrocities, and it soon sinks into unmitigated, coldblooded murder. . . ."

This was a Quaker view, and the Milhouses were leaders among the Quakers, who so far opposed the War of the Revolution that they would not support it in any way.

From one Chester county meeting, Judge Blackburn

enlisted, early in the war, and was subsequently disowned, as were his relatives Joseph, Thomas, and Anthony, when they too joined the army.

The position of the Friends was against war, flatly and simply. They called themselves friends of liberty, they wanted to maintain their civil rights, but they did not want to do so by "illegality and revolution." They were unwilling to help the British, but determined that they would take no part in the war itself. When the war became a fact, the Quakers in Philadelphia issued a statement of neutrality. There were some Tories, and some revolutionists among them, but the vast majority would take no part in the war.

The revolutionary government of Pennsylvania did not appreciate this attitude on the part of the Friends, and decided that if they would not fight, they would pay for the privilege in heavy war taxes. The Quakers refused to pay the taxes. So their property was seized to the value of the taxes and fines levied on them. Typical is this incident involving George McMillan, a Quaker of York county:

"On the 22nd of 1st Month, 1778, between one and two o'clock in the afternoon came Henry Lewis, James Perkeson, and John Witherow to my house and Lewis told me he had an Execution for me for substitute money, telling he would take my horses if I did not pay him. Producing an Execution bearing date 22 of 1st month, 1778, for 100 dollars with cost and cost accruing for substitute money alleged to be laid out for me the while. I refused to pay. He seized on two of my horses and bore them off for sale, which was done 26 of Instant January and one sold the other returned —worth £30 silver money. . . ."

Poor Quaker McMillan was fined and attached again and again:

"6 month 1778—Came James Perkeson and John Moody to my house . . . and then searched my drawers and took 3 pound ten shillings. . . .

3 month 1779—Came John Moody and opened my

desk in my absence and took for a state tax £5, a muster
(tax) 1. 3 12 s and an Indian substitute fine, £4. . . .

11 month 1779—the same Moody came and searched
as before and found 37 dollars and took it in my absence. . . ."

It went on, wheat, money, hay, sometimes by the wag-
onload, twice in 1780, three times in 1781, twice in 1782,
and again in 1783, 1784, 1785—but the farmer never for-
swore his principles or gave willingly.

The Milhouses stoutly refused to support the war, and
were active in the formation of the Committee on Conference, whose duty was to advise and encourage Quakers to
resist. The committee collected the records of suffering by
the Quakers and reported on them to the monthly meetings,
visited the authorities and tried to reason with them in behalf of the Friends. The members also met once a month
with the quarterly meeting (district) to confer on united action.

William's brothers John and Thomas Milhous served
on this committee for eight years, visiting even General
Washington to state the case of the Quakers, and encourag-
ing the resistance to the war.

They suffered for their adherence to conviction. The
New Garden Quaker community was distrained of more
than 1600 pounds worth of farm produce, animals, and
food, during the year 1781. Thomas Milhous alone lost four
head of cattle, four sheep and eighteen bushels of oats,
taken by the authorities. And the forced taxes continued
throughout the war. They came from both sides. There is no
record of what the Milhouses or others lost to the British
who long occupied the area, but it was at least as much as
was taken from them by the revolutionaries. All this time
they had provided for their own people who were left desti-
tute or harmed by the demands of the army. They had seen
their lands fought over as the battle raged through and
around them.

Finally the struggle came to an end, and the Quakers were able to settle down once again and live a more normal life.

With the peace, the Milhouses, or some of them, began to feel the same pressures that the Nixons felt in their lands over in Delaware, and to respond in much the same way. William and Hannah had spent the war years raising their family of nine. Little Mercy had been born in 1768; Sarah in 1771, Samuel in 1773, Rachael in 1776, Joshua in 1778; Hannah, 1780; William, 1783; Phebe, 1785; and Jane in 1790. That latter year was also a year of tragedy for the Milhouses, because son Joshua died.

The older children of William Milhous married and began to raise families in Pennsylvania. Thomas's son, William Milhous, remained on the family farm for a while, but in 1805 he moved to Belmont county, Ohio, taking the children who were young enough to still be dependent.

William Milhous, Jr., who was to become a President's great-great-grandfather, went with his family to Belmont county, although he was then twenty-two years old and could have remained behind had he so chosen.

The Milhouses bought land in Colerain township in Belmont county, although when they went there it was not yet organized as a township. The land had been settled as early as 1788, and by 1798 there were enough people farming in the area to justify the establishment of a tannery. A year before the Milhouses came, John Harris built a flour mill of logs, and a little later Burton Stanton built another.

The Milhouses came here because they found the area was being settled by Friends, some of them from the South, who were moving this way to escape the evils of slavery. The Pickerings came from Virginia, Howards and Steels from North Carolina, Milhouses, Vickerses, and Malins and Whartons from Pennsylvania, and after they built their rude log houses they built a meeting house. It was new country, heavily timbered then, and consisted of rolling hills and deep ravines. It was drained by Indian Wheeling Creek

on the south and west, and by the south branch of Shoot
Creek on the north and by Glenn's Run on the east. The
farmers were lucky, beneath the land and cropping out here
and there were veins of bituminous coal. The Quakers
marked off their lands with rail fences to keep the animals
confined, planted their grain, and kept their way of life.

The Milhouses wrote enthusiastically back to Pennsylvania about the land and the freedom they were finding in
the Ohio country. Two years after they had established the
farm, William Junior went back to Chester county and
married Martha Vickers, the daughter of a neighbor and
Friend, and then they returned to Ohio.

Many other Friends came west at this time, and settled
in this region of Ohio, including several Milhous relatives.
They kept in close touch with many letters and visits back
and forth as often as weather and work would permit. A letter of this time, from one of the Milhous women, gives an
indication of life in this frontier land early in the nineteenth
century.

". . . the house is one of the roughest kind of cabins
(we are at no loss for fresh air during the coldest parts of
winter, it was rather too plenty). . . . all in one room
though we intend to have a partition run through it. It
stands low on the side of a hill. The spring is down in a
gully some 10 or 15 feet with perpendicular banks. In
muddy weather it is a difficult task to get it out. But by digging we can have water in the kitchen if we choose—"

The family had cleared some four acres around the
house, which was the subsistence farm. The rest would have
to wait.

The Milhous cabin door faced the south, into a garden
fence with posts and a rail fence to keep the stock out. That
winter the mistress of the house was anxious for spring to
come so she might be at work, planting sweet potatoes and
"other worldly comforts."

But her mind that winter was not all on worldly things.
She longed to see Hannah. Her letter continued: ". . . we

could spend our time very agreeably climbing about over the hills and rocks just for the sake of being romantic. I think we could compose a very good novel between us in these hills. . . ." These were not rough country people like Ohio's Nixons; the Quakers were sensitive, intellectual people who chose to live simply on the land and to brave the frontier. With them to this far country they carried books, and after the meeting house was built (often in it) the Friends arranged to have a school for their children, where they were taught the ways of man and the ways of God.

Another basic difference between Milhouses and Nixons was their attitude toward family. When old George Nixon left Delaware for Pennsylvania, he passed out of the Nixon family picture. Five years after he was gone from New Castle county, when James Nixon died in Brandywine Hundred, no one there knew exactly where George was. The Ohio Nixons later lost track of the Pennsylvania Nixons. But this casual attitude toward family didn't exist with the Milhouses. They kept in close touch with one another.

And their thoughts were of simple happiness: ". . . I often think of evenings how pleasant it would be to be transported to your cheerful fireside for an hour or two," wrote Mary Milhous to her sister-in-law Hannah Milhous. "I could then talk ten times more than I have written in the same time. But so it is and must be. I should like to hear of thee coming to the wise conclusion of changing thy name, at least the last of it. If so I shall begin to look for an invitation to the wedding. But it is not altogether self interest that makes me wish it. It is for thy own happiness and comfort. I feel now is the time, my dear sister, to make a choice of a companion for life. It may be hard to give up the enjoyments of a single life, but depend upon it thee will be fully rewarded and overpaid for any little sacrifice of that in the enjoyment of domestic happiness and the comfort of home. All thee has to do is to choose wisely. Do not look to the exterior, look to the heart. Look to the disposition and if thee

chooses wisely one suitable to thy own the result will be a
happy union. . . ."

This particular letter was hand-carried by Mary's husband, who was coming to visit William Milhous, Jr., and his
family, who now lived in Concord, in Belmont county.
Mary closed hastily, noting that she had made molasses
("but it has been a very poor season for it here") and had
been making candles from tallow given her by her mother.

The winter weather in Ohio was a difficult cross for the
Milhouses to bear, it was so much colder and somehow
seemed more damp than their native Pennsylvania.
". . . as cold days as I have ever felt," Mary Milhous had
written. "The cold was no way backwards about coming
into our cabin, but putting on something a little less than a
cord of wood on the fire and turning first one side then the
other we contrived to keep both from freezing. . . ."

At thirty, William Junior was already suffering from
"rhumation" or rheumatism, which gave him much pain in
the winter months. The family treated his ailment with
sympathy but with the dedication of the Quakers. From
Pennsylvania, William's sister Rachel Lightfoot wrote the
Milhouses stoically: "Often, very often I think of you and
wish your welfare in every way, and feel a great deal for my
poor afflicted Brother, and hope the suffering he has to endure may wean him from things here below and set his
affections on things above, believing when time is no more,
he may (if rightly engaged) find a rest eternal in the heavens, which is more to be desired than any thing this world
can bestow with all its pomp and grandeur. . . ."

The War of 1812 came, but it did not seriously affect
the people in these backwoods. There were nothing like as
many calls upon them by their neighbors as there had been
in the War of Independence, and the Friends could keep to
themselves (as they did) and keep their opposition to the
conflict from becoming a community irritation.

At the end of 1813 the senior William and Hannah

Baldwin Milhous took a trip back to Pennsylvania to visit relatives. It was a difficult and expensive (a hundred dollars) journey of two weeks, by way of Washington, Pa., made by a company of eight Friends, using boats and coaches, and when they arrived in Chester county, Hannah was exhausted and remained indoors for ten days to recover. They stayed with the Lightfoots and began visiting their grandchildren.

Hannah wrote home to Ohio about several important matters. First, they had to have their "certificates" from the Concord Meeting. Even though the Milhouses were well known in Chester county, that was the rule. Who in the local meeting would know if they might have fallen from the path and been disowned by Friends in the west otherwise? Friends were trusting of each other, but not in matters of religion. When the certificates came there was difficulty because in the shortage of paper daughter-in-law Martha Vickers Milhous in Ohio had taken the liberty of writing a letter to them on the back of the papers.

Wrote Hannah: ". . . we discovered the great mistake of writing on the back of the certificate, and concluded by all parties that it would not do to draw them on other paper. Some proposed pasting paper on the back, others were not quite satisfied with that, at length it was agreed that a careful hand might scrape it out, and J. Gibbons [her son-in-law] undertook it—after drawing off the letter which kept him several hours, it was neatly done, a stranger would not perceive there had been any writing on it, he said he would rather draw a deed than do such another job. . . ."

The war had created many financial problems. In recent years many banks had been issuing their own currency, and while nearly all money was good in the West, the Western money was not accepted, or was highly discounted in the East. William and Hannah Milhous encountered serious financial difficulties on the way. ". . . thee may recollect we proposed changing in Washington notes from different banks such as would not pass where we were going, on offering when there we were a little surprised to find we had none worth changing. . . ."

Life in the East these days was difficult for those who did not believe in the war. Thomas Vickers, who was William Junior's brother-in-law, wrote to describe the troubles:

". . . A mob in Baltimore lately have carried on the highest that ever was known than before. Indeed they proved themselves even worse than the savage . . . They killed two and wounded many of the others some of whom they left for dead. [One] . . . they beat while they could perceive life in him. Then they stripped him, tarred and feathered and carried him through the streets in a cart after which they set fire to the tar to see if there was life in him, upon which he told them and begged them to shoot him or cut his head off and not torture him in such a manner. He only pretended to be dead in hopes they would leave him. . . ."

The pinch that the Milhouses expected with war, from their old experience, had not yet come too severely in 1814. Rachel Lightfoot wrote:

"We feel little disadvantage from the war as yet. Jamy is off the muster roll by age, and the legislature has paid our taxes this year, every article we have to sell brings a good price, but sugar and salt is double what it used to be. Tea and coffee almost so, in those articles we feel the greatest pinch as we use a good deal of them. I understand fowls have been 1 dollar and 11 pence the couple this winter, and sheep skin as high as five or six dollars, butter has been half a dollar a pound."

The elder Milhouses spent the winter with the Lightfoots. They had their own bed-sitting room, and the children brought in firewood and served such meals as the old people did not wish to take with the family (William was now seventy-six years old). He wrote home to Ohio, complaining only that "I am sometimes afraid that I shall fall into a kind of habitual Indolence, for want of more exercise. . . ." But they were enjoying themselves, and William

Junior at home was taking care of their considerable estate, which included a section of land at Beaver. Young William collected his father's debts and paid off his creditors. Financial affairs were very tricky in these hard times. Young William had to be careful to have money paid into the bank at Washington, Pa., where they kept an account that would enable him to draw a draft on a Philadelphia bank. Then William Senior could cash that draft in the East, whereas Ohio and western Pennsylvania notes were ever more heavily discounted.

Old William predicted an almost immediate new emigration of Friends west. ". . . Land here had advanced in price enormously, for $50 to $300 per acre, which I believe in part owing to the vast quantity of bank notes now in circulation . . ."

Faced with such prices, and disaffected by the demands of war, the young of the Friends were choosing to move West where land was cheap, and William Milhous then knew of several young families who were preparing the move.

When peace came in 1815, it brought welcome relief, at least from high prices, to East and West. The print calico that had sold for eighty cents a yard now fell to twenty-five cents, and the price of good wollen dropped by half. Flour went to seven dollars a barrel and stayed there. But the Friends were still being punished for their refusal to join the service; William's brother-in-law Thomas Vickers wrote that Friends ". . . are fined $60 each for not marching last fall, some are fined as high as $96. They have let none go clear that I have heard of even though they had the most reasonable excuses, such as not being able to march, etc. which they proved when they were tried before the court martial. . . . I think they will find it difficult to collect the fines. There will be great opposition, if they do undertake it, which there is no doubt, but the . . . Friends have almost universally (those that were drafted and many others) associated to oppose their proceedings as unlawful, respects those that have never mustered. J. Hersey has applied to an attorney in Philadelphia who says that a person that has never mustered or voluntarily appeared in the ranks can not according to the Constitution of the U.S. (not the constitution of the state of Pennsylvania) be tried by a court martial. We are going to have it tried before the Supreme, and if they give it in our favour, Friends will come off clear in this state. . . . I have got a clearance from military duty for life on account of my ear. . . ."

Surprisingly, perhaps, in days when travel was so difficult, the Milhouses did a good deal of it. In the East Martha's brother and his wife made a trip to the Jersey shore, taking four weeks. They went by wagon and barge and sailboat, they stayed in a cabin full of fleas, and shot birds to eat. And as for the Western Milhouses, they came back East, usually with other Friends who were traveling. In the summer of 1817, Martha went home to Chester county to visit her parents, traveling with another Quaker, John Hutchinson of Ohio, who was going that way. Young William could not leave the farm that summer. Times were changing, even in Pennsylvania. And specifically Chester county was changing, not for the better as far as the Friends were concerned, as outsiders moved into the Quaker areas: a Milhous cousin wrote with shock and horror of a robbery of the house, and noted that there had been many robberies in their area. From these Milhouses the thieves got "all the plate," two gold watches, and other valuables. They did not go into the bedrooms, so they did not get the household's money.

In the West there were many changes, too, but these were for the better. When old William Milhous died in Belmont county, in 1826, young William was a prospering farmer with a growing family. William Junior's children were well educated—it was a sign of the growth of Ohio that daughter Jane was sent to a Friends boarding school in Mt. Pleasant, not far away, to finish her education. The Friends had always had a higher regard for education than most of their neighbors in America. Now the Milhouses could indulge it.

But if in the changing times the standards of the Friends in America and particularly those who moved West were to unbend a little, that is not to say the Quakers failed to keep the high stock they put on morality and the appearances of morality. For some reason, William Milhous, Jr., felt constrained to warn his daughter after a deviation from the narrow path.

"Thy time at the school is now about to expire, and I feel much satisfaction from the hope and belief that thee will return home with a pretty good degree of erudition. Indeed it would be a very humbling reflection on me if I had a daughter who attached no higher value to her character than some girls, who it appears from reports circulating through this neighborhood, much to their discredit, have done. A girl possessing delicate and refined feelings would spurn such advances or proposals from young men, let them be who they would, as an insult to their dignity, and could thee be made aware of the humbling estimation with which thy character is viewed in consequence of such conduct even by the young men themselves, if aware of these, no consideration would induce thee to deviate so far from the path of rectitude and respectability.

"Burn this when read. . . ."

Times had changed, but not that much.

16
Joshua Milhous
and Indiana

Joshua Vickers Milhous, who was to be the great-grand-father of Richard Milhous Nixon, was born in Colerain township, Ohio, in 1820, and was a twin. He and his sister Jane were the sixth and seventh of the eight children of William Milhous, Jr., and Martha Vickers Milhous.

Joshua's first teacher was his mother. From her he learned to read and write. Then he went to the local Friends school, where his teacher was Joshua Cope, the husband of his eldest sister. Young Joshua was a thumb-sucker, a habit he continued until he went to school. One day schoolmaster Cope found his young charge sitting in his rude seat, placidly sucking his thumb. The teacher pulled out his pocketknife, and opened the blade, drove it into the plank desk before the boy, and tied his thumb to the blade. Young Joshua turned scarlet. He vowed that as soon as he was big enough he would lick that old teacher good, but he stopped sucking his thumb.

In school and at home Joshua soon became aware of one of the burning issues of the day—the American dilemma of slavery. Nat Turner's Insurrection had come in the summer of 1831, to shock the nation. The Anti-Slavery society had been formed in New England; in Ohio the Lane Theological Seminary in Cincinnati had been destroyed by a quarrel over slavery, and the new Oberlin College formed by the liberal teachers had become a center of abolitionism. The slavery question split Ohioans, because many in the southern part of the state came from slave states, had relatives in slave states, and favored slavery; many others detested slavery, and the discussion of the question never ended. There was talk about passive resistance, which appealed to the Quakers, about resettlement of the Negroes as colonists in Africa, about outright abolition. In Illinois in 1837 an antislavery editor named Elijah Lovejoy was killed in an attack on his office. Two years later, Theodore Weld published an exposé of slavery, *American Slavery As It Is*, a horror story of death and torture, which shocked the nation.

The Milhouses often discussed slavery and the moral issue it raised. One of William's sons wrote while on a trip, "I have got to be almost an Abolitionist." They read abolitionist and proslavery literature avidly, constantly weighing the moral issue. That was their way. The Quakers still lived with one eye on the hereafter, as one of Joshua's cousins made clear in a letter home from a trip in Michigan, where he admitted to actually enjoying the change and the scenery—all evidences of worldly life. Almost guiltily, the cousin wrote about bad health in William's family (another worldly matter).

"Thy patience and fortitude will need daily strengthening . . . and I sincerely desire with thee, that this season of solicitude may prove to be of mutual improvement, a period of serious reflection and close self examination. . . . To be made sensible of the uncertain tenure by which we hold all our earthly enjoyments—though this may be by the disappointments of our schemes, and the blight of promised happiness, often proves a salutary lesson, and when we are thereby enabled to turn our desires and hopes to more permanent good we may indeed esteem such dispensations as messengers of love, intended by Divine Mercy to wean our affections from the perishing things of time, and raise our views to that far more exceeding 'weight of glory' which is the promised portion of the righteous. May we then remember that we are but pilgrims and sojourners bound to a better country, where sorrow and separation are no more known. Everything connected with this world, is from its very nature, perishing and evanescent—the sweetest enjoyments of this life, its pains and its pleasures will soon be past forever from us—let us then be diligent to obtain a more enduring inheritance, while the privilege is yet afford us—let us seek daily for the blessing of Divine Goodness. . . ."

These Quakers approached all problems thus, except the young did not. At about this time, the Milhous youngsters, who were going to the Quaker school at Mt. Pleasant, met several children of the Amos Griffith family of Washington, Pa., who were also attending the school there. Jess Griffith struck up a warm friendship with young Jane Milhous, and Joshua Milhous became very interested in Jess's sister Elizabeth. These interests were encouraged, along the proper lines, by the families involved, and took the form of letters for some part, and those letters indicated that the young were far more interested in the affairs of the world than in the never-ending contemplation of their immortal souls.

The youth worried about the primary American social problem in the fall of 1843, slavery. Intelligent and thoughtful young people, which these Quakers certainly were, gave as much consideration to abolition as their heirs of another century would give to civil rights and social change in the 1970s. Special interest was triggered by a breach in the Indiana district of the Friends society. One group of Friends broke off from all the rest, in disgust over what they regarded as abysmal conduct toward slavery by the inactive majority. This group termed itself the Anti Slavery Friends of Indiana, and began bombarding other districts with letters and pamphlets. The young Griffiths and Milhouses were intrigued. They did not accept the position of the Anti Slavery Friends, for they could not believe the harsh charges these people in their exuberance laid against the more conservative group. But they had food for thought. The Anti Slavery Standard of the dissidents could be put up against the Review of the Declarations of the "si mon pure" Indiana Friends.

Jess Griffith wrote Joshua's sister Jane Milhous, in serious discussion of the matter:

"So thou sees I had document against document, and it was 'tis so' and 'taint so' and it was so and it wasn't so, and when I read them both attentively I concluded they were both false. For surely thought I, a single individual would not openly, publicly and positively contradict a community in so many things if that community had not misrepresented a few things. And on the other hand, I thought a congregation made up of respectable members of a religious society would not and could not lay so many charges to the other party, if many of them had not been true. . . .

". . . I do think the Antislavery Friends should have put on faith and patience and borne with a few more hard thumps before they separated. That Friends of Indiana were too overbearing and treated the subject of Abolition, as well as those who advocated it with too much contempt, who will deny. I think they should have clung together a little longer and submitted to the privations it may have caused them for the cause is worthy. It does really seem to me that the testimony Friends pretend to bear against slavery has dwindled down to a cold sentimentalism . . . We must not go beyond . . . or we will be stigmatized as seditious characters that are going astray. . . . But to keep to the point I think separation will not be without its good points. It will have the tendency to arouse the attention of Friends to the subject. . . ."

The younger Friends, particularly, *were* distressed and concerned about the overriding issue of slavery. Jess Griffith reported with pleasure that the York Yearly Meeting had considered seriously the issue of using slave produce. They came to no strong conclusions, but he said that earlier they would not even have considered the problem—". . . the person who would have introduced such a thing two years back would have been taken as much notice of as a child crying. . . ."

In their correspondence, Jane Milhous made sure that Jess received the most current abolitionist literature, which was plentiful in the Milhous household.

Jane and Jess Griffith remained close friends—but the friendship of Joshua Milhous and Elizabeth Price Griffith ripened into something else, and when in the spring of 1845 the eighteen-year-old Elizabeth finished her studies at Mt. Pleasant and went home to Washington, Pa., she and Joshua kept in close touch. She taught school in Washington county for two years, then in the winter of 1847 Joshua came to Washington and he and Elizabeth were married. It was a marriage of two prominent families of Friends, for the first Griffith had come over to Pennsylvania on the ship with William Penn himself, and had been a key figure in the early development of the Pennsylvania colony.

In January 1848, the young Milhouses returned to Ohio, where they set up housekeeping and farming in Colerain. The children began to come along. The first child was Franklin Milhous, born in November 1848, who would be the grandfather of a President. Second son was Jesse, and then came little Edith. Elizabeth Price Griffith Milhous was a good mother and a distinctive individual. Her marriage with Joshua, like so many marriages of the Quakers, was a true partnership. And in matters of religion, Lizzie was the leader of the family and one of the leaders of the Friends community. Very early, she showed a "calling," or an aptitude for Faith, and became a minister, presiding at christenings, burials, and visiting the sick and watching over the poor—doing all the tasks that paid ministers did in other faiths. She also churned the butter and milked the cow and took care of the chickens and cooked the meals, while Joshua built fences, plowed, cleared land, and kept the farm.

The Milhouses stayed in Colerain, happy on the farm, for several years, but in the 1850s the westering fever struck them. Rather it struck Joshua. Again it was the question of land and a future for the children. Joshua Milhous was a very ambitious man for a Quaker, and wanted to improve their lot. So in the spring of 1853 he left home on a trip West to find a suitable place and buy some land so the family could move on. He went first to Toledo but found nothing in that area. He stayed with friends and relatives there for a few days, then took the Southern Michigan Railroad 250 miles to Chicago. The train passed through Indiana, where he saw rich, rolling land and improved farms.

One neighborhood appealed to him particularly, a small rolling prairie in Laporte county, Ind. He wrote home full of enthusiasm:

"It is a handsome town of several thousand inhabitants, a stirring business place, and is improving rapidly. The country round is splendid farming country. The prairie is small, some five or six miles across, surrounded by excellent timber and is very rich and productive. It is beautifully rolling, is said to be well watered and healthy. If I owned a half section of land on Deer Prairie I would feel that I was a rich man and just as soon as I could do it I would leave hilly Concord and move there. . . ."

But there was a problem—the cost of land again. Five years earlier, Joshua said, he could have bought land for ten or fifteen dollars an acre. Now it was twenty-five to fifty dollars an acre. So, reluctantly he gave up eastern Indiana. "But I am told that a large portion of the northeastern part of this state is very much like it in appearance and can be bought at a reasonable price. . . ."

He had intended to go to Minnesota, but the look of

the land in Indiana dissuaded him. Also he had relatives near Bridgeport, Indiana, and knew there was a community of Quakers there. He was committed to a trip to Iowa, but he kept looking back. He knew the kind of land he wanted, and it was a question of finding it at a price he was willing to pay.

Elizabeth, in the manner of women, was far less eager to move on West than her husband. Her roots were in Ohio and western Pennsylvania, and they ran deep and firm. Joshua reassured her that he was not going to do anything rash, but his letters showed his determination to move on.

He went to Chicago, but was so much concerned with business that he saw little of the city. The train arrived in the evening after dark, and he left the city again the next morning at half past seven.

From Chicago, Joshua traveled ninety-two miles by train to Rockford, then took a stage eighty-one miles more to Galena. The train arrived at Rockford at I P.M., the stage left a few hours later for the West, and what a difference in travel. By stage it took until noon the next day to make the eighty-one miles, over the roughest roads.

Joshua Milhous was now in Nixon country again, the Rock River land where old George Nixon, the Revolutionary soldier, had come with some of his children and grandchildren a few years before. But Rock River country did not appeal to Joshua Milhous—"too much prairie and too little woodland"—and too little water on the land.

He was definite. "I think it is rather a rare occurrence to see a tree in Rock River country away from the running streams large enough to make more than one rail cut, and the largest portion that I saw would have required to have been spliced to do that. I only inquired one place how far they had to haul their firewood. They told me seven miles. Rock River is not the country for us to move to; that's certain."

Joshua wasted little time in Galena, then, but took a hack to Dubuque, Iowa. Later he realized that he should have taken a boat, and chided himself. From Ohio to Dubuque he had spent twenty-five dollars for living and transportation.

So Joshua Milhous searched the countryside. He did go on to Muscatine county, Iowa, and looked around. But no matter how far he went, the vision of the Indiana lands stayed in his mind, and when he came home from the trip West, it was Indiana that drew him, and Jennings county in the south, where he found the combination of open country and wooded land that he desired.

He returned to Ohio, then, and sold off the farm and went ahead to Indiana to buy land.

Elizabeth went to live with relatives and was sorely tried by the whole process of moving, not least because they encountered sharp and even backbiting resistance from Friends of the old meeting. The others accused the Milhouses of worldliness—"breaking up a meeting for the sake of speculation." It is clear that Elizabeth was most reluctant to leave Ohio, but Joshua was insistent. He spoke of the poor quality of the land, compared to the rich land he had found in Indiana, and he would have it no other way. She was only half resigned.

"But we did what we did for the best and if wrong, we have need of deeper humility, and increasing watchfulness into prayer lest another step in the dark plunge us into irretrievable ruin. . . . I have felt (irrespective of the opinions of others) that here we could live very well if we were concerned *more* for our best interest and the prosperity of truth than anything else. . . . Indeed the simple *circumstance of moving* has introduced my mind into the sharpest conflicts I have ever felt. . . . I almost wish that thou will not think of buying even the *prettiest farm* in the west, but stick to the first reason, to rid thyself of so much bodily labor, and take more time to enrich thy mind and strengthen thy hold on eternal things. . . ."

The wrench was indeed great, for Elizabeth was far more spiritual than Joshua, and she felt the change with emotion akin to panic. And yet, so great was her love for her husband that she would go. ". . . although our friends here seem anxious that we should go no further in pursuit of a Home, yet if this is no *Home* for thee, remember that we all wish *thee first to be happy in thy choice,* and then we will try to accommodate ourselves to it."

While she waited, Elizabeth visited the old farm, and could have wept. "Our garden looks well for such poor ground, and everything around seems to look more cheerful than I feel now. . . ." She spoke of their old horse, who had gone lame, "fat and lively," and said of the farm, contradicting herself, that she "did not feel charmed with its beauty."

She went to quarterly meeting, and visited friends and waited. Then came the word. Joshua had bought land and was determined to settle in Jennings county, Indiana, not far from the town of Butlerville. The die was cast.

17

The Worldliness of Joshua

Jennings county, Indiana, had been settled around 1815 by hardy pioneers, who quickly put up cabins and mills along the Muscatatuck River and established a community whose religion was largely Baptist. A brick courthouse was built in the county seat of Vernon in 1818, and civilization progressed so far that in 1853 when Joshua Milhous came to look at land, the county was on its second jail.

The town hoped to become a flatboat port, and the settlers ran rafts down the Muscatatuck with produce that eventually reached New Orleans by water. The mills prospered, the farmers came in to market, and the place grew to be a town, incorporated in 1851.

The incoming settlers were a mixed lot, Methodists and Presbyterians and members of the Christian sect, and Friends, many of these latter people located in Campbell township.

That township began to flourish around 1850. One of

the first settlers was a man named John Morris, who came to Jennings county earlier as a peddler, then established a store at the crossroads of the Madison-Zenas, Vernon-Versailles roads. Then came a farmer named Bryant Trickey, who lived at Butlerville, Ohio, bought eighty acres of land here in Indiana, and started what became the town of Butlerville, when he got the place its own post office and had mail delivery once a week from Vernon.

Storekeeper Morris went back to Ohio, where he met John Burdge, who became interested and then brought other relatives of his named Burdg to the area. William Burdg's wife was a sister of Evan Cope, and of course the Copes were related by marriage to the Milhouses. Campbell township began to grow—this was the manner of settlement of the American West.

By the time that Joshua Milhous came to Jennings county one might expect that it would have been well-settled country, but the West was still raw frontierland. The staple meat was venison, the country was heavily forested, and most land uncleared. The people lived along the streams or housed near springs, and the roads followed the waterways. Most travel was by barge or boat. The place was civilized: the bears and wolves and wildcats and Indians had been driven out, but there were plenty of deer, wild turkey, pheasants, and squirrels for game. Wild pigeons were then so plentiful that a flight of them could cover the sky from horizon to horizon—before they were killed off to disappear forever.

At about the time the Cope family came and Joshua Milhous decided to settle here, many other Friends from Ohio and Kentucky came West. The Kentuckians were coming, largely to get away from slavery. Soon there were two hundred families in Jennings county, most of them in Campbell township.

The Milhouses came and lived in a rough cabin, but not for long. They built a clapboard house, as did their substantial friends in the area, and Joshua Milhous brought apple, peach, plum, and quince trees from the old place. Soon they had a big barn, and a wagon, and a simple carriage. Joshua spent his efforts improving the farm. He saw the need for a nursery in the vicinity. He established one on the farm and it prospered. In season he would go East and buy cuttings and young plants, bring them back and husband them, then take the fruit of his labor out by flatboat and wagon to sell. He was away a good deal of the time, but he loved his family, and he was with them as much as he could be, a friendly genial father. On Saturdays the family would drive into town behind Old George, the wagon horse, and as they came back from market in the evenings, Joshua would air his erudition in the matter of astronomy, pointing out with his whip the North Star and the planets, giving their names and locating them in the heavens for the children. He explained the Big Dipper and the Milky Way, and sometimes he got carried away. Once the lines flopped against the dashboard, and onto Old George's back, and he ambled to the side of the road, carrying one wheel into a ditch. Elizabeth spoke up sharply, telling her husband to watch his driving. "Why, Mother," he said, "if we hadn't gone into that ditch we would never have known how deep it was."

In the beginning of their life in Jennings county there were not enough Friends to make a real meeting, although they built a little meeting house and called it the Grove Meeting. Really these Friends were part of the Blue River Monthly Meeting and remained that way until 1861 when Grove Meeting was chartered after enough Friends had settled in the region.

But from the beginning, Elizabeth Price Griffith Milhous predictably took an especially active part in Friends affairs here. She came by this calling quite naturally. Her mother was even then an active minister. Edith Griffith was still living in Washington county, Pa., where she had been exercising her "gift" since the 1830s. She visited all the Ohio yearly meetings, and even went to the Baltimore and

Philadelphia yearly meetings. Since 1848 she had been running a Sabbath school, which she did with great enthusiasm, in the belief that even Friends were backsliding in these modern days. "I have long believed that we have suffered very serious loss by lack of the early and careful training of the children in the knowledge of the Bible. . . ."

Joshua, for his part, would get up in the morning, come to the table for the big family breakfast to start them off on the right road physically, and he would then read a portion of the Scripture, closing with the 8th, 19th, 34th, or 91st psalm. But he was silent in meeting, while Lizzie got up to make the statements, and to preach.

Elizabeth also organized the first school for the Friends children, and since there was no one else with experience, taught the school herself for the first two years of their residence in the new country. She was paid for her labors, a dollar fifty a day, a goodly increase over what she had received as a girl when she "boarded around" in western Pennsylvania for eight dollars per month.

These years after 1854 brought their trials. More children were born to Joshua and Lizzie, a baby coming just about every two years. Franklin and Jesse and Edith were joined by William and Charles and baby Jane. But Jane died when she was six weeks old, a crushing blow to the loving family.

Perhaps through her normal love of teaching, perhaps through the tragedy of loss that sharpened her compassion, Elizabeth grew constantly more concerned with matters of the soul.

In the absence of a strong group of Friends, Lizzie's depth of interest in the ministerial calling was much appreciated. Blue River Monthly Meeting was seventy-five miles away, nearly a week's journey, and it was the home of the nearest other minister of the faith. So more often than not she was called on for christenings and funerals. One day she was asked to preside at the funeral of an unbeliever, and said she could not do it. But Joshua told her it was her responsibility to the Lord to give such solace to the family as she could, and she managed. This act of faith enhanced her reputation, and she became the leading theological figure of the Friends in this large area.

The Quakers of this part of Indiana had very strong feelings on the subject of abolition, and by and large they were shared by the Jennings county community. Not far away was Newport, the home of the first Anti Slavery Society in the state. Indeed, it had been the New Garden Meeting here which had first split on the subject of slavery, the split that had attracted the attention of the young Milhouses years before.

In the late 1850s as the crisis neared, slavery distressed the Quakers more than ever. The law of the State of Indiana provided that no man could hold slaves in Indiana. That meant that if a slaveholder came to the state and brought his slaves, they became freedmen. But a slave could be taken through the state legally if the master did not buy property and make Indiana his residence. For a long time there had been trouble about slavery in Indiana, because it bordered on slave states. Slave dealers came into the state looking for runaways, and they were not above kidnaping black freedmen and selling them back into slavery. Thus tempers began to rise in the 1840s over this issue. The Quakers were famous—or notorious, depending on point of view—for helping the slaves escape to the North. A "ferryman" was stationed on the river at Madison, and the black fugitives he ferried were brought through Jennings county and kept at various houses, then moved on to Indianapolis and north to Toledo, Detroit, and finally to the safety of Canada. As Indianians lined up, for slavery and against it, those who conducted the Underground Railroad were quiet enough about their work, particularly by the time the Milhouses arrived in Jennings county, because the Law of 1850 had strengthened the provisions for return of runaway slaves and made real trouble for those who helped them.

*The Milhous family around 1890.
The man with the white beard seated
in the center is Joshua Vickers Milhous.
His wife, Elizabeth Price Milhous, is seated
beside him (right). Franklin Milhous, Richard Nixon's
grandfather, is standing second from left, in the back.
His wife, Almira Burdg, is seated next to Joshua (left).
The small child standing between Almira and Joshua is
Hannah, Richard Nixon's mother.*

Left: Amos and Edith Price Griffith.
Right: Elizabeth Price Griffith Milhous—Richard's great-grandmother.

Below: Joshua and Elizabeth Milhous with baby Frank—Richard's great-grandparents and grandfather.

Left: Frank Milhous, Richard's grandfather.
Right: Almira Milhous, Richard's grandmother.

Below: Frank and Almira Milhous and their children.
Almira is in middle row, left. Frank is in middle row, right.
Hannah Nixon, the President's mother,
is at right in top row.

Left: Frank Milhous in top hat and moccasins on his honeymoon.
Right: Frank Nixon as a streetcar conductor.

Below: Frank Nixon with his Sunday school class.

The President's mother at the age of ten.

*Above: The Richard Nixon birthplace
in Yorba Linda, California.*

Right: Hannah Nixon as a young woman.

Main street, Yorba Linda, circa 1915.

*The Nixon family. Frank and Hannah, and the children,
left to right: Harold, Donald, and Richard.*

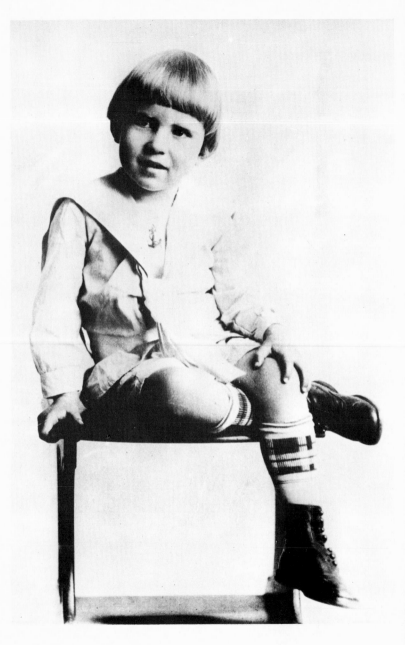

Richard Nixon, four years old.

Right: Richard and Harold Nixon.

Left: Richard Nixon, at age eight, with baby Arthur in Yorba Linda.

Below: Miss Williams' seventh-grade class. Richard is second from right, top row.

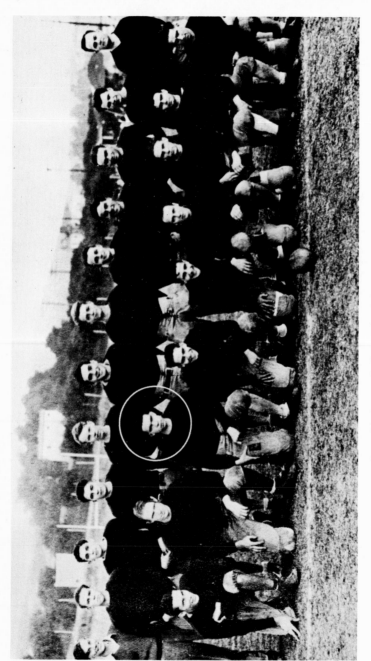

The Whittier football squad. Richard Nixon inset.

Above: Richard as lieutenant commander.

Below: Richard in the South Pacific.

Richard and Pat Nixon.

Richard and Pat Nixon on the beach.
Courtesy Mr. and Mrs. Jack Drown

Left: Richard and his mother, 1946.

Right: Frank and Hannah Nixon, 1952.

*Below: The Nixons, January, 1953. From left, Donald, his wife
Clara Jane; Frank, Hannah, Richard, Pat, Edward.*

The Nixons and their friends Jack and Helene Drown,
Nassau, 1954. Courtesy Mr. and Mrs. Jack Drown

The Nixons at the cottage of J. Edgar Hoover,
La Jolla, California, 1955.

The Quakers of Jennings county were sturdy idealists who continued to help the slaves; yet not all of them could bring themselves to break the law of the land. The philosophical and moral problems for the Friends were very serious, and the dispute created even more serious problems for those in the West, where conditions of frontier life tended to erode some of the stern beliefs and practices of Friends in the old settlements of Pennsylvania.

Vernon had a Negro settlement called "Africa," where freedmen lived. "Africa" was a haven for escaping slaves. Many came across the Jefferson county line, and to the old Edwards farm. On the southeast corner of this place the old slave trail wound through the woods, along the creek, by an old stockade, and to the woods beyond. The slaves hid here in the woods during the day, and traveled at night to Vernon, and to Hege in Geneva township.

One hiding place was Egan cave, above Graham Creek, north of the Edwards farm. Slaves were often kept here for a day or so—even longer when it was known that slave hunters were combing the neighborhood. Farmers also sometimes dug hidden basements beneath their barns, one was sixteen feet by eighteen feet, and deep enough to accommodate six men comfortably. The slaves would come there and the women of the farm would cook for them and care for any wounds or illnesses they might have, then send them on their weary road north. There were stations at Madison and Eagle Hollow and Hanover. In Bigger township, Thomas Hicklin was the manager of the "railroad."

The moral issue of slavery was in part resolved for the Quakers of Indiana with the coming of the Civil War, but then war raised anew the matter of nonviolence and conscience. Nor was the question confined to the North. There were many Quakers in the South as well; indeed one branch of the Milhous family, stemming from the first Thomas Milhous's brothers, had settled in North Carolina. Some Quakers had made their way North rather than live with slavery, but many had stayed, and the Milhouses now learned of their plight. One Southern Milhous relative wrote from Willow Grove, Virginia, in November 1861, of family affairs:

"Dan sold his horse for fear they would come and seize it. Mother is afraid they will come and take her yet. . . . They talk of selling the wagon for they think somebody will come and take it anyhow. Dick Bright is doing some of his big talk again. He says he reckons he will have to take one man at a time and take them to Jail. Furry was standing by, he says you better not try to take one of his boys or he would be a dead man. Mother heard in person that they had taken Dan Plyer, Sam Bolton and one of the Smaltys, George or Bill, prisoners in Richmond. She heard too that they had raised a black flag at the junction. That is a sign they intend to kill all they get. You boys had better watch and not let the Yankees get you for they will do the same. . . . Somebody come after Thomas yesterday and took him to town. They didn't give him time to tell anybody good-bye. . . ."

In the North, Quaker Milhouses faced the old dilemma. Fortunately the children of Joshua and Elizabeth were too young for this war. In 1861, Franklin, the oldest boy, was just thirteen. But cousins were directly affected, and one of them, William Milhous, joined the Union army and became a captain. He was captured and sent to a prison camp in Salisbury, North Carolina. In an earlier war, by a strict Philadelphia-oriented meeting, this William would have been disowned by the Friends, but these were different times. How could a man be morally wrong if he was willing to give his life to stamp out a moral wrong? It was a fit subject for theological debate within the Society, and it was debated endlessly, and often hotly by the Friends, but the result among Westerners in particular, was a softening of the old mores, a change in the hard-nosed pacifism of the past.

A company of the Sixth Indiana Volunteer Infantry was mustered in Vernon that year, and other young men of

the community went off to fight for the Union cause. But
the war was far away, not like the revolutionary struggle
which had been fought figuratively in the backyards of the
Milhouses and the Nixons. Or it was far away until the
summer of 1863.

The Battle of Gettysburg had just ended, and Private
George Nixon of the 73rd Ohio Volunteer Infantry was
lying, dying among the discards of that dreadful struggle,
when Confederate General John H. Morgan began a ride
northward to strike the Union in its soft parts in the West.
He was heading for Jennings county and particularly for
the towns of Vernon and North Vernon, which were important rail centers.

Union soldiers came pouring into Jennings county on
July 10, and centered around Vernon and North Vernon.
Next day Morgan came. His men moved through the countryside, taking food and horses and tack as they went. The
general arrived before Vernon and sent a flag of truce.
The commander of the 61st Michigan regiment, which held
the town, refused to surrender and asked for an hour to
evacuate women and children. To the Union men it appeared that a siege was coming. But Morgan knew that
Union cavalry were not far behind him and he had no time
for siege, so while continuing the threat, he moved his forces
on. Next morning the word was in Butlerville and throughout the county; the Milhouses learned that the countryside
was again safe from the marauders.

Morgan headed east, and went into Ohio, northwest of
Cincinnati on July 13. His troops continued across Ohio,
terrorizing the countryside. They reached Wilkesville in
Vinton county, where the Nixon family lived, on July 17.
They fought a battle on the eighteenth with a superior
Union force, and lost heavily, then headed back across Vinton county to Vinton Furnace and Elk Fork, very near the
homestead of the George Nixon family. They moved to
within one mile of McArthur, then crossed and headed
northeast, having given the Nixons and other citizens of

Vinton county as great a fright as they had given the Mil-houses.

That was the war in Ohio and Indiana, a sort of high-water mark for the Confederacy, to remind the people of the North that they were not safe.

By the time war ended in 1865 the Milhous family of Jennings county was well along in Joshua's worldly drive to comfort and prosperity. Young Frank was now seventeen years old, and had secured all the education his family and the Friends school in the region could afford him. The Mil-houses were prosperous enough to send Frank to Moore's Hill College near Cincinnati. There he completed his edu-cation, and even taught German for a time, and then came back to help with the growing family properties. The main property now was the nursery, and it was known as J. V. Milhous and Sons.

Butlerville, which was the Milhous marketplace, was growing very fast. It had mail twice a week and two hotels. The Ohio and Mississippi railroad line (which would become part of the Baltimore and Ohio postwar re-organization) ran from Cincinnati to Seymour to Indianapo-lis. The oaks of Jennings county were cut for the ties, and to build new roads in the county. Immigration here had stopped for the most part and for the usual reason: the ris-ing price of land, which sent settlers past Indiana and into the unclaimed lands further West. But the Joshua Milhous family was far too prosperous to pick up and leave; their in-vestment in land and the nursery business was quite profit-able enough to support all the boys.

Campbell township grew steadily. The town of Ne-braska was laid out, with a railroad station. A sawmill was built, with a village around it, called Oakdale, which meant there were *three* towns in the township.

This burgeoning civilization brought its problems; one was occasioned by the railroad. Since most farms were not fenced other than by rail fences to protect fields from the stock, the cattle and horses wandered along the railroad right of way, and pigs rooted around the lines for acorns and beechnuts. The trains were forever hitting them, causing delays and damage, until the farmers were pushed into fencing the land.

All things considered, the household of Joshua Milhous could not have been more happy and contented than it was in the spring of 1866. Two more children had been born, the last, Walter, in 1863. But as the Quakers half feared, half expected, when worldly pleasures drew them, human tragedy lurked behind the door—to bring men back to a sounder understanding of their place in the scheme of life. That spring in 1866 spinal meningitis came to the neighborhood, and two of the Milhous children were stricken, almost as by lightning it seemed. Ten-year-old William fell ill. So did baby Walter. William died one day and baby Walter died the next. They were buried together.

This swift tragedy nearly broke Elizabeth Milhous's heart and health. Her spirit could be mended, and was, by her intense faith in the goodness of God. She aroused herself from her weeping to say "Thy will be done" and found that she could believe her words. But the blow to her health was more serious; it took all her strength to support the tragedy and go on. She ate little and lost much weight, and by fall she was thin and pale.

Joshua worried about his wife all summer, and when the harvest was in, he decided to take her home to Ohio to visit Father William, Mother Martha, and have a change. The boys were left at home with a relative, to prune and fertilize and oversee the farm. The girls and Lizzie were loaded into the family's two-horse carriage, and Joshua set out for the adventure of driving back to Ohio. It *was* an adventure, impossible until the end of the war, but now there were roads, and they could make as much as thirty or forty miles in a day.

The trip was a success, all the more so because Lizzie's mother and father, Amos and Edith Griffith, had moved to Mt. Pleasant, Ohio, a few years earlier, so it would be possi-

ble to visit all the immediate family at once. Edith was a
great comfort to Lizzie in her time of need, although the
mother was even more completely immersed now in the
affairs of the Society of Friends than was Elizabeth. Edith
and Amos were planning a trip to England and Ireland the
next year, during which they would visit many meetings, so
many that they would remain abroad until the summer of
1869.

When Joshua and Elizabeth came home, they found
some changes. Among them was a new vehicle which their
son Jess had bought and brought back to the farm. It was a
sulky, a very modern rig with only two wheels, like a cart,
and long tapering shafts. It was, said Jess, the latest thing,
quite the rage of the East. Lizzie clucked over the worldliness of the boy, and Joshua said he had no patience with the
sulky and that Jess was a fool to spend his money on it. He
wouldn't be caught dead riding in this rig, Joshua said.
He'd rather walk.

But when the boys were gone and Lizzie and the girls
were safely in the house, tending to women's chores, Joshua
saw the sulky sitting in the barnyard, the shafts resting up
on top of the rail fence. He decided it wouldn't hurt to sit in
it, just to try it out. Not that he had changed his mind or
anything like that. So he climbed up and in. His weight
overbalanced the delicate shafts, and the sulky tipped over
backward, landing Joshua on the ground on his back, with
the rig on top of him like a tent. Just then someone came
out of the house . . .

Joshua recovered—it was his aplomb that was injured
and nothing else—and when the boys came home they
hitched up the sulky to a horse, and he tried it out on the
road. Even Joshua had to admit it beat riding the roads on
a horse—and he bought the sulky from Jess for his own use,
worldly or not.

Poor Joshua was in constant battle against his worldliness, which was Elizabeth's particular worry about his soul.

She was forever chiding him. He tried to conquer himself. He wasn't always successful, but, oh, how he tried.

Since Joshua had been ten years old he had been chewing tobacco. When he married Elizabeth this disgusting habit became one of the sources of annoyance in the household. Lizzie was forever after him to quit chewing. One day, when Joshua was out on the farm looking over the sheep pasture, he turned his back on a big old ram, who proceeded to ambush him and knock him head over heels down the slope of the hill. Joshua picked himself up lamely and went back to the house, where he was seeking a little sympathy as well as medicine.

Elizabeth listened to his woeful tale about the ram and went to get the arnica bottle. "Yes," she said, "he smelled the tobacco."

That was all the sympathy poor Joshua got that day.

Lizzie's strong feelings went back a good long way, to Ohio—in fact, to the first years of their marriage. Joshua had promised in the honeymoon days that he would give up smoking and chewing, and he had been true to his promise. Then, when Frank was born they wanted to enlarge the house and some carpenters came to work, and boarded with them as was the custom.

Each night after supper Lizzie would clean up the kitchen, and the men would go outside and sit on the fence and smoke and tell stories. Joshua, the soul of helpfulness when they were alone, would go out with them. And the men would light up cigars, and Joshua would look uncomfortable. Finally he confessed to the carpenters that he had quit smoking because his wife wanted him to, and they began twitting him, telling him that he was under his wife's thumb and that he ought to stand up and be a man and do as he pleased. No such thing, he said, and to prove it, he asked for a cigar and lit up. Poor Lizzie sat in the house next to the window, listening, crying and feeling utterly forlorn, betrayed by the beast she had married, and wishing she were back home in Pennsylvania with her family.

So Joshua continued to smoke and chew, and his addiction continued to be a source of irritation between them. Finally, when the boys were growing up, he realized that he was setting them a very poor example, and said he was going to quit tobacco. His brother Vickers lived nearby, and Vickers' wife heard of Joshua's reform movement, so she made her husband promise to quit too, if Joshua could. So the men entered into a pact to quit chewing, and if either fell back into this particular worldliness, the other was to have his pick of the backslider's horses. And that is how Joshua Milhous quit chewing. He took three chews a day for the first week, and two chews a day for the second week, and one chew a day for the third week—and then he quit cold and never used tobacco again in his life.

But as for Vickers—a month or two went by and then came the word from Vickers' farm. "Come and get your horse."

Lizzie Milhous was relieved and then proud of Joshua for his will power in the matter of the devil weed. But she still lamented Joshua's worldliness, and he continued to give frequent cause for complaint in other manifestations of concern for life on earth.

The Friends, for years and years, had eschewed any kind of popular music as the work of the Devil. It had been so in the days of George Fox back in England, in the days of Thomas Milhous in Pennsylvania, and it was so in the days of Joshua and Elizabeth in Jennings county. But secretly Joshua Milhous loved music, and when he went to Butlerville or away from home and found someone playing, he was one of the first to gather around. Such are the things he never told Lizzie.

One evening after the railroad came West and the roads opened up from Indianapolis, a peddler driving his wagon came to the door of the Milhous farm. In the fashion of the times the peddler got down and asked if the family could put him up for the night, and offered to pay. Joshua asked him in. At supper the family learned that the peddler was an organ salesman and had a demonstration organ in his wagon.

Joshua's eyes brightened and he suggested that the peddler bring in his wares and show them off. Lizzie frowned, but it would not do to start a family argument in front of a stranger, so she and the girls busied themselves in the kitchen while Joshua and the boys helped the peddler lift down his organ and carry it into the parlor.

There the peddler gave a concert. He played one tune after another, and when he played "The Old Musician and His Harp," Joshua threw caution to the winds, looked straight over Lizzie's head and told the peddler he wanted an organ.

Lizzie put her foot down and said she would not have that instrument of perdition on the place. She raised her voice, and the girls looked at each other in panic, for it was not their parents' way to quarrel over big things or small. The peddler went away next day without his order, but Lizzie, if she was satisfied that she and Faith had won, was basking in the satisfaction of only temporary victory.

For in a very short time Joshua found it necessary to go to Indianapolis, and while he was there he was again overcome by worldliness, and he actually bought and paid $260 for a Mason and Hamlin organ to be delivered to his house.

There, it was done! When Lizzie found out, she was furious, then aghast. What if the neighbors heard about it?

Joshua was contrite, and perhaps a little ashamed, but he *would* have his organ. He was willing to compromise: when the crated organ was delivered to the Vernon station, Joshua made arrangements to have Jesse bring it from there by wagon after dark so the neighbors would not see and begin to wag their tongues.

On the appointed day, Jesse came by night, as ordered, unloaded his package, set it down in the parlor. Lizzie stood in the doorway and cried for the shame of it, then turned and escaped to her room to pray for the good Lord's forgiveness of her erring husband.

The youth of the family, of course, were delighted. They could not wait to sit down and play, and also to tell their friends at school about the new acquisition. But next morning, a stern Lizzie absolutely forbade anyone in the family even to whisper to their best friends that they had an organ in the house. It was the family's shame, she said, and they must bear it alone and as best they could.

No word was said by a member of the family. Lizzie passed the parlor a dozen times a day, but the door remained firmly shut, and she pursed her lips each time she passed. Poor Joshua began to wonder if possession of his dream was really worth the trial of living with an angry wife. But he was a stubborn man—it was and would be a characteristic of the Milhouses that they *would* have their way if their minds were made up. So he persisted in keeping the organ. Lizzie persisted in her anger, and the household suffered.

How long this might have continued and what might have come of it is debatable, but there was another force at work, quite uncontrollable by the Milhouses. Their neighbor, Brachen Burdg, had seen the wagon come by his road on the night of the delivery of the organ and it had aroused his curiosity to know what had gone to the Milhouses that night. He asked Joshua and did not get what he considered to be a satisfactory answer. So he came to call, and somehow the parlor door was open—and Brachen Burdg saw the organ.

Within a week the news was all over Jennings county. At meeting next First Day Lizzie knew the women were eying her and whispering, and Joshua sensed that even his closest friends were edging away from him. No one said anything outright, but he knew they knew, and they knew he knew they knew.

Lizzie was full of I-told-you-sos, and the girls complained that their best friends were not so friendly. Several families forbade their children the Milhous house. But that was not the worst of it. Lizzie found that her influence in the meeting was threatened. There came a letter from Elder Thomas Armstrong, a chiding, bitter letter. "It was the darkest hour that ever came over the meeting," said Elder Armstrong, wondering how in the name of the Lord Joshua could have gone so far astray.

If secretly Lizzie hoped that this chiding would bring her husband around and cure him of his worldliness, she did not know him well enough. For Joshua Milhous saw no evil in music. These were modern days and he was a modern man, and he would stick with his organ, and let the Devil take the objectors.

Joshua did stick with it, unpleasant as meeting days became, and cold as remained the atmosphere in his own household. The matter might have become more serious— he might have been called before the meeting to explain and be judged. But Joshua was right, and his critics were wrong—these were modern times and he was acting in the spirit of them. Other Friends, farmers in Jennings county, shared Joshua's courage, even though coming late, and within a matter of a month or so several more organs came to Jennings county, so many that the elders were hushed by numbers. Within a year they were even allowing singing in the meeting!

18

Frank Milhous and the Call of California

Although the Joshua Milhous family of Jennings county, Ind., maintained close ties with the Milhous and Griffith families in Ohio, eventually these ties were loosened by the deaths of the parents. Amos Griffith was the first to go: he died in 1870, a year after returning from the hallmark trip to Ireland and England. His wife, Edith, lived three more years, and died in February 1873. So Elizabeth Price Griffith Milhous lost her parents.

Three months later, Martha Vickers Milhous died. As is often the case in marriages that are real partnerships, with Martha's death, her husband lost interest in life and fell ill. William Milhous, Jr., took to his bed. His sight failed, and he began to see Martha in dreams and hallucinations. He prayed much, and the relatives who looked after him heard him saying he hoped he would soon meet Martha in Heaven.

During his waking hours, he would ask for her, and when told she was not there, he was astonished.

"Why, I have just seen her and talked with her. It is very strange if she is not here," he would say.

He grew weaker and asked for Martha more often.

"Is my wife here?" he would ask. And the person sitting with him would say no.

"I am sorry for that," the old man would say, "for we have not been together much lately."

Sometimes he would repeat the questioning two or three times within half an hour, and then he would fall back into a doze. He lingered thus until the spring of 1874, and then he too died, breaking the last strong bond between the Milhouses of Indiana and those of Ohio.

Family was now represented by reunions of the Milhouses and Griffiths and other kin in the Western country. As Joshua grew older and the children began to move away from home, his greatest joy became the "homecomings," when there was bustling and feasting that would have shocked the good elders of the New Garden Meeting back in Pennsylvania.

The first child to leave was Frank, the oldest boy, and grandfather of Richard Milhous Nixon. In the summer of 1872 Frank married Sarah Emily Armstrong. They had three children; the first died an infant, the second was a girl, Mary Alice, and the third was a boy, Griffith.

There were homecomings then, in the Campbell township farm, at the house where Frank had grown up.

Joshua was often in trouble with the more conservative members of the meeting for what a later generation would call a progressive attitude, but what some of Joshua's peers saw as his curse of materialism. He was the first to buy a carriage, and my, how tongues wagged over that. He was the first in the area to install a telephone, between his house and Frank's, which was three-quarters of a mile away. He was the first to build a bathroom in his house, although he had more trouble with that development. The carpenter did not understand what all this folderol was about, and did not put a door on the bathroom because it was not mentioned in the specifications. Joshua also was the first among his acquaintances to install "manufactured gas" in the house for lighting. He manufactured the gas by burning coal in an outbuilding, and then piping it into a six-foot gas tank in the cellar. It worked beautifully—the gas jets gave off a handsome blue-white flame and quite outdid the kerosene lanterns in every way. There was only one difficulty. The gas tank leaked, and the fumes came up through the floor so strongly that even Joshua agreed that the experiment had to be abandoned. Lizzie was delighted—she had just been waiting for the whole contraption to blow them to kingdom come.

Frank's marriage did not separate the families. Joshua had a huge library with cases of books that reached to the ceiling. The children came to borrow books on religion, science, history, drama, poetry, romance. He had the works of Charles Dickens and Sir Walter Scott, and a technical library on horticulture. He also had a greenhouse with glass sides and a heating system.

And the children and the grandchildren came to play the organ. Frank Milhous spent a good deal of time on the road selling the products of the nursery, and Emily decided she would give him a surprise. Once when he was on a trip, she went to her in-laws' house and practiced on the organ, day after day, until when Frank came home she could take him over there, sit him down, and play "Jesus Lover of My Soul."

And Charles, who went off to school in Lebanon, Ohio, came back and astounded all the family because he could play "Rock of Ages," *with two hands.*

Joshua took it all in. He invited every comer to play the organ for him, and when they were ready to quit he would say, "Now play my piece before thee stops," and the knowledgeable would play "The Old Musician and His Harp."

The Milhous place nearly burned down in the summer of 1872 while Joshua and Elizabeth were away attending the Western Yearly Meeting of the Friends at Plainfield, Ind. The children were all at meeting on the Sabbath when the fire started, and the barn burned. Neighbors came and saved the house and other outbuildings that time. The house itself did burn down a few years later, and was rebuilt.

Five years after Frank's marriage, tragedy again visited the Milhouses of Indiana. Frank's wife Emily died that summer. A year and a half later he was married again, this time to Almira P. Burdg at Grove Meeting House.

Almira Burdg was a mature woman when she married Frank Milhous. She had been born in Columbiana county, Ohio, but had come with her parents to a farm near Butlerville. Her father Oliver and her mother Jane were members of the Hopewell Meeting of the Sand Creek Quarterly Meeting, and she had grown up attending Hopewell Meeting and Friends school. She was a frontier girl; she rode to school on horseback most of the time. When she finished her education she began to teach school, and taught for ten years in Hopewell and Shelbyville, until she met and married Franklin Milhous.

Frank built a house on a 108-acre farm adjoining his father's, a big brick and board house surrounded by trees and meadows, with a creek running nearby. The house was on a hill, and was reached by a long lane that wandered through the pine woods from a big red gate on the pike.

He continued in the nursery business with his father and his brother Jesse. His brother Charles became a druggist and moved to Seymour.

North Vernon was competing with Butlerville for Jennings county trade in this last half of the nineteenth century. A German immigrant named Wolf Gumble started a department store there, where the Baltimore and Ohio terminal would later be, and the three Tech brothers came to town to open a competing store. The county was large enough in population and prosperous enough to keep them both in business. And factories came to town, one to build spokes and hubs for wagons, and another to make sheet-metal products. The Milhouses took eggs and milk to sell in North Vernon and in Butlerville, heating bricks on the stove to keep them warm in winter on the long carriage ride.

J. V. Milhous and Sons nursery moved with the times. By the last quarter of the century they were shipping thousands of young fruit trees and even ornamentals around the state and into several neighboring states. They experimented with varieties of peach, cherry, apple, and pear trees and installed whole orchards for some farmers.

They were staunch Republicans, these Milhouses of Jennings county. Joshua was a man of substance in the community, too, although most of his effort, like that of his fathers, was concentrated within the community of Friends. He was a major supporter of the local academy, an elder of the meeting, an overseer, a clerk, and a committeeman. He did his duty from time to time as a juror in court cases. He was chosen by the State Fair Board as a judge in the fruit competitions.

So the big old Milhous place was busy enough, all the time. Edith grew up and married a young preacher named Lewis Hadley, and they moved away. Martha, or Mattie, as she was called in the family, grew up and taught school before she married Wilmer Ware. Because of Joshua's early intransigence in the matter of music she learned to play the organ and also became a music teacher. Before the end of the century there was an organ in the meeting house, too.

Frank and Almira Milhous continued the tradition of the big family, with seven children: Edith, Martha, Hannah, Ezra Charles, Jane Burdg, Elizabeth, and Rose Olive. Hannah, who was the mother of Richard Milhous Nixon, was born in 1885 in the big two-storey house in Biggers township, and like the others she went to school at Harmony Hill, the little red schoolhouse built on a corner of the family farm. The Milhouses also served their community in the broader sense. Elizabeth, who was ordained as a Quaker minister, became superintendent of a nonsectarian Sunday school that met at the schoolhouse, and as time went on the family transferred to the Hopewell Friends church that replaced the simple meeting house. The manner of worship was still much the same as in the past: the men sat on one side of the building and the women on the other; prayer was largely a private matter, with guidance and some reference to Scripture by the minister, whose final job was to say the benediction and close the services. The Friends still dressed soberly, at least for church, in gray bonnets and plain dresses, and they still used the plain language of thee and thou.

The children grew up in a happy home, virtually unmarred by friction. In later years Hannah could only remember having been punished once. When she was five years old, she told her two-year-old brother that he could go wading in the creek, and when her mother discovered what she had done, Almira switched her daughter's ankles. "The switching didn't amount to anything," said Hannah, "but I felt terrible about it." As for her father, he never punished the children. A scolding was quite enough. The children played at home, and went skating on Graham creek in the winter. But changes were coming to the area and some of them were troublesome.

The Friends of Grove Monthly Meeting had decided shortly after the Civil War to build a college about three miles south of Butlerville, and had acquired the land and put up a forty- by fifty-foot stone building. Talbot Ware, Joshua Armstrong, and Hiram Burdg were trustees. Joshua Milhous was a heavy contributor, and Amaziah Beeson undertook to board many of the students who came from smaller places to attend this Quaker college.

When Frank and Almira Milhous began raising their family the college was flourishing. Yet as new lands opened in the West and roads and rail lines increased, the college ceased to prosper and was closed down in 1882.

As the 1880s drew to a close and the children grew, Frank and Almira Milhous talked time and again about the future. The West—now California—beckoned once again. Many Quakers from the district had gone West and settled in southern California, particularly in a little town called Whittier, after the famous Quaker poet. The letters that came back reported glowingly on the winter climate, the possibilities of orchards of oranges, lemons, and avocados, and the existence of a strong and thriving Quaker community with a burgeoning academy.

Franklin Milhous went to California to investigate, and visit relatives who had moved there, and came home saying the West was everything it was claimed to be. He suffered from bronchitis in the humid air of Indiana, and it was greatly relieved in the drier air of the West. Frank Milhous made several trips back in the next few years, and began buying land in southern California. He was still deeply involved in the family nursery, but now had another interest. In 1893, Joshua Vickers Milhous died, and then Frank began thinking even more seriously about moving West.

In 1895 the Santa Fe Railroad ran two daily overland trains equipped with Pullman Palace cars and tourist sleeping cars from Chicago to Los Angeles. There were plenty of hotels in the vicinity. One might put up at the Hotel Lindley or the Corfu or the Virginia on Olive Street, where Mrs. J. C. Philbrooks presided. That was a first-class family hotel "convenient to all streetcar lines, businesses, and places of amusement"—all for $1.25 a day.

When Frank came to look over Los Angeles, he headed for Whittier, the Quaker community east of the city, for he was looking for a congenial and intellectual environment that would suit his family. In many ways, he found that Whittier fitted the bill.

The place was completely dominated by the Quakers. There were no saloons or beer halls in the town, no atmosphere of harum-scarum that characterized so much of the Los Angeles area. The people who settled here at the base of the mountains were God-fearing Friends, the kind of people among whom the Milhouses had moved for six generations. There was no absolute way for the Quakers to insulate themselves against a rough and thoughtless society, but the Friends controlled Whittier.

Frank's interest was nurseries, and he found nurseries here, but of a different kind than his own. Here the hot sandy soil would grow pomelos (a kind of citron), apricots, peaches, oranges, olives, lemons, and palms, and those were the features of the East Whittier Nursery and the Railroad Nursery and the Ferguson Nursery. There was very little opportunity against these going concerns for a stranger to come in and opt the field, and Frank Milhous was thinking along different lines. He would have a nursery, but he was nearly fifty years old. Back home he and his brother had a very comfortable business and he had capital to spare. He was not in a mood to start all over in a strange business, nor was there a need in the manner that previous generations had felt to make a great success. He was looking for a simple life, perhaps even a little less pressure than the thriving business in Indiana brought.

So he paused to look around Whittier. The Friends academy—Whittier Academy—was in its fourth year. It offered academic subjects that would lead to college entrance, perhaps at the University at Berkeley or at Stanford, and the more prosaic studies of bookkeeping, stenography, and typewriting. But it also offered courses in painting, drawing, and music.

"Few places excel Whittier in beauty and location, healthfulness of climate and freedom from immoral influ-

ences," said the advertisements for the academy. "Could
anything be more perfectly lovely than our California land-
scape views?" asked the Chamber of Commerce. (It had just
rained for several days.) And the city fathers were en-
tranced with "their clear air, bright sunshine, the sharply
defined outline of hills and blue mountains and the deepen-
ing robe of green that covers mesa lands and valley."

Everywhere there were signs of promise and success.
The Whittier Fruit Exchange one day got orders for two
carloads of oranges. This caused the exchange to install new
packing facilities, including a modern Woodward grader.
Land companies were selling plots briskly just now, in the
Puente hills east of Whittier for sixty to seventy-five dollars
an acre, in the Leffingwell tract, and in the La Habra valley. All this land was located in what they called "the frostless belt."

Frank Milhous looked around for a few days, and
bought several pieces of land. Obviously, the way the land
was going it was a good speculation even if he never came to
live on it. Then he went home.

Frank made several more visits to California, and then
in 1897 he decided to move the family there. They packed
their household possessions and put together door frames,
windows, and good Indiana lumber for a house. They
loaded their horses and some other animals in a boxcar, and
a black farmhand named John Rickman went along to care
for the animals on the trip. Then the Milhous family moved
to California.

Perhaps one of the deciding factors in the move was the
promise of the extension of Whittier Academy. That year it
increased its offerings, and began calling itself Whittier College. There would be a three-year course fitting students to
enter Berkeley or any other higher school with two years of
bona-fide college work.

So the Milhouses came and built their house on a farm
on the south side of what is now Whittier Boulevard, the

house located in what is now a huge shopping center, at Painter and Laurel streets.

One of the first properties that Frank owned was a thirty-acre walnut orchard at Walnut Street and Whittier Boulevard in La Habra. He did not keep it very long, but sold it and invested in other real estate, in Whittier, Yorba Linda, and farther north. He did not sell out his interest in the nursery back in Indiana, but made trips back several times each year to confer on management problems.

The Milhous place was ideally suited to the family's needs. It was located close to both the focal points of interest: it was a mile from the Whittier academy and college and a mile from the Whittier Friends Church. The smaller children attended Evergreen grammar school, the girls began to go off to the academy, and the whole family attended the meeting.

The family lived very comfortably. They kept a carriage and horses. John Rickman took care of the horses, and his wife Ella took care of the family inside the house. In the manner of Quakers, there was not the slightest feeling of discrimination against the Rickmans either because they were servants or because they were black. The children grew up without the taint of racism; the Rickmans ate at the table with the family and so did any other workmen who happened to be at the place. So there were often Mexicans and Chinese and Japanese and blacks eating in the big house. A reader ought to pause and consider this unlikely situation for a moment, for it is important in the understanding of the character of Richard Milhous Nixon to know that the influences on him were so far removed from the general American scene. Dealing with the Milhouses one would not know that American society was race- and class-conscious. Like other Quakers they followed their consciences and their beliefs and were very largely insulated from the general stream of that American society. The Milhous position in life, later put into words by Hannah, was that "a person has to stand on his own two feet in this world, and it's what you make of yourself and not what your family was that counts."

So the children went to school, but they also worked around the farm, helping to care for the young plants and learning even to graft. As in Indiana, Frank Milhous quickly earned a reputation as an honest nurseryman. If a plant turned out to be sick, or to be other than as advertised, he would replace it free of charge. He guaranteed the pedigree and hardiness of his plants, too, which was not always the case with California nurseries.

Daughter Hannah followed the Milhous pattern of life: hard work, prayer, and concern for the immortal soul beyond that of ordinary men and women. In 1902 she was ready to begin her studies at Whittier Academy. Every day she went up the hill to the old Founder's Hall. She finished the work at the academy with good grades and then began attending the college. She was in her second year of college work when she met Frank Nixon.

19

The Milhouses
Absorb Frank Nixon

When Frank Nixon came to California in 1907 and looked around, he decided to become a motorman again. No frozen feet in this climate. So he found a job with the Pacific Electric Railway Company, which had opened a suburban line.

The line ran from Los Angeles south to Long Beach, Huntington Park and Maywood, through the countryside to Santa Fe Springs and Whittier. It was a fifty-minute trip, and Frank Nixon was paid eighteen cents an hour to guide the car. He worked as a motorman for nearly a year, and then he hit a car that was crossing the street railway track. That was the end of Frank's railroad career.

If he couldn't work on the street railway, he at least knew how to farm, so he got a job on the old Judson ranch east of Whittier, worked as a ranch hand, and began chasing girls. He met Hannah Milhous at a Valentine party.

"I immediately stopped going with the five other girls I

was dating," he said later, "and I saw Hannah every night."

One incipient complication existed in their courtship: Frank Nixon had been raised a Methodist, and Hannah was as devout a member of the Friends Society as any person in the Milhous family. The difficulty was overcome when Frank agreed to accept Hannah's religion, and on June 25, 1908, they were married and went to live in a cottage on the Judson ranch.

What to do? Frank Nixon was a hard worker, but he had no capital, and although southern California was still frontier country, it did not represent the farm frontier of the old days when land was cheap. On the contrary, land was extremely valuable and growing more so as citrus growers prospered in the area. John Gales of East Whittier sold his five-acre orange grove to J. M. Randall for $12,000. Down the valley a twenty-acre berry ranch went for $30,000 the same week. The eleven-acre Peters ranch, which grew Valencia and native oranges, sold for $25,000. Frank Nixon, obviously, could not compete in that land market.

He continued to work for Judson for a while longer, but early in 1909 it became apparent that Hannah was going to have a child, and the family insisted that she come home to the Milhous place for care and confinement. Little Harold was born there in June.

The Milhous household was crowded, and as busy and nearly gay as a Quaker house could be. But its members were never allowed to forget for a day their purpose on earth and their responsibility that transcended the flesh. Each morning the breakfast bell was rung, and then the family filed downstairs, to wait quietly at their places until every person in the house was seated. Woe to the last straggler—all eyes were upon him. Then Father Milhous, or Mother Milhous if he was out of town, would read a chapter from the Bible. Grandmother Elizabeth sometimes led. She had come to live with them in 1906. Each person around the table would say a verse, or a prayer. And then the day could start.

It was a sharp departure from the kind of life Frank Nixon had lived, but he became accustomed to it. He joined the family on outings to the beaches and the mountains, for Frank Milhous had inherited a certain worldliness from his father, and liked particularly to travel and see new places.

Frank Nixon now found that he was virtually inundated by Milhouses and Milhous relatives. Frank Milhous's brothers Jesse and Charles and his sisters Edith Hadley and Martha Ware all came to live in the Whittier area, and the number of aunts, uncles, and cousins who could be assembled was astounding. They *were* assembled, too, particularly on Elizabeth Price Griffith Milhous's birthdays, which became family reunion times, no matter whether she was staying in California with Frank or back East with another relative.

In the absence of his own family, then, Frank Nixon was "adopted" by the Milhouses, and became a part of that circle. One could not say that Frank and Almira Milhous lost a daughter. Instead they gained another son and a grandson. The family was very well known in Whittier by this time. Ezra Milhous was going to the academy, and he and Jennie Milhous were very active in scholastic and social affairs. They were surrounded by Friends they had known back in Indiana, including the Beeson family and the Wares. Indeed, back in Indiana circles it was sometimes said that the Milhouses had caused an exodus to California, and there was some truth in the statement. A few years after they left the area, the Quaker colony around Butlerville diminished and died.

Frank Nixon was not one to stay idle when there was a living to be earned, and he became restless in Whittier. Frank Milhous offered him an opportunity: why did he not take the little family and go up to Lindsay, where Frank Milhous had bought some land? Young Nixon could farm the land, test it out, as it were, plant some groves if he wished, and they could straighten out their financial complications later. Frank Nixon took the opportunity and did take Hannah and the baby to Lindsay, where he planted an orange grove. They stayed there for about a year and a half, but did not find it to their liking, so they came back to Whittier, and then Frank Nixon and Frank Milhous invested in a piece of property in Yorba Linda.

Frank was a fair country carpenter in addition to his many other skills, and he built the house they were to live in there, a small frame house with a peaked roof.

Frank Nixon was carrying out the Nixon tradition when he came to Yorba Linda, for in 1911 the place was scarcely a settlement at all. The name commemorates Bernardo Yorba, descendant of a soldier of Spain, who was given some 25,000 acres in land grants by the Mexican government early in the nineteenth century, with the hacienda located about three miles from what is now Yorba Linda's Main Street.

In 1888 there had been an abortive attempt to lay out a town in the area, and call it Carlton. It was a promoter's dream, and like so many of these dreams in the West it died aborning. Some streets were built, wells dug and driven, and twenty-five buildings erected. But the people did not come, nor did the promised railroads. And so Carlton died, and by 1896 it was literally deserted, with several buildings bodily moved to the thriving center of Fullerton, and the rest vandalized for their valuable properties. One of the main reasons for failure was water—the wells were too shallow, the water turned brackish, and the settlers lost faith. It was, if nothing else, a good object lesson for the settlers of California in the matter of water, the most valuable commodity in this arid land.

The land of the modern Yorba Linda was sold by Porfirio Yorba in the year that Frank Nixon came to California, and soon fell into the hands of the Janss Investment Company of Los Angeles, which fixed upon a land and town promotion here. The main theme of Janss' promotion was that the land was "absolutely frostless," in spite of the fact that once in a while it did freeze. (There are modern pictures of eighteen-inch icicles to prove it.) Still, the claim was given a good deal of credence in the big frost of 1913, when the temperature in the Pomona Valley dropped to twelve degrees, and the fruits on the trees split open. Actually there was frost then from Porterville to the Mexican Border, but Yorba Linda was least harmed of any area, and little but nursery stock died in the freeze. The reason was the dry warm Santana wind that blows from northeast to southwest, and warmed this particular place while La Habra, virtually next door, was freezing badly.

The promoters of Yorba Linda promised a great deal, and the most important promise they made was to provide water, 777,600 gallons every thirty days, on each ten acres of land—with the land at $150 an acre. It was rangeland, very nearly desert land, covered with sage, greasewood, and native grass, rolling for the most part. To the southeast you could see Old Saddleback, and to the north, the San Bernardino mountains, where Old Baldy wore a crown of snow in winter. Technically, the soil was known as Ramona loam, excellent for citrus trees, with a clay subsoil. The trick—the secret of success—was to secure a piece of land with topsoil deep enough to nourish the roots of the citrus, and those who did so found the Janss brochure to be very reasonable in its claims.

Dr. Peter Janss, the principal promoter of the area, was a teetotaler, and his deeds prohibited the sale of alcohol in any form. It was just the kind of town the Quakers would like, and so many of them began spilling over here from Whittier and East Whittier and La Habra. They were joined by the Methodists, who had equally strong views on the subject of temperance.

When Frank Nixon came to Yorba Linda, the ten acres on which he settled were planted in barley. But Frank Milhous had advised him to plant a lemon grove, and made the plants available from the home nursery in Whittier. So a lemon grove was planted on the ten acres. They bought a cow, and a horse to pull carriage and wagon, and some chickens for eggs. Hannah cooked on the old wood stove, not only for the family but for the road gang that built the first road through the area.

Once the lemon trees were planted, Frank's citrus farming consisted of fertilizing and irrigation, and waiting the five years for the trees to grow until they bore fruit. So he had to have another way of making a living in the interim. He had two ways. First, he laid out and planted citrus groves for other farmers. Second, he used his skills at carpentry to help build other people's houses, and stores and buildings in Yorba Linda.

Yorba Linda was a place with about two hundred people then, congenial settlers for the most part, and intensely loyal to the community they were building. One friend of the Nixons was Ben Foss, a Quaker who shared the interests of farming and railroading with Frank. Ben Foss had a fourteen-acre lemon and orange grove on Buena Vista Street, and he was also a conductor on the Pacific Electric line which connected the settlement with Los Angeles. Ben Foss was a favorite of the youngsters in the town, because he often let them ride with him from Yorba Linda to the end of the line at Stern, then turn around and ride back home. He was also Yorba Linda's greatest booster, head of the school board, and of the infant citrus board. On duty with P.E. when his car came swaying into town he would announce: "Yorba Linda, the capital of the world."

Other friends of the Nixons—although they were Methodists—were George and Fannie Corbit, and their son Hoyt, who was about eighteen years old, and went to work for Frank as carpenter's helper and in the orchard-planting business. Frank combined forces with another rancher and bought the first caterpillar tractor in Yorba Linda, to help with the work.

Frank helped build several of the town's buildings, in-

cluding a schoolhouse on Olinda Street that was used by the
Friends and others for church services in the early times.
The Pullen grocery store was nearby, and the Buckmaster
hardware store near that. One by one the buildings went up
until the street began to acquire the character of a village
center, with a horse fountain of concrete, a blacksmith shop,
a masonic hall, drugstore, and the other structures of civilization. The town's mail was first delivered from Fullerton,
but in 1912 Yorba Linda got a post office of its own.

Close relatives and other family connections continued
to come into the area. Just across the great Anaheim water
ditch—the principal irrigation source for the area—lived
the Eldo West family, who were closely related to the Nixons through the Milhous line. Grace West had been Grace
Milhous, daughter of Jesse Milhous, son of Joshua Milhous
and brother of Frank. In other words, Grace and Hannah
were first cousins. And the relationship did not tell the
whole story: Frank Milhous had gone back to Indiana on
one of his business trips, which were also his proselytizing
trips, and he had persuaded the Wests to come to California
to settle.

After the Wests came, Eldo managed the water company, but that was saying very little about his life in Yorba
Linda. He became a member of the school board, and a
mover and shaker in the little community. They saw a good
deal of the Nixons, visiting back and forth.

Frank Nixon embraced his wife's religion wholeheart-
edly, and helped to organize and build the Friends church
in Yorba Linda. The Friends had support from Whittier's
church, which gave eight hundred dollars for lumber. The
Pasadena Friends church donated, and the Janss company
was persuaded to give the land. Then Frank Nixon and
other volunteers, not all of them Quakers, gave their labor
to put up the building. The monthly meeting was organized
in 1912, and the Nixons were listed among the organizers.

The first meeting was held on August 11, 1912, and it
occasioned some comment from visiting Friends who came

for the affair. Theodore Stanley, an Ohio Quaker, began to complain when he saw that Frank and the others had put a steeple on the meeting house. Worldly. Then Quaker Stanley's conservative heart was thoroughly shocked when he went inside, and discovered that the Yorba Linda church possessed an organ. Shades of the Devil! He began to speak out, and was only shushed by his wife, who was more tolerant of the wild and woolly ways of these Westerners.

The meeting was modern, with a *paid* minister who preached, instead of the old silent prayer—another departure that brought frowns to Quaker Stanley's face. And after the meeting, instead of repairing quietly to their homes, Frank Nixon and the others stood in the street and talked politics, arguing the merits of Teddy Roosevelt, William Howard Taft, and Woodrow Wilson. Frank, as was his custom, talked long and seriously, this time in favor of Roosevelt Republicanism. Indeed, in the days to come Frank was to be known as a portentous political arguer.

Hannah Nixon settled quickly into the community, too. She was a charter member of the Yorba Linda Federation of Women in 1912. The club devoted itself to practical matters for the most part: how to get electricity into the community (they managed), how to get a park (they did).

At the meeting of November 14, 1912, someone moved that since Hannah Nixon was expecting, and was the first member of the federation "to have anticipations of a little one in her home," the ladies give a surprise party for her. (Apparently Hannah was absent that day.) The matter was discussed but the party was rejected as unseemly, and the ladies voted to give her a book instead.

Richard Milhous Nixon was born on January 9, 1913, a time notable in Yorba Linda as the season of the worst freeze the area had ever suffered. Frank Nixon was working a crew of young men, planting an orchard, that day. Hoyt Corbit and the other young men assembled at the house early in the morning as was their custom, and they were met by Frank, who was very excited. He threw his hands in

the air and danced around the yard. "I've got another boy,"
he shouted. And all that day he could scarcely contain himself.

During the big freeze another event of importance occurred in Yorba Linda—the emergence of Fuerte Avocado,
which proved to be one of the greatest boons ever to come to
southern California agriculture.

John H. Whedon, an Angelino, was preparing a five-
acre avocado grove that winter. He had ordered forty small
trees from the West India Gardens Nursery. But, alas, that
January freeze killed off the forty trees set aside for him at
the nursery. The nurseryman did, however, have another
variety of avocado, Mexican trees from Atlisco which the
nurseryman called *fuerte* (strong), and oddly enough these
little trees had survived the freeze where larger ones had
not. With a poor attempt to conceal ill temper, Mr. Whedon took the second-choice trees and planted them in his
grove. He really had no choice: the nurseryman had lost so
much money he could not make a cash refund; it was either
the Mexican trees or nothing.

A few years later Yorba Linda suffered another freeze
and more avocado trees died, but not these trees. One tree
in particular did not seem to be bothered at all, and the
next season produced phenomenally well.

Farmer Whedon then realized that he had something
unusual in that tree. He began cutting buds, or scions from
the tree, and one season he sold six thousand dollars' worth
of buds. And the tree grew and grew and produced huge
luscious avocados, all the while. Soon the tree was famous,
and was known as the Mother Tree of the Fuerte Avocado
in California. The Yorba Linda Chamber of Commerce
honored the avocado by placing a picture of its fruit on the
Chamber's seal. That tree has had its picture in more newspapers around the world than anything else that came from
Yorba Linda except Richard Milhous Nixon.

20

Enter Richard
Milhous Nixon

As a baby, Richard Milhous Nixon was known in the family as a screamer. Harold, the first-born son, had been a quiet baby and he was a quiet boy, but Richard possessed a healthy set of lungs and he let the family know of his existence. But a year later, when his brother Donald was born, Richard had quieted down. Perhaps it was the Quaker atmosphere, triumphing over his father's "more effervescent" Methodist inheritance.

The Nixons were very active in local church and educational affairs, and if Frank used bad grammar and did not have any education himself he respected it in his wife and others, especially brother Ernest, who had made his way through advanced college studies, and was becoming a professor. Hannah was chairman of the Women's Federation's education committee and instrumental in getting a library for the town, located first in the little schoolhouse. Frank taught Sunday school at the Quaker church. Jessamyn West, daughter of Eldo, who was to become the fore-most American Quaker novelist, remembered that Frank was a strong, forthright and very effective Sunday school teacher. A man of character, no doubt about it. And if he was irritable and had a bad temper, which he did, it was usually controlled by Hannah, who was known throughout the community as the mistress of the soft answer. She was a gentle, good-hearted woman, to whom violence of thought or action was anathema. She was never too busy to do favors for others, or to work for her church or community. While Frank Nixon was respected in town as a sober, industrious man who paid his bills on time, Hannah was loved. While Frank was obeyed by his children, lest they feel the rod; Hannah was adored.

These disparate personalities lived together comfortably in the little frame house in Yorba Linda, and Richard Nixon's childhood was spent in the atmosphere of a big family: Harold, Richard, Donald, and Arthur, born in 1918. Besides this immediate family, there was constant visiting among Hannah's relatives, in a very informal fashion. Jessamyn West recalled staying with the Nixons, and sleeping in the bed with Frank and Hannah when she was a little girl. These were days when families worried more about food and less about Freud.

Richard Milhous Nixon also grew up in the atmosphere of a small town. The children accompanied the family to church, two or three times on Sunday and on Wednesday nights. They went fishing in the lake on Buena Vista Street, and they waded and sometimes swam in the Anaheim Union Water Company ditch that went by the house. (Hannah recalled years later that she lived in constant fear that the ditch would claim one of her children one day.) They stole watermelons (a popular youthful sport), and one time Harold and Richard were driving in the family wagon and helped themselves to some grapes from an arbor of a neighbor. They were so foolish as to still be eating grapes when they arrived at home. Where did they get the grapes? They confessed. Hannah was furious. She sent Richard into the house to get the pennies he had been saving, and then she forced them to go back and confess their theft to the farmer, and offer to pay.

A mature Richard Nixon recalled those early days in a sort of kaleidoscope:

". . . We were poor," he once said. "We worked hard. We had very little. We all used hand-me-down clothes. I wore my brother's shoes, and my brother below me wore mine and other clothes of that sort, but we remember the little things. I recall, for example, a Fourth of July. We were the only ones in the neighborhood that . . . didn't have the money for firecrackers. In those days you could get them. But my mother wanted to do something, so she . . . got some bunting and I remember she fixed the table with red, white and blue bunting and my father went out and got some ice cream and what a feast we had.

"We had our arguments within the family and there were times when I suppose we were tempted to run away and all that sort of thing. None of us ever did. . . ."

The overriding recollection that Richard Milhous Nixon preserved from those earliest days was a sense of a happy family, poor but honest, dignified by hard labor and community effort. It was, in other words, the noble American frontier family of the nineteenth and early twentieth centuries, honoring the homely virtues. Here are words about the family that came to Richard Nixon's mind when during the campaign of 1968 the Republican National Committee made a filmed interview for the presidential campaign: ". . . proud . . . effervescent . . . drive . . . self-supported . . . devout . . . strict . . . deeply devoted . . . self-sacrifice . . . challenges . . . crises . . ."

And while he loved and respected his father, the Milhous tradition ruled the family. Cousin Jessamyn West later remarked that the Milhouses (of which she counted herself as one, although she was also a West) regarded Richard Nixon as a Milhous, not a Nixon. There was an arrogance about the Milhouses that tended to swallow up the marriage partners—reinforced by the size of the family and the unrelenting spirit of togetherness that Elizabeth Price Griffith Milhous and Almira Milhous levied.

Two stories indicate the highly disciplined farm-family air in which Richard grew up. Once, when Richard was visiting Aunt Jane Beeson and her husband, he and the Beeson boys got involved in a barnyard prank that left corn all over the floor—wasted. The uncle took his *own* boys into the house for a good strapping, and Richard told his aunt he ought to be punished too. "Not on your life," said Harold Beeson, "I wouldn't dare touch a hair of Frank Nixon's son."

Frank had another reputation within the family, particularly among the girls of the generation of Jessamyn West. He was what they called a "hot man." When Jessamyn West was of mature age she and one of her cousins were discussing Frank one day.

"Didn't he ever pinch you?" asked the cousin.

Jessamyn said no, but she recalled Frank after that with a new interest, and remembered he was very careful to keep a good distance from the young and attractive girls of the family, although they might be kissing cousins. Suddenly she knew why Frank sometimes seemed aloof and very controlled around the women. But in other ways he was not controlled. He was furious with Hannah in 1916 when she voted for Woodrow Wilson. (She had believed Wilson's claim that he would not send American boys to fight abroad and that was her basic justification.) Even his Quaker pastor called Frank "brusque, loud, dogmatic, strong-willed, emotional, and impatient."

As for Hannah, she never raised her voice. Once when little brother Arthur was caught by a neighbor woman (neighbor lady, said Richard Nixon) smoking cornsilks, Hannah Nixon was informed. Arthur asked Richard to intercede, and to have his father give him a spanking. "Don't let her talk to me," he said, "I just can't stand it." The emotional experience was too grave for the youngsters; they much preferred their father's hand.

Frank Nixon brought a non-Quaker influence to the family in another, indirect way. His half-brother Hugh Nixon came to settle in Yorba Linda, and during World War I, Hugh Nixon enlisted in the army, in the Nixon family tradition of military service. It was true that such California Quakers as the Milhouses had become far more liberal than their Eastern brethren. The Hicksite movement had spread West, leavening the strict beliefs, and the New Quakerism of Joseph Gurney had followed. It could be said that the Grove Meeting back in Indiana had become somewhat Gurneyite, and the Hopewell Meeting very definitely so, until its discontinuance in 1912. But Elizabeth Price Griffith Milhous was a pacifist, and so were Almira and Frank Milhous. Uncle Hugh's enlistment brought a definite contradiction of traditions.

The matter of the Nixon poverty is not precisely supported by other evidence. From time to time the Nixons had a "hired girl," although Hannah did not like that term, never used it, and in the Milhous and farm tradition had the girl eat with the family. Frank did not prosper as a lemon farmer, but relatives indicated he had chosen his land badly, a piece where the topsoil was not deep enough. He did work successfully as carpenter. For a time the hired girl was Mary Elizabeth Guptil, and she tucked the boys in bed at night and read to them (James Whitcomb Riley, for example) and listened as they said their prayers.

The boys played near home for the most part, and one of their favorite games was "train." Richard particularly liked to be fireman, and his great ambition in those early years was to get a job on the railroad. The Southern Pacific engineer who ran the train from Los Angeles to Needles was his ideal.

As a very small boy he was very nearly scalped one day. Hannah had driven to town, taking a relative to the Placentia station and was coming back to Yorba Linda.

Baby Donald was on her lap, and Mary Elizabeth Guptil was holding a very squirmy Richard on hers. Suddenly Richard escaped the girl's hold and fell out of the wagon, under an iron tire, which split his scalp open. Hannah picked him up and rushed him to the Quigley farm nearby. They had the only automobile in Yorba Linda, and they drove twenty-five miles to the hospital that day, where a doctor sewed eleven stitches in Richard's scalp. Richard recovered quickly enough and was soon back swimming in the irrigation ditch against family orders.

Except for his father, Richard Milhous Nixon grew up in a family heavily dominated by women; both paternal grandfathers were dead by 1919. The Nixon family, living in Ohio, had very little influence on the life of these Westerners, but Grandmother Milhous's place in Whittier was a center of the lives of all her children, and their children.

When Richard was old enough to go to school, he went to Yorba Linda's grade school, and did well enough there. He was quiet, and behaved himself as his mother had taught him to do. He was bright and he was a willing pupil. He also gave his first indications of political interest in these times. During the election of 1920, aping his father, seven-year-old Richard argued fiercely on the street in behalf of Warren Harding.

Harding "normalcy" did not turn out to be of the prosperous sort; indeed Harding's administration suffered from the economic hangover of the First World War in a way that the Nixon administration would later suffer from the hangover of a war atmosphere that extended from 1940 until the 1970s. The year 1922 was particularly disastrous for farmers in America, with inflated prices of merchandise and services and depreciated prices of farm produce. Frank Nixon's fruit ranching did not survive the recession. His lemon trees had been producing for more than three years, and they gave no signs of supporting the growing family. Frank had been offered $45,000 for the property by an oil speculator, and he had turned it down. (No oil was ever found there.) But he did decide that the lemon grove was not for him. He moved the family back to Whittier.

Frank Nixon had a chance at fortune then. Some property was available in Santa Fe Springs, and Hannah wanted to buy it. Frank did not. Oil was later discovered on the property.

The Whittier to which Frank and Hannah returned was growing, partly as a result of this southern California oil boom. In November 1922, new wells were brought in in Santa Fe Springs to add 10,000 barrels of production to the total—now 60,000 barrels a day—making it the "hottest" field in the West. That week George Getty brought in the Mitchell well, an 800-barrel producer, and Standard Oil brought in several wells.

Frank built a house for his family, and then for two years he worked in the oil fields. The pay was good but the future was limited without capital. One had to own the land or the leases to get rich in oil. So Frank Nixon began to look around for other opportunity.

He considered the automobile business, which was booming in southern California. You could buy a new Nash for $1250 then, or better yet, a Hupmobile for $450 down and $63.33 a month. But there were half a dozen successful automobile dealers in Whittier already. C. I. Dorn was the Buick dealer, George Mitchell had the local Ford agency, Al Hinnen handled Cadillacs and Dodges, and James A. Miller sold Darts and Maxwells. There were dealers in Paiges, Studebakers, Chandlers, Peerlesses, and Columbias. No, the automobile business was fairly well taken up in the area in 1922.

But the gasoline business was not. The St. Helens Gasoline and Petroleum Products company service station was located at 341 Whittier Boulevard, but there was no other station between Whittier and La Habra, which meant there was an opportunity in East Whittier. So Frank established a service station at Whittier Boulevard and Santa Gertrudes.

Business was very good. The family lived in a house be-

hind and Frank kept the service station in front, and prospered, selling gasoline and oil and tires. It was not very long
before people began leaving boxes of produce at the station
for sale, and this idea persuaded Frank to expand into a few
more items himself. Thus a country store was born.

As he grew a little older, Richard became notably
more the student. He played sandlot football, and he did his
chores. But he was happiest when he was curled up with a
book. He read the newspapers—he was reading newspapers
with understanding and interest at the time the Teapot
Dome scandal broke in 1924. He announced grandly then
that he had forsaken his dream of becoming a railroad engineer and would be an incorruptible lawyer.

He showed at this time, too, one attribute of character
that he would develop: the ability to concentrate. One summer day he was lying on the lawn "stargazing," his Aunt
Olive Marshburn said, when she called him to come in and
attend to some chore. He paid no attention. She called him
again and again. Still no answer. Finally she went out and
shook him, and then he responded. He had been a thousand
miles away.

At home Richard "helped out." He particularly hated
washing dishes, but it was a chore to be done. He would go
into the kitchen and pull down the window shade lest some
outsider see him doing this woman's work.

He learned to work in the citrus orchards, to irrigate
and work in a packing plant. He helped in the station, and
sold goods in the country store, and pumped gasoline.

When Richard was in seventh grade in Whittier
school, he went to stay for six months with his Aunt Jane
Beeson in Lindsay. Richard's mother wanted him to study
music. He had already taken some lessons from his uncle
Griffith Milhous, but Aunt Jane was a graduate of the Met-
ropolitan School of Music in Indianapolis and a professional music teacher. It was 1925, and he was twelve years
old.

Richard proved himself to be industrious and adaptable. He played with his cousins Joseph Alden and Richard Sheldon, but not for very long at a time. He was too busy, studying for good grades in school, and working at his piano. In six months, his aunt said, he had accomplished as much as other students of hers did in three years. Of course living with the teacher did not hurt, but it was an early mark of Richard Milhous Nixon's drive and determination to succeed at whatever he turned his hand to.

Not long after Richard came home in the summer the Nixon household was sorely grieved: seven-year-old Arthur contracted tubercular encephalitis and died in a week.

In the spring of 1926 Richard Milhous Nixon gave the first indication of success in his unrelenting pursuit of that goddess. He had done well in grade school, and he finished his year by being chosen outstanding member of his class and also class valedictorian. He was a hard-working, tight-lipped, serious boy, and he put everything he had into his studies.

The Nixon household was not so happy now. Everyone in the family worked in the service station and store, and later Richard estimated that they worked about sixteen hours a day. Frank and the boys would argue at dinner until Hannah would cry, "Now hush, all of you." Frank would feel rebuked: "You make them hush," he would say, "and I'll hush."

Frank was a "thumper"—he would snap his index finger against the boys' heads when they angered him. And the other boys angered him frequently, while Richard, who observed his father closely, managed generally to stay out of trouble. He tried to persuade Donald and Harold to his way—"don't argue with him"—but he was more successful than they, and took fewer lumps. Hannah stood on the sidelines and kept peace. She was, said an old friend, born to endure. Frank was often jealous of the time she spent with other people, but that did not prevent her from baking pies for the busy, visiting the sick, and helping the poor. Like her mother, Almira, and her grandmother, Elizabeth, who had

died in 1923, Hannah was a devout member of the East
Whittier Friends Church, a firm believer in the Golden
Rule, and in the virtues of self-improvement and hard work.
In her last years, to be more useful to society, Elizabeth
Milhous had learned to be a nurse and had spent much
time nursing sick friends and members of her family. Like
her mother, Almira insisted on being useful. After Frank
Milhous' death she occupied herself by reading, keeping
abreast of current affairs in religion and the world, by hard
work around her own house—she tended her plants, fed her
chickens, picked her own oranges, and grew flowers with a
passion. She traveled to Hawaii in 1919 for a visit with her
daughter Edith Timberlake, and she was forever organizing
trips to the seashore or the mountains. It was the family tradition to combine travel, search for knowledge, and recreation. The Milhouses of Indiana had visited Niagara Falls
and international expositions, and nearly every point of interest in the Middle West.

"Work" was still king of Richard's life and always
would be. Schoolwork, music, homework, family chores.
When the East Whittier Friends Church decided to abandon the old meeting house and build a new church, Frank
bought the old building, and what had been a country store
and gasoline station became a much more sophisticated
store. There were others in town, the Whittier Market at
108 West Philadelphia and the Square Deal Grocery at 301
South Greenleaf, but none others near the Nixon place in
East Whittier. By extending credit and promising delivery,
Frank secured a good bit of business, including much of that
of the Leffingwell ranch, one of the area's most important
industries. The boys, of course, delivered the groceries, and
this took Richard's afternoons. He learned at a very early
age to budget energy and time in a way that might seem
mechanical.

In the fall Richard Nixon went to the high school in
Fullerton; he could have gone to either Fullerton or Whittier, but there was a problem. They lived a long distance

from both schools, so Richard went to live with relatives
while he went to high school. For a time he lived with Walter Nixon, a brother of Frank's who had come to try his luck
in California.

Now, going to high school in Fullerton, Richard began
to shape his interests. He liked football and played sandlot
ball with the neighborhood boys, Lincoln Dietrick and his
brother, Akton Miller, and the Burnett boys. They built a
tennis court behind the Nixon store, leveling a dirt patch
and marking out the lines. When he went to high school,
Richard tried out for football, and the debating team, and
played in the school band. His family rather hoped that he
would become a professional musician (shades of Thomas
Milhous!) and his aunt Jane said he had the talent for it.
But the world began to get in the way.

As a sophomore at Fullerton, Richard played on the B
team, which honed the varsity for the games against other
schools. He was a fair scholar, and he distinguished himself
even at Fullerton as a debater. He had begun public speaking in the seventh grade, and learned very quickly that by
applied scholarship he could achieve a good deal of his aim,
which was victory in the debate. One of his first debating
assignments in grade school had been the affirmative on the
topic "Resolved that insects are more beneficial than harm-
ful." He consulted a knowledgeable uncle (the virtues
of a large family) who guided him to the positive facts
about insects, and when he appeared on the platform, his
argument overwhelmed the enemy and his side won the
debate.

There are people born with a platform presence but
Richard Nixon was not one of them. Dr. Lynn Sheller, who
was his debating coach at Fullerton, recalled Richard as a
shy boy, serious about his work, but with no natural ability
as a speaker. "He wrote his speeches with a great deal of
care and memorized them," said Sheller. He marshaled information and worked so hard at speaking that he achieved
a certain success in spite of his natural handicaps. In his

sophomore year he represented the school in the National Oratorical Contest on the Constitution, an affair sponsored by the Los Angeles *Times*.

After two years at Fullerton High School, Richard transferred to Whittier High School. Frank Nixon had an old Ford car; he bought another car and gave the Ford to the boys to get them to school and back.

Richard continued to study hard at school and produced satisfactory results. Later in law school he would be known as "iron butt" because of his ability to sit and grind at the books for long and weary hours. It was a habit he acquired in the high school days; he was a serious young grind of a student, cautioned by Mother and Father that he must make his own way in the world.

At Whittier High School, in his junior year, Richard Nixon distinguished himself as a debater. This year he was able to eschew the use of notes. Progress. He was still unsure of himself on the platform, physically, but then he always would be, and in spite of the next forty years of public speaking he would never achieve the ease of gesture and comfortable look of a man who really enjoyed the process of communicating with an audience, face to face.

Yet in spite of this nervousness and insecurity on the platform, Richard Nixon at sixteen was an accomplished public speaker, good enough to win first place in the district contest against South Pasadena. It was his preparation that did it, not his platform presence. His topic was "Our Privileges Under the Constitution," and his approach at sixteen to the freedoms of Americans is interesting in view of the mature philosophy of President Richard Nixon.

". . . the framers of the Constitution provided for the highest type of justice. No citizens of the United States can be tried for a capital crime without first being indicted by a Grand Jury. If he is indicted, he is given a public trial by an impartial jury. He may obtain counsel and witnesses. He is not compelled to testify against himself as in times past, nor is any evidence obtained by compulsion. . . ."

"During the struggle for freedom, our forefathers were in constant danger of punishment for exercising their rights of freedom of speech and freedom of the press. Again the cause of their danger was the intolerance of men in power toward others with different views. The framers of the Constitution provided that we, their descendants, need not fear to express our sentiments as they did. Yet the question arises: How much ground do these privileges cover? There are some who use them as a cloak for covering libelous, indecent and injurious statements against their fellow men. Should the morals of this nation be offended and polluted in the name of freedom of speech or freedom of the press? In the words of Lincoln, the individual can have no rights against the best interests of society. Furthermore, there are those who, under the pretense of freedom of speech and freedom of the press, have incited riots, assailed our patriotism, and denounced the Constitution. Consequently, laws have justly been provided for punishing those who abuse their Constitutional privileges—laws which do not limit these privileges, but which provide that they may not be instrumental in destroying the Constitution which ensures them. We must obey these laws for they have been passed on for our own welfare."

One might call the sixteen-year-old Nixon's view a conservative one, not much different from the views of President Nixon.

Naïveté—both of the sixteen-year-old and of the educational system of the 1920s—showed in Richard Nixon's appreciation of the constitutional provisions for freedom of all the people.

"In the United States," he said trustingly—for this is what his history books said and what his teachers told him —"the people themselves are the rulers. Gone are the days of inequality and servitude. We derive our powers from the privilege of suffrage. Let us see how it has been established in the Constitution. When this document was first adopted, the privilege of suffrage was held by all free male citizens.

Three quarters of a century later the curse of slavery was forever removed from this nation, and the ballot was extended to all men regardless of race or color. In our own time this privilege has been fully established by the Constitution and has been extended to all citizens regardless of sex. . . ."

He chastised those citizens who had not gone to the polls. "Does it seem right that in the Presidential elections of 1920 and 1924 little over fifty percent of the eligible voting public went to the polls, and that in our last election little over 65 percent cast their ballots? . . ."

Next in importance to the right of voting, he held the right to hold office. "In times past the right to hold office was given only to those of the nobility, we however, have our Lincolns and our Jacksons—men who needed only a chance to prove their worth, that they might rise to the highest office in the land." (He identified himself, obviously, with Presidents who had pulled themselves up, unblessed by the advantages of privilege.)

"Truly," said Richard Nixon, high school junior, "it is a great privilege to hold office, but it is also a great responsibility. The office holder is elected by his fellow men who expect him to represent them wisely and justly. It is his duty to give his service willingly, no matter how insignificant the position; to perform his work to the best of his ability; and to defend, maintain, and uphold the Constitution. . . ."

Now at Whittier High School Richard Nixon was undergoing the pressure of deciding on a career. In those days a junior in high school had to declare himself, and Richard said he was a pre-law student. He was already making decisions that would shape his future. He worked for the high school paper. He joined the Latin club. He was involved in high school campus politics, and ran for president of the student body. He lost the election to an opponent who made a vigorous personal campaign of handshaking. He did not forget it.

In Richard Nixon's senior year at Whittier High
School he was president of the scholarship society, still active in the Latin club, feature editor of the newspaper, and
general manager of the student body, a job that took a mod-
icum of discipline and hard work.

Once again, he distinguished himself with his public
speaking. Again he entered the *Times'* contest and this time
he spoke on "America's Progress—It's Dependence Upon
the Constitution." This time, too, he very nearly won the
contest—he reached the finals by comparing American
progress with that of Latin American nations under their
diverse systems of government.

Richard had hoped for total success. He was bemused
by success early and in a very worldly way. He brought
home from the school library a copy of Dale Carnegie's *How
to Win Friends and Influence People* and the whole family read
the book, on his urging. Its formula opened new vistas.

Richard Nixon closed his high school career very satisfactorily. He was popular; in his yearbook, the admiring
scrawls of fellow students, male and female, indicated that
he was held in considerable respect for his attainments. He
was friendly and his teachers regarded him as a self-starter.
He was showing the influence of his mother, of whom it was
later said that "her humanitarian Republican liberalism
was based on self respect, self regulation, self restraint, and
self attainment." It was the old Milhous Quaker theory of
standing on one's own feet and doing the best one could.

Richard Nixon had done his best, and in practical
terms it helped him considerably. He won a Harvard Club
scholarship to attend Harvard College, but it was out of the
question for him to go so far away. Not only were the times
hard, but the Nixons had another child, Edward, born in
the spring of 1930. Richard applied for, and received, the
Frank and Almira Milhous Scholarship to Whittier College, financed from the $50,000 or so that Frank Milhous

had left to Whittier over the years, a fund established for the education of deserving members of the Milhous family. Once again, the Milhous connection was shaping the future of Richard Milhous Nixon.

21

The Horatio
Alger Tradition

The oldest Nixon boy, Harold, was discovered that summer to be suffering from an advanced case of tuberculosis, and Hannah Nixon gave up her work in the store to devote her time to nursing her son. Frank sold part of the land on which the store and service station were located, and Hannah took Harold Nixon off to Prescott, Arizona, where the dry air was supposed to be a specific treatment for tuberculosis. She opened a boarding house there and took in other tuberculars. When they could, her other children and husband came to visit her. During the summer Richard spent time in Arizona. He worked at a swimming pool for a while as janitor; he was barker in a carnival game. He earned money and prepared to go to college.

Until Harold fell ill, Hannah had usually supervised the running of the store, the relationships with customers in particular. Frank's peppery temper cost them business in the early days, and so he agreed to take over the chores of supply and maintenance. He would drive into Los Angeles in the small hours and pick up fresh produce, and he would cut the meat and stack the cans and keep the inventory up. But with Hannah's absence in Arizona, it fell on the boys, Richard and Donald, to take over much of the work at the store. Donald became the butcher, and Richard became the produce man. He arose in the dark, drove to Los Angeles in a "beat-up touring car" converted to a pickup, and bought produce, returned, dumped it into a vat out back to wash, and then separated and culled and arranged the fresh fruits and vegetables. He hated the work cordially but he did it cheerfully.

The store took the family's time in these years, and Frank rented out the gas station. For a while it was rented by Merle West, Richard Nixon's second cousin. In 1925 the Wests had moved, too, from Yorba Linda to Anaheim. Merle and Richard renewed acquaintance then. Merle came into the store to gossip, as on the day that Richard was helping grind hamburger and cut his finger. The blood ran into the hamburger, and Donald, disgusted with his brother, prepared to throw away the whole platter.

"Don't throw that away," said Richard. "That's the reddest hamburger you'll ever see."

So Richard did have a sense of humor, which he displayed to his intimates.

There were few of these intimates, even in high school and college days. Richard simply did not have the time to get involved socially. Store, schoolwork, and extracurricular activities made him a very busy young man. Occasionally he and Merle West would go to Los Angeles on a double date. Occasionally they would even go to the burlesque theater. But not often—the priorities of a young, ambitious man, working his way through college precluded many such excursions. And Richard Nixon's ambition and curiosity knew no bounds. From the Leffingwell ranch and the area south of Whittier Boulevard a number of Spanish-speaking people drifted into the Nixon store. Richard thought it would be a good idea to learn a little Spanish, so he got hold of a Spanish grammar and studied it at home, on the side, until he could say a few phrases at least. It might not be intellectuality, but it was interest.

In the fall, when Richard Milhous Nixon began his studies at Whittier College, he entered an environment reminiscent of the extremely devout Quaker background in which he had been raised. He was a "birthright" Quaker. That was a new concept among the Friends since Franklin Milhous's day, for until nearly the twentieth century young people lived within the religious community on sufferance until they were grown, at which time they were told to consider their relationship to God and to accept Christ or not. The acceptance was a formal part of their religion, and was often dated in the family Bibles and records.

Times and the West had changed the Quaker faith in California. As noted, the Nixons and Milhouses of southern California were far more lenient in their views of worldliness than the Quaker fathers. In another way, their religion demanded more of them. The young Nixons sometimes attended three church services on Sunday at the East Whittier Friends Church. Sabbath school began at nine forty-five. At eleven o'clock the pastor or a visiting minister conducted the worship service. At six-thirty in the evening the young people went to Junior, Intermediate, and Senior Christian Endeavor meetings. At seven-thirty the pastor or another gave the evening sermon. And there were prayer meetings during the week.

As was the church changing, so was Whittier College. It had been founded as an extension of the old academy, to give the Friends who settled this community a moral and congenial atmosphere for the education of their children. But as Whittier changed, so did its college. In 1925 the college had 281 students; four years later it had nearly five hundred. When cousin Jessamyn West had gone there to school a few years before Richard, Whittier's student body was largely Quaker, largely composed of youngsters from the Whittier area. By the time Richard would graduate, more than half the students would be from other areas of California and out of state, and while he was in school there, the number of Quaker students was only 17 percent of the total. So it might be said that these formative college years threw Richard Nixon into a new atmosphere—not so totally as if he had gone to, say, Harvard College.

Certainly a liberalizing spirit was hovering over Whittier College in these days. One change had come in 1925 with the establishment of a joint council of control, which consisted of six students and four faculty members, whose task was to define standards of campus conduct and recommend penalties for violations. There had been prohibitions against smoking, drinking, card playing, and dancing. These were softened to such an extent that when President Dexter of the college wandered into a new dormitory one day and encountered four young men playing poker, he simply wandered out again. (One of the gamblers was the son of a Quaker pastor.)

For years, chapel had been compulsory at Whittier College, three times a week. That, too, fell away.

These changes did not come without repercussions. Some Friends meetings refused to support the college from time to time. And 1930, Richard Nixon's freshman year, was marked by what to a young Quaker was an exciting confrontation.

Guy Fitch Phelps, a Methodist fundamentalist preacher, came to Whittier to conduct revival meetings at the Nazarene Church. Perhaps to stir up interest, the preacher issued a challenge to debate to the college's leading professors. The subject: Resolved that the Theory of Evolution Is Unscientific and Absurd.

The challenge did what the Rev. Mr. Phelps had hoped it would do—it filled his pews to overflowing for the next few revival meetings. He warned them about the evils being performed on the young up on college hill by godless professors, and the town began to buzz. A bastion of the college establishment, Professor John R. Wilkie, came to the next meeting accompanied by Dr. Albert Upton, a younger teacher. They listened as the Rev. Mr. Phelps rebuked the professors of the college for teaching evolution while they were supposed to be teaching the Bible.

This day—because word had spread of the confrontation to come—the place was filled with college people. Professor Wilkie stood up to reply to the preacher. But before he could speak two big ushers closed in, grabbed him, and hustled him out of the church.

The preacher smiled benignly. "Now things smell better," he said, and proceeded to lambaste the college and its teachers anew. Next day the students' representatives asked the Rev. Mr. Phelps to come up to the campus and talk. President Dexter announced a lecture on evolution by the new head of the biology department, Dr. S. Arthur Watson, a devout Quaker who believed in evolution.

The Rev. Mr. Phelps did not show up. Instead, he sent a letter to Professor Wilkie, declaring war until "the church of Peace has fumigated you infidel vermin out and put real scholars in your stead."

This was the year of the fundamentalists, to be sure. Dean Coffin of the college had published a new book, *The Soul Comes Back*, a discussion of personality with a special definition of the soul as "the self conscious level of personality," and he had gone into the matter of the soul's relationship with the cosmos, God, and other people. He concluded that the soul was not an inherent part of man, but something to be achieved.

This book had been reviewed scathingly by the Rev. Mr. Phelps during his perorations in Whittier, and the Friends churches in the area were a-buzz with discussions of the matter. The Whittier Meeting appointed a committee to investigate, and while Dean Coffin was finally exonerated of what amounted to heresy, even to be charged was embarrassing.

That fall of 1930, town and gown were having their

troubles. The Rev. Mr. Phelps had left the citizens with the uncomfortable thought that there might be a considerable amount of hanky-panky going on up on college hill. He had insinuated that the college was alive with sexual immorality and gambling.

Good moral Whittierites, watching the apparent decay of the civilization around them in Greater Los Angeles, which was as freshly washed in bathtub gin as any other city, hearing the blare of saxophones and the swishing of the Charleston, were ready to believe almost anything. Fundamentalists among the Friends continued to believe that dancing was "impure, polluting, corrupting, debasing, destroying spirituality, increasing carnality" and attempting to accomplish something in a public place that was best accomplished in a bedroom.

President Walter F. Dexter of Whittier College and his faculty, however, knew something the good burghers did not—that most of the youth of Whittier College indulged in dancing off campus. They did not go into what else occurred at these parties, but they came to the conclusion that if dancing was part of the new way of life of the young, it ought to be brought to the campus and supervised, rather than left off with the students breaking the rules of the college every weekend, in spirit if not in letter.

A quiet little investigation disclosed what President Dexter suspected: the older people in the college community (trustees and the like) abhorred dancing, and the younger people (students and young faculty) adored it. So in September 1930, when the student body held its annual reception, President Dexter gave the students permission to hold a dance at the Wardman gymnasium. The place was decorated with palms and lanterns and leis (Hawaiian motif) and everyone came to the party. There was a grand march, led by President and Mrs. Dexter, all found partners, and *everybody danced.* Later some *played cards.*

The Whittier Meeting told the college board of trustees that dancing and card playing were improper social amusements, and that this matter would be taken up with the California yearly meeting, which controlled the college. Permission for these sinful activities had been granted in violation of the college bylaws. Luckily for President Dexter the board of trustees of the college was split on the matter of dancing. But in view of the hullaballoo the board decided that dancing would not be permitted on the college campus. So the next college reception was held at the Whittier Women's Club, three blocks off-campus, and featured dancing in the ballroom, and games downstairs.

Whittier College's announced purpose was undergoing some changes, too. In the 1920s the college authorities had established an integrated program, seeing that their student body was changing character, and now they concentrated on providing the students with a Christian philosophy of life. It was higher education with a very definite Quaker overtone, and it was expected that most graduates would become teachers, preachers, or social workers, and that a lesser number would go into the professions. For the most part the student body was relatively poor; in Richard Nixon's first year 83 percent of the men earned at least part of their expenses, so he was in the company of his peers in every sense during these depression days.

Since the college had doubled in size in a few years, some social changes were in order, too, and Richard Nixon found himself in the middle of them. Whittier had no national fraternities or sororities, but it did have the equivalent in a men's society called the Franklins. The membership was limited, and some who were left out were not very happy about it. One such was a sophomore by the name of Dean Triggs. He was older than the usual college student, having spent several years "knocking around" before he went to college. He began the year 1930–31 looking over the college and for an opportunity to organize a new group.

One person immediately caught his eye. It was Richard Milhous Nixon, who had come to the college and settled in immediately, playing freshman football (there were only eleven freshmen on the whole squad, so everyone played every game) and getting elected class president in the first flush of the fall. Triggs approached Richard Nixon and found him interested. They both approached Professor Upton, who agreed to sponsor the new society. Then they began finding members, and soon had enough takers to form a respectable group. They found a name, *Orthogonian* (square dealers, from the Greek), and the square became their symbol (beans, brawn, brain, and bowels being the corners). Professor Upton gave them a symbol, the boar's head—the symbolism being that the European boar was a snake killer and the Orthogonians would stamp out evil, and a motto in French *écrasons l'infâme*—which means the same. The boys wore sweaters with big O's on them, and assembled once a month at Sanders' café in Whittier to eat beans and spaghetti, their symbolic feed. They had a song:

> All hail the mighty boar
> Our patron beast is he . . .

(words and music by Richard Nixon)

And Richard Milhous Nixon was elected first president of the Orthogonians, because he was an organizer of the first water.

Who cared if the Franklins laughed and called them "the big pigs?"

> Écrasons l'infâme
> Our battle cry will be,
> We'll fight for the right
> And win the victory.

22

A Young Man in a Hurry

Richard Milhous Nixon's first year at Whittier College was satisfactory in every way. President of his class. President of the Orthogonians. He wrote and played the lead in the slightly risqué (Whittier standards) Orthogonian play, and he had a role in the freshman class play. He was among the most enthusiastic players on the freshman football team. He contributed to the *Quaker Campus*, the student newspaper.

At the end of the year a classmate wrote in his yearbook, "You sure have been a keen Orthogonian president, class president and everything else. The funny and keen part of it is you have just gotten started—Eddie."

And with a touch of paternalism, outgoing senior and student body vice-president Claire Jobe wrote: "Keep up the good start you've made, Nixon. You sure are a good leader."

There were poems and friendly little notes from classmates, young women and young men. One could hardly say that Richard Milhous Nixon was either shy or unpopular. "He was a real enthusiastic guy," said Kenneth Ball, classmate, fellow history major (there were four in the class), and Nixon partner on the freshman debating team.

One aspect of debating that was to stand a future politician in good stead: he had to be prepared to take the affirmative or negative side on almost any question, and then make an argument that would indicate that he believed what he was saying. On the freshman debating team, Nixon and Ball once argued the negative on "Installment Buying Is a Detriment to the Country," and whipped their opposition. And Nixon could now crack a joke in a debate. "Malthus, who made himself famous warning the world of over-population, was what I would call a hypocrite. He got married and had twelve children."

In view of later presidential positions, some of Richard Milhous Nixon's debates are interesting in retrospect for their subject matter. His team defeated the University of Southern California team that year defending the position: "All Nations Should Adopt a Policy of Free Trade," and beat California Christian College defending the theme "Tariff Is Detrimental to the Prosperity of the World."

For a college boy, Richard Nixon was dreadfully, dreadfully serious. He was known sometimes as "the boy with the intellectual look above the eyebrows" and of course what that meant to his peers was that he studied very hard, got good grades, and took the academic world seriously. He taught in the East Whittier Quaker Church Sunday school that year (the young marrieds class), if other testimony is needed as to his seriousness of mind and the hold the religion of Friends held on him then. He played piano in the Friends church. He was dedicated to the Horatio Alger principle. He was greatly respected in the community of his peers and by adults for his achievements. That used to be a legitimate basis for respect of youth. He was a square—the Orthogonian mystique summed up his character very nicely—but he was a square among squares, and there were no hipsters in evidence even for comparative purposes, nor any sophisticated members of the Eastern-oriented establishment much nearer than San Francisco. Richard did not even know of the existence of the Eastern establishment; he was an innocent among innocents. Except among the handful of rich men's sons and the odd recipient of a scholarship, that establishment's tentacles in the West in the 1930s and 1940s were as wispy as those of a Portuguese man-of-war. Westerners thought very little about Eastern schools and Eastern ways, and were so naïve as to not even know they were different, or that here, in what was then the New York-Philadelphia-Washington axis (later expanded to include Boston), was the domain of the movers and shakers of American economics and thus of American society.

Study and forensics produced in Richard Milhous Nixon a habit he was to carry through his political career. He read avidly and catholically, and he took notes on little index cards as he did so, *aides-mémoires,* which he kept and kept and kept. The value to him of his system was proved: the *Reader's Digest* held an Extemporaneous Speaking Contest in southern California (and probably everywhere else). During a specified period the contestants were to read the *Digest*; part of the game was that their speech topic would be assigned on their appearance at the contest, and their success depended on their homework and their ability to reconstruct an article, given the title of it. This kind of work was precisely down Richard Nixon's alley. He applied himself to the *Digest*, and when the day came, aided by memory of the notes he had taken for so long, he won the contest handily. His success as a speaker was due as much to preparation as to platform performance. For Richard Nixon, even in college days, knowledge was power.

In his second year at Whittier, Richard Nixon was elected to the College Knights, an honorary men's organization. He went out for football, and attended practice faithfully, but he was not big enough, fast enough or skillful enough to make the starting lineup, or to do more than sit on the bench and lend his visible enthusiasm to the warriors on the field. He did finally make the all-interclass team of 1932.

Richard Nixon's scholarship that year was nearly impeccable. He had learned in his freshman year that he did not want to be a journalist (his only C's in college were in journalism) and his interest in the student publication waned and then ended altogether in his sophomore year. He got A's in nearly everything else, except French, where he was a B student. There was a pattern to his grades: they got better as he went along, and as he engaged in more and more outside activity.

In his sophomore year he was elected to membership of the executive committee of the Whittier student body, he continued in the Orthogonians as a member, he worked harder than ever in the store, yet he found time to make debating an even more important part of his life than the year before. One might examine that interest for a moment, since it became so important to Richard Milhous Nixon; there are indications that it shaped his style. What were the principles of debate? One was to marshal facts, an army of facts. One was to present these facts in pyramidal fashion to overwhelm the enemy. One was to undercut the enemy's pyramid with slashing attack on his facts or reasoning. And one was, having won or lost, to be free to forget the whole vigorous battle and start over again next time.

The team this year consisted of Richard Nixon, Ed Miller, Joe Sweeney, and Joe Bosio. They debated California Christian College for first place in their intercollege league. They won the Allison Speech Trophy. They gave up their Christmas vacation to travel 3500 miles in seventeen days, through the Pacific Northwest, debating Redlands University, and several others, and ending at Linfield College in McMinnville, Oregon. In February, at a southern California contest, Nixon and Miller defeated the national champion debaters, Dean and Frost of Redlands University.

Richard Nixon's college career never faltered after that. In his junior year he was a member of the executive committee of the student government again, a member of the joint council of control. He was a debater, and repeated the long Christmas trip this year, with the added excitement of being snowbound en route for four days by a Rocky Mountain blizzard. He played a "heavy" role as an English innkeeper in John Drinkwater's *Bird In Hand*—complete with sideburns and a pipe. He appeared in a one-act play, a "serious study" of the mining country of Scotland. And in the spring he was elected president of the associated students of Whittier College for the year to come. His senior year was a cap to all that had gone before. He had a girl, Florence Welch. As Number 23 on the football team, he tried hard, and practiced indefatigably but never achieved anything more than a status as prime bench-sitter and enthusiastic team supporter. It was the only activity in which Richard Nixon also stood and waited. He was in the glee club and in the honor society. He won the southern California intercollegiate public speaking conference contest in Los Angeles that year: "Resolved that the Power of the President Should Be Increased As a Matter of Settled Policy."

When the end of his college career loomed, his peers summed up his year of leadership: "Always progressive and with a liberal attitude he has led us through the year with flying colors."

He had actually earned the accolade in several ways. The Orthogonians had opened the way for other young men, who established two more fraternities, the Lancer Society and the William Penn Society. And Richard Nixon, a fast man with an issue, had seized upon a natural—the desire of the student body for dances on the campus instead of in the half-light of the town, blocks away. Whittier men and women wanted open social life. Richard Nixon campaigned on that issue for his student body presidency, and won, and by the beginning of his senior year had persuaded the trustees to not only permit but help pay for dances which would hereafter be held once a month.

And square though he might be, President Nixon was willing to stick his neck out in a good cause. A coed by the name of Marion Hawk was organizing one of the proms, and she needed flowers for decorations of the hall. Nixon took a gang of students out to Grandmother Milhous's place and she let them raid the garden where she labored so hard. But there weren't enough, and Marion Hawk saw the peach blossoms in bloom in the little park across the street from the Whittier theater. Nothing would do but they must have peach blossoms. So, President Nixon and his gang went off to get peach blossoms. They were in the act of taking them when down swooped the minions of the law, and they were lucky to be let off without being clapped into durance vile for destroying public property.

But that was Richard Nixon's way. He was eager to please. Sometimes he held meetings of the Orthogonians at his grandmother's house—where Almira and Hannah prepared the ritual food of beans and spaghetti by the crock. Sometimes he took his debaters home. He was known to have brought the football team home to dinner on occasion, or at a party to show up with a freezer can full of ice cream. It was all part of his effort to be a good fellow, perhaps to overcome his own natural introversion. Having a hand in a family grocery did not hurt in the natural alimentary orientation of college youth.

The store played the major role in the lives of the senior Nixons—store and church. Frank continued his peppery ways, and Hannah soothed customers and suppliers and even her children on occasion, avoiding the hair-trigger of Frank's temper. Hannah was a remarkable woman in many ways, kindly, deeply religious in the fashion of her family, and never sparing of herself. In the spring of 1933 her eldest son Harold died of tuberculosis—there was nothing anyone could do about it apparently; she watched for months as he wasted away, distressed in the knowledge that he, too, knew that he was going to die. It was a wretched period for the family, etching them all with a kind of tragedy that then touched many families. Yet through it all Hannah remained gentle and patient with the world around her.

At this time she was deeply troubled when she discovered that the store was being regularly robbed by a customer who was a shoplifter. She told Frank, who leapt to the side of law and order, and insisted that she have the woman arrested. Hannah demurred, and after a family argument they consulted the pastor of the East Whittier Friends Church. The pastor tended to agree with Frank, and so did all the family except Richard. He sided with his mother, and told her to stand fast and handle the problem as she saw fit. She took his advice—it coincided with her own compassionate disposition. She gathered her courage, spoke to the offender, and reduced the woman to tears and the promise to repay. Richard backed her all the way.

He was a strange concatenation of shyness and aggression. Much has been made of his football days and his perennial position on the bench. He might have gotten into action with the football team, except that Whittier's "Poets" had too much at stake in 1932 and 1933. The team won its first two games, lost a game to Occidental College, and then steamed on to win the conference football championship for the first time since 1921. The coach, Chief Newman, was scarcely going to jeopardize any victory by throwing in the weaker men. The next year was not quite so successful; the team managed only to tie for second place, but the pressure was on all year. No Nixon appearances. He was so low on the totem pole that he was not even privileged to make trips with the team, so when Whittier went to Tucson to play he and two friends drove over on their own to cheer the boys on, and watch them lose, 45 to 0. Even the snowstorm of the day did not dampen his ardor.

It was his never-ending drive that amazed all on the Whittier campus. As student body president, he arranged picnics, staged plays, and brought bands to the campus. He worked hard on the annual homecoming program. And, of course, he won scholarship honors and more public speaking and debating victories. He graduated in the spring of 1934 with many honors, including scholastic ones. But for those last there was a real need: if he hoped to go on to law school, which he did, then he had to have a scholarship and a very complete one at that. He applied for several such grants, and was backed by his professors. It was a bad time, 1934: the nation was thrashing in the swamp of depression. But Duke University off in North Carolina was trying to establish a law school and welcomed bright young men from the West. Duke granted Richard Nixon a scholarship.

23

Student,
Debater, Politician

Richard Nixon finished his college career as satisfactorily as he could have wished. Dr. Dexter, the President of Whittier, recommended him to the dean of the Duke law school "because I believe that he will become one of America's important if not great leaders." His history professor, Dr. Paul S. Smith, regarded him as one of his best students. But some of Nixon's teachers thought he cared too much about winning, and the Quakers among them wondered if he did not justify his means to achieve good ends. As for his peers, he was respected for his achievements, held in some awe for his tremendous drive, and regarded as not quite one of them.

This drive for success was notable even in the family. Aunt Jane Beeson remarked on it later in a letter: "I never will forget," she wrote, "how he used to go all out to win when we were having games at parties. He sure put his whole soul in everything he did."

And now, in 1934, Richard Milhous Nixon had decided to study the law, and would put his whole soul into that endeavor.

He headed for Durham that summer and discovered on arrival that there was no place for graduate students in the campus complex, so he joined forces with a fellow student, William Perdue, of Macon, Georgia, and found a room for $5 a month in Duke Forest, about a mile from the campus. He had $35 a month from home, a tuition scholarship of $250, and a National Youth Administration job that paid 35 cents an hour.

There were forty-four students in his class, from thirty-seven states, and nearly all of them were on scholarship. In order to build a big reputation in a hurry, Dean H. Claude Horack of the law school had evolved a squeeze system—there would be fewer scholarships available for second-year students than there were for first-year students. So the pressure was on from the first day.

Nixon, the small-town boy in a strange and often hostile environment, was frankly scared. He told an upperclassman, William Adelson, that he was worried about his ability to keep up. He had counted thirty-two Phi Beta Kappa keys in his class.

The talk occurred in the Duke library, where Nixon was studying late one night. Adelson was sympathetic, and that is where the "iron butt" story came from. "Listen, Nixon . . ." he said. "You've got an iron butt and that's the secret of becoming a lawyer."

Richard Milhous Nixon was admirably suited to the grind. He sought few amusements except to watch Duke football, which he favored with as acute an interest as he had shown for Whittier football in the years before. There was no put-on or fakery about it. Richard Nixon was a good student of football, and would remain so, knowing names, records, and achievements in an unusually thorough fashion. But as for the rest, he had neither the time nor the money to do much more than study. Here he was generally in the same boat with serious law students everywhere, except that most law students of the thirties had a reputation for "raising hell" on vacations. Not Richard. There was a certain amount of horseplay with his fellow students, but that was all. Occasionally he and other students were invited to the house of the dean or one of the professors for dinner. But generally he was so deeply involved in work and study that his classmates called him Gloomy Gus.

One of Richard Nixon's jobs was in the law library, where he came under the stern and usually reproving glances of the law librarian, Miss Covington. Other students did not regard working for Miss Covington as a desirable occupation, but Nixon never complained. He worked in the law library after school, got his dinner, went back to the library to study at night and was usually one of the last to leave. Then, in the morning, he was one of the first to arrive.

In spite of his gloomy fears, or perhaps because of them, Richard Nixon secured good enough grades to have his scholarship renewed for his second year—which meant he could go back to school. Otherwise it would have been impossible. During that second year he roomed with Carl W. Haley and two other divinity students who had taken a house. One of them was married, and his wife kept house for the crew. They borrowed each other's shirts and jackets and socks, and went to the movies occasionally. Again in the fall there was Duke football. Otherwise it was more grind.

In this second year, the courses were harder, and there was always the implied threat of withdrawal of the scholarship if a student did not succeed in maintaining at least a B average. Nixon did. His average was very nearly A, through grind, grind, grind. But he was still worried, and when school was over for the year, and the dean's office seemed dilatory in releasing the all-important grades, he and William Perdue and Fred Albrink decided to raid the office one night and discover the awful truth. So they did—the others hoisted the skinny Nixon through the transom of the locked office, he moved with the finesse of a cat burglar, got what they wanted—a good look—and got out, and was never captured.

That summer Nixon, Albrink, Perdue, and Lyman Brownfield decided to room together. They found a place in Duke Forest, in the home of a widow, which they christened Whippoorwill Manor. They took one room, and paid fifty dollars for the year. They had two double beds and very little else. The room had no light and no running water. They used an outhouse and to heat their room they had a sheet-metal stove, but scarcely enough money to burn anything in it but crumpled newspapers. The trick was to get up in the morning early enough to get to school and use the lavatories there to wash and shave. Then, after a day of classes, to go to the gymnasium for a shower.

Those were the days when Nixon arose at five o'clock, about an hour before his roommates, and set off alone, because he felt he needed that extra hour in the library. Iron butt again. Probably better than any of his contemporaries, Richard Nixon was conscious of his own limitations. He *knew* that he had to study hard to achieve what he wanted. His roommates observed with some wonderment this driving self-demand that characterized Nixon. Years later Fred Albrink still recalled the law scholar Nixon as the hardest working man he had ever seen.

He had a sense of humor, but it was a very private one, shy, and in a sense studied. At the Senior Beer Bust he was a real wow—he mounted a picnic table and gave a deadpan parody of a talk on Social Security—which he called Insecurity. But that was just once. He was asked to repeat the performance and he demurred; he had neither the time nor the inclination to become known as an entertaining fellow.

He worked for the *Law Review* and Duke Bar Association Journal, and wrote one article published under his own name on the subject of auto insurance law. He worked for the school's legal clinic, which meant doing legwork among citizens in the city of Durham, and by that much he was exposed to the South and Southern culture. Yet his was a rarefied exposure at best, the law grind had little time to consider the special problems of the South.

In his senior year at the law school, Richard Nixon achieved the same kind of honors that had marked his career at Whittier, the kind that can be won by super-drive. He was elected to the Iredell Law Club, one of two honoraries. The other was Phi Delta Phi, the national fraternity. He was elected to the Order of the Coif (the top three men were taken, and he was third in his class).

The Veterans of Future Wars, an organization of Young Turks in the law school, decided to pick the senior who would go furthest in their class, and they chose Robert T. Bean of Louisville as the man most likely to succeed, which in their terms meant to become a candidate for President of the United States. Drive did not seem to count in that popularity contest. But there was another kind of contest, for president of the student bar association, which was the equivalent of the student body. Phi Delta Phi put up a candidate, and Iredell Law Club put up Richard Milhous Nixon. There was a vigorous campaign, with Richard Nixon working hard. He was elected. As president of the student bar association, he persuaded Thurman Arnold, the liberal Democrat who had made a reputation as "the trust-buster" to speak before the Duke students. Richard Nixon was very much impressed because Arnold was "one of the biggest men in law in the country. He's pleading cases before the Supreme Court now."

As the fall of Nixon's last year in law school drew on, leisure hours were devoted less to football and more to thoughts about the future. Some of the students intended to go home and pass the bar (hopefully) and hang out their shingles. Some intended to join family law firms. Richard hoped to go to what he considered the top of the profession, to join one of the big New York corporate law firms. The class was down to twenty-six, and he was third. With Harlan Leathers and William Perdue, Nixon set out during Christmas vacation to visit New York firms, and they appeared for interviews at half a dozen of them. Leathers got a job with Millbank, Tweed, Hope, and Webb, one of the most important firms in New York. Perdue got a job with a big oil company. The shy, aggressive boy from Whittier, California, did not make that kind of an impression on the princes of his chosen profession. The firm of Donovan, Leisure, Newton, and Lombard expressed some interest, but no job was forthcoming. Richard Milhous Nixon had suffered his first rebuff from the genteel Eastern establishment.

Back at Duke he picked up the pieces of his shattered ambition, and tried again. He applied for a job with the Federal Bureau of Investigation, which was very much in the public eye for its celebrated "gangbusting" activity. Dean Horack wrote a strong letter of recommendation. But June came, and graduation time, and no response from the FBI. Richard Nixon had not intended to return to California. Suddenly, he had no place else to go. He had been away from the state for three years, and had not registered as a voter, although he was twenty-four years old. It was questionable if he would be allowed to take the California bar examinations that spring, and he was worried enough about it to have Dean Horack intervene, to secure the necessary permission. It was worked out favorably.

Almira Milhous was eighty-eight years old and still living in the house on Whittier Boulevard and conducting her busy life. She was a member of the Women's Christian Temperance Union, the Whittier College Auxiliary, the East Whittier Women's Improvement Club, and, of course, the church. She was busy and zesty and sharp as always. For years she had been living with Olive and Oscar Marshburn, her daughter and son-in-law, and the house had continued to be the mecca of the Milhous clan, with pilgrimages made there on birthdays and holidays. For three years Richard had not attended; he had not had the money to come home, but he had kept in touch, and Grandmother Milhous had sent him little gifts of money from time to time. Now when Richard was going to graduate from law school, Hannah and Frank announced that they were going to take some time off and drive to North Carolina for the ceremony. Almira announced that she was coming, too. So she did. Richard got his sheepskin. Then they all went home to California.

24

The Young Lawyer

Whatever private thoughts he might have had about his rejection in the East, Richard Milhous Nixon settled down to make a life for himself in his home town. Whittier was then a center of about twenty-five thousand people, serving what was still very much a rural area of orange and avocado groves. As a lawyer Richard Nixon would have several advantages here. For one thing he was well known in the community from church and college activities. For another, he had a large family that was very prominent in Quaker circles. To be sure the Quakers were now outnumbered in the town, but they were a potent force.

Richard might have gone into business. His cousin Merle West was doing very well. Although Merle had never gone to college, he had left the Nixon gas station, gone into the fruit spraying business, then into raising avocados, and would finally establish himself in the rug-cleaning business in Whittier. Richard's brother Donald, after a stint at the

University of Southern California, was taking more responsibility in the family grocery store. But Richard's best bet was to get into law practice.

So one day in the fall of 1937 Richard Nixon appeared in his blue suit at the law offices of Wingert and Bewley in the Bank of America building in downtown Whittier. He knew Thomas Bewley, junior partner in the firm, for Bewley's grandfather and Frank Milhous had been acquainted back in Butlerville, Ind. So a connection, humble as it might be, got Richard Nixon a job. He was lucky; 1937 was a recession year, following close on the heels of a long, deep depression, and many young men of promise had no jobs at all.

As for work, Richard was put to doing what young lawyers do. He handled collections for the firm. He handled accident cases. He handled divorces, but he was not very good at divorce suits because his Quaker background caused him to try to persuade the parties to reconcile. Soon he began to handle trial work.

After about a year, Wingert and Bewley made Richard Nixon a partner, and he had more important law business to transact. The reason for the partnership was the need for a trial lawyer, and Richard Nixon was ideal for the task. Indeed, Nixon's whole educational career seemed bent in this direction. Examine it: his forensic ability, which involved thousands of hours of practice at presenting a "case"; his histrionic ability, which involved the learning of parts and the ability to project apparent emotion; and above all, the "iron butt," the ability to spend long hours preparing the case. Apparently had he continued in California law, Richard Milhous Nixon could have enjoyed a successful and enriching career as a trial lawyer. "He always seemed to be way ahead of the witness," said Thomas Bewley, "and could anticipate what answers the witness would make."

But it was a general law practice and Richard Nixon handled estates and taxes and corporations, too. He did a good deal of work for the Leffingwell ranch and the Citrus

Water Company. He became very much interested in business, so much so, in fact, that he organized the Citra-Frost Company, and persuaded businessmen in town to invest ten thousand dollars in it. The idea was sound—involving surplus oranges in southern California that year—fruit that could be bought very cheaply. Citra-Frost undertook to freeze the orange juice, and found some large customers who were interested. But the Nixon group never solved the preservation and packaging problem, perhaps because they used whole juice rather than concentrate. Whatever the problem, in a year and a half the company was out of business, and so was Richard Nixon.

He did much better as a lawyer. He opened an office in La Habra, to serve the four thousand people of that community, and divided his time between La Habra in the mornings and Whittier in the afternoons. He could often be seen in the firm's office on the sixth floor of the bank building, long after others had left, having a hamburger and a pineapple malted milk for his dinner.

He was very busy at first, and he took very little time for any kind of recreation. He did not play golf, he had long since abandoned tennis, and he had no interest in liquor, and no particular female friend. He liked to sit around the office talking shop at the end of the day. On Saturdays in the fall it was different. Then he went to football games, and since there was usually a football game somewhere in the Los Angeles area every Saturday and sometimes on Sunday, he had plenty to amuse him. But then as forever, amusement was really incidental to Richard Milhous Nixon. His eye was on the main chance.

Nixon was still very poor. Rather than spend twenty-five or thirty dollars for a desk for the La Habra office, he built one in the family garage by the grocery store.

He was full of theories about government. He believed it ought to be run like a business, and that it could be run like a business if more businessmen would give up time and money and engage in government.

Once again Richard sought activity, and his drive led him to leadership. He became a member of the twenty to thirty club, a group of young businessmen, and was elected president of the club. He became a member of the Junior Chamber of Commerce, and then president. He was president of the Duke alumni association for California. He was a member of the Whittier College alumni association, and he became president of that organization, too. He was elected trustee of the college—in his twenties the youngest of them. There were problems at the college after Dr. Dexter left under rather trying circumstances, and a move began to promote the election of Richard Milhous Nixon as president of Whittier College. It was a serious move, backed by a number of younger faculty members.

Nixon retained the friendships he had made at Duke, although they grew progressively dimmer with the years. His classmates from law school were scattered: New York, Baltimore, Hartford, Portland, Napoleon, Ohio, for example. But he kept in touch, particularly with his old roommates, by letter, and they reported on their triumphs and their marriages. One of his divinity school friends, Edward Miller, had gone to Cornell, and he wrote from Ithaca asking Nixon if he did not need a good young Quaker lawyer in his firm, ". . . a young fellow here active in the Meeting, finishing his law work this June. I've been struck by the Christian earnestness of him. . . ."

He was also active in the Friends church of East Whittier, particularly with young people.

Obviously this young man had a certain charisma in his own community, although the word had not yet been developed into a cliché. He represented very fully qualities that were honored in the 1930s in southern California: honesty, piety, ambition, dedication, and purpose. His purpose at that time, unrevealed to many, was to work his way up and then move to a big city where he could become a bigtime lawyer. The rebuff in New York had obviously hurt, but the spirit that had kept Nixon going out for football for three long years with nothing but his own hope to let him believe he might ever win a letter in the sport now kept him plugging with the same intensity at everything he touched.

For the first two years in Whittier, Richard's ambitions left no time for romance; one might belong to many organizations, but one got to be president by working harder than anyone else, and that meant doing things that no one else wanted to do, exercising leadership.

But a young bachelor tends to keep his evenings occupied, and Richard found social intercourse in the church and by joining the Whittier Community Players. His first role was as Señor Ortega in *First Lady*, in December 1937. The next season he had a part for which he was cut perfectly: that of District Attorney Flint in *Night of January 16th*, which involves a trial. Mrs. Clyde Baldwin, director of the theater, liked his portrayal. Mrs. Baldwin also regarded Nixon as a very handsome young man. She was not dismayed, apparently, by the ski-jump nose, which had already marked Nixon for caricaturists as early as the Whittier College days.

A year later, Richard Nixon tried out for a part in *The Dark Tower*, a play written by George Kaufman and Alexander Woollcott. So did a young teacher from Whittier High School named Pat Ryan.

Except for family and religion, the backgrounds of Thelma Catherine Patricia Ryan and Richard Milhous Nixon were strikingly similar. Both came from poor families. Both had worked their way for what they had received, although Pat's situation was much more difficult than Richard's. Both were young and on their own.

Pat Ryan's father William was born in Connecticut of a Connecticut family, and he shipped out on a whaling vessel when he was a youngster. He led an adventurous life, as a sailor and a surveyor in the Philippines, and in Alaska, where he had been lured by the dream of gold. He did not strike it rich in Alaska, and made his way to the Black Hills of South Dakota, where a brother was engaged in mining.

He did not strike it rich there either, but he learned mining engineering in the field.

William Ryan met a woman in the Dakotas. She was Katherina Halberstadt Bender, a widow with two children. She had been born in the German principality of Hesse, but had come as a girl of ten to live with an aunt in America and had grown up in the United States. When she was twenty years old she married a shop foreman, and had two children, Matthew and Neva. Katherina's husband died in a flood before Neva was born, and she was left to face the world alone. Then William Ryan came along, a mature man of forty-one, who offered marriage and protection. They were married. It was not long before the word came that men were striking it rich in Nevada, and William Ryan picked up the family and took them all to the tent city of Ely, where he got a job as a mining engineer. Here his and Katherina's children were born, William, Thomas, and little Thelma, as she was called at birth. In 1916, when Thelma was four years old, Katherina persuaded William to stop the dangerous business of mining and move to a piece of ground near Artesia, California. In the East it would have been called a small truck farm (eleven acres). In the West it was called a ranch. It was about twenty miles southeast of Los Angeles, and the house there was a small frame structure, not unlike the Nixon house in Yorba Linda, only a few miles away.

The two oldest children, Katherina's by her first marriage, were soon gone—but so was their mother. She died when Thelma was thirteen years old. Thelma was a little girl no longer. She cooked and sewed and kept house for the three men of the family, and went to school and nursed her ambition to go to college. At Excelsior Union High School, Thelma was known as a vivacious redhead. She was vice-president of the school dramatic club and played in the senior play *The Rise of Silas Lapham*. Because of the vagaries of their life after their mother died, her two brothers were in the same grade in school at the same time she was. When her father fell ill with silicosis, Thelma graduated from high school, but gave up the idea of college and nursed her father for two years. Then he died.

Shedding the name of Thelma, she christened herself Pat, and set off into the world to make something of herself. Pat Ryan's life now was much more difficult than Richard Nixon's had been at the same age. He had a family behind him, and if his family was not wealthy, at least he could count on his parents and grandmother for various kinds of support, moral no less than financial. For all practical purposes, Pat Ryan was alone. Her two brothers were off in Los Angeles, working their ways through college. If she wanted education she must do the same.

She continued to live at the house in Artesia, and began studying at Fullerton Junior College. She supported herself by working part-time in the First National Bank of Artesia as a teller. But after a year she left Fullerton Junior College. An elderly couple she knew wanted to go to New York, but did not want to drive there. They offered Pat a return bus ticket to Los Angeles if she would drive them to New York in their Packard sedan. She succumbed to the adventure, then when she reached New York decided to stay. Another girl might have been daunted by the obvious depression in New York. This was 1932 and men were selling apples in the streets. But Pat Ryan found a job as a secretary at Seton Hospital. She took a course in x-ray, and became a technician. She remained for two years, leading an active social life, but not getting the college education she wanted, and eventually this life appeared her a dead end. So Pat took her bus ticket and went back to Los Angeles. She moved into the apartment with her brothers Bill and Tom, and they helped her get established as a student at the university. She would, of course, have to work her own way. Richard Nixon had a scholarship to Whittier, and he lived at home, which cost nothing; but while Pat's tuition was virtually free, there were still books and fees and self-support. Her way was much, much harder than that of her future husband.

She worked in the school cafeteria, and in the library, and as a movie extra when the opportunity arose. She worked as a salesgirl at Bullock's Wilshire department store. And, like Richard Nixon, she graduated with honors. She found a job teaching shorthand, typing and bookkeeping at Whittier High School. She was very popular as a teacher, with students and with the faculty. She knew how to handle the students (friendly but firm) and the older women teachers (industrious and self-effacing.) Then came the tryouts for *The Dark Tower.*

Richard Milhous Nixon was very much impressed with the new young teacher. "Some day I'm going to marry you," he told her, driving her home from rehearsal one night. Pat was less impressed with the young lawyer. "He's a bit unusual," she confided to a friend. And while Nixon pursued her avidly, the far more sophisticated Pat continued to see other young men.

Richard Nixon took Pat Ryan dancing. He was not much of a dancer, but he learned. A new skating rink opened in Artesia. He took her ice-skating. He skated on his ankles, but he went. They went hiking and to the beach. They went out to dinner—usually to parties at someone's house because none of their crowd of young people had very much money. Pat was making $190 a month as a teacher, and this was very good pay for the late 1930s. With the enthusiasm of the young, they amused themselves and they laughed a lot. Pat Ryan recalled that Richard Nixon was usually the life of the party, telling more jokes and funny stories than anyone else.

She grew progressively more impressed. Tom Bewley was city attorney of Whittier and he appointed Richard Nixon as his assistant. And the law practice brought in more money every year. Richard was a rising young lawyer, and he could think about getting married. It was a mark of the changing times that he did not seek his bride within the Quaker community as Quakers had nearly always done in the old days. Nor was there any family trouble about it. Richard had taken Pat home to meet Hannah very early in the game, when they were playing in *The Dark Tower*. Hannah's reaction was that she was beautiful, but she seemed a little frail. And as the courtship became serious Pat cemented her relationship with her mother-in-law by helping her. Hannah baked all the pies they sold in the Nixon grocery, arising very early in the morning to do it. And one morning Pat showed up to help her, stayed as long as she could, and then went off for a full day of school. That was the kind of doing that endeared a future daughter-in-law.

With marriage in the air in the spring of 1940 Richard Nixon set out in his own fashion to examine his mind and feelings. He went on a brief trip to northern California with his brother Don, and kept Don up half the night discussing the merits of various engagement rings. "A man only buys a ring once in his lifetime, and that should be a ring his wife would always be proud to wear," he said. He had already done his homework—checked with a member of his twenty to thirty club who was a jeweler. The trouble was that Richard Milhous Nixon did not have enough money to buy Pat the kind of ring he decided she ought to have.

That spring Richard Nixon asked Pat to marry him and she agreed. They solved the problem of the ring by combining resources to buy a better engagement ring and matching wedding ring than Richard could have afforded on his own. It was all delivered to Pat on May Day in a May Day basket, and the happy couple announced the engagement to the senior Nixons by appearing at their house and showing them the ring.

Pat and Richard were married, then, on June 21, 1940. Pat's religious background was rather uncertain, and she agreed to be married in a Quaker ceremony, but it was not performed at the East Whittier Church. Instead they were married at the Old Mission Inn in Riverside. These were modern times, and while Richard was a birthright Quaker, he was a modern Quaker in every way, and a Western Quaker at that.

Richard and Pat had decided to pool their money and take a two-week honeymoon in Mexico. If they were careful and if they "ate in" a good deal they could manage it. So they had laid in a supply of canned goods to take with them. During the wedding festivities, thoughtful friends removed all the labels from the cans, so they ate interesting meals.

After two weeks of spaghetti for breakfast and canned grapefruit for supper, the Richard Nixons returned, to set up housekeeping in an apartment over a garage. They were young, poor, and very gay, and they had friends who were also young and poor and equally happy. Special among these were Jack and Helene Drown, whose situation was very much like that of the Nixons. Jack Drown had been a football player and was now attending the University of Southern California law school; Helene was a fellow teacher at Pat's school; so they had a great deal in common: young marrieds, football, law school, and teaching. The Drowns were to become the Nixon's closest friends.

There was not much money, but the Nixons' tastes were simple. For amusement they went to San Juan Capistrano and Santa Monica beach with the Drowns quite often. Sometimes they went swimming at midnight. At night they would go dancing, to the Cocoanut Grove at the Ambassador. This could be an expensive place—but not if one went to the bar and ordered a drink, and then nursed it half the night while dancing. They went to the opera and sat in the gallery. They went to the movies, and had more parties at home.

Richard continued his law practice, and Pat went back

to teaching as if she had never been away. Richard read the newspapers and followed the progress of the European war, which raised so many questions in the minds of the Quakers of Whittier. What would they do if the United States got into the war?

25

What Richard
Nixon Fought For

When the Japanese attacked the United States Pacific Fleet
at Pearl Harbor, Richard Nixon decided he had to do
something more than stay on as a small-town lawyer. His
ambition had been pulling him away from Whittier even
before the war began. He had talked with Jack Drown
about going into practice together in Los Angeles. He had
made a trip to Havana and even considered setting up
there. The war caused him to put aside all that ambition for
the moment but it did not change his desire to make a
move. As a birthright Quaker, with his family and religious
background, he could have registered as a conscientious ob-
jector and sat out the war. But he decided otherwise.

His first step was a compromise with his heritage—he
went to serve as a civilian with the federal government. In
January 1942, Nixon applied for a job with the Office of
Price Administration in Washington. The officials considered his record at Duke and in Whittier and gave him one

easily enough. It was not much of a job—he was willing to accept about sixty dollars a week, and that is what he was paid to start. He was put to work in a "bull pen" handling tire rationing problems. Almost immediately Richard Nixon showed his superior abilities. He began to organize and simplify and struggled manfully against red tape. In six months he had two raises in pay, to ninety dollars a week, and was supervising the activity of several attorneys and secretaries.

Nixon found OPA dismal. Coming from a small, self-satisfied, and heavily Republican community, he discovered that he was working among Democrats and radicals who had strong feelings that the business community could not manage its own affairs. As a college boy and law student Nixon had dreamed of slaying dragons in government; now he was frustratingly bogged down in a self-serving federal bureaucracy. Further, Washington was full of men in uniform, and a young civilian there was very self-conscious. He began consulting with Pat and his conscience.

The Milhouses, guardians of the Quaker tradition, had seen many changes in America and to some extent they had changed with the times. Almira Milhous was a determined pacifist, and so, in a more quiet way, was Hannah. Yet when Richard Nixon decided to apply for a commission in the navy, they did not try to interfere. "He was always guided by his convictions, which I never questioned or discouraged," said Hannah Nixon.

Friends from the East Whittier Church regarded Nixon as active in church affairs, but as a young man not particularly devout and in no sense one of the "spiritual" members. There was a definite break with the past in this enlistment, but it had come gradually, and Nixon himself did not realize it until long after the fact, when someone asked him if there was not a time when he felt he was entering another world from the one in which he had grown up.

"I think the war was probably the breakpoint," a mature Nixon remarked. "It seemed to me to be the right thing to do. . . . I could have engaged in other activities during the war, such as my uncle and others had during World War I, Red Cross and other activities. But I just had a different attitude toward the great problems that confronted us at that time. I was a student of history in my own right. I didn't just take everything from my mother and grandmother and my father and their ideas. . . . I was convinced that with this great threat of world-wide aggression that was sweeping across the globe, that no one could stand aside."

Nixon's application was accepted and he was commissioned a lieutenant junior grade in the Navy and sent to Quonset Point, R.I., for training as an administrative officer in the naval air service. Here he learned something about the navy, and when he had been indoctrinated, he was sent to Ottumwa, Iowa, to a new naval air station. He found an apartment at Fourth and Green streets and brought Pat to live there. In his application for naval service Nixon noted that his wife was self-supporting. Indeed, she got herself a job as a teller with the Union Bank—this was not unusual, for she was used to supporting herself.

Nixon served as aide to the executive officer and as legal officer of the new base until the spring of 1943, when he was assigned to the overseas duty he wanted. He had applied for sea duty, but he was going to be assigned to establish a land base in the South Pacific. He and Pat went to San Francisco, where she found a job as an economist for the Office of Price Administration and he made ready to ship out. After the usual waiting, he did ship out on the USS *President Monroe*, and landed at Espiritu Santo, the headquarters of naval air. Aboard ship there was not much to do, but Richard Nixon did one thing—he learned to play poker, and with his usual concentration on anything he tried, he became a very skillful poker player.

Lieutenant Nixon's naval career was useful if not spectacular. He was assigned as operations officer to the South Pacific Combat Air Transport Command. SCAT, as it was called, set up air strips on South Pacific islands and supervised the air transport of supplies and people. It was not exactly a combat job, but in the South Pacific combat had a habit of coming to the men everywhere, and from time to time Lieutenant Nixon's unit was subjected to Japanese bombing, more in the beginning, less as the South Pacific campaign was won.

When Nixon went to the South Pacific he drank little and smoked less, he read the Bible and he did not swear. But informal military language was infectious and soon he was using it, and he was smoking cigars at the poker table. Indeed, the navy did mark a change in Nixon's way of life.

He took good care of the men in his command (begging hams for their dinners for example). He opened Nixon's Hamburger Stand, which was widely known in the area as a place where you could get something decent to eat. It was supported by scrounging and trading Japanese battle flags and other souvenirs for things to eat, and even beer and sometimes whiskey. It was a good command, which won citations from the navy, as well as a promotion for its leader. He had all kinds of men, a boy from the slums of New York, the son of a railroad engineer, a farmer from Nebraska, a Mexican, an Indian, and an Italian. When things were dull he taught a course in business law, and played poker in the evenings. He was not a plunger but a very conservative player who seemed to end up thirty to sixty dollars ahead just about every night. And when he was not busy with duties, he did a lot of reading, and took notes on what he read, in the fashion he had followed since school days.

He read to learn and draw conclusions. He read a magazine article about a Fulbright Resolution in the Senate to create appropriate international machinery to establish and maintain a just and lasting peace, and he so noted. He read an article in *Liberty* by Maurice Hindus on German atrocities. Result, said Nixon in his notes: Russians hate Germans *as such*. He read about heart disease: overeating was worst, mild exercise was good. He read about childbirth: it was best to have children at two-year intervals and mothers should nurse their children instead of bottle-feeding them.

There was a sort of pattern to the reading he wanted to remember, and thus annotated. There was the war, of course; but he was equally interested in the postwar world to come. He noted from the *Kiplinger Magazine* an article that indicated a postwar trend to conservatism and encouragement of initiative, a temporary six-month recession after the war, and then five to ten years of prosperity, with emphasis on housing and consumer products. He was interested in self-help, and wrote down a list of rules for success in administration, compiled in a magazine by Harold Smith, director of the federal budget:

1. Be trained for job.
2. Have passion for anonymity.
3. A good and merciless judge of men willing to sacrifice personal prestige, loyalties, and friendships to the success of the job.
4. Stick to the administrative job and leave policy to the politicians.

From Bernard Baruch he learned: A speculator is one who observes the future and acts before it occurs.

Somewhere he picked up an axiom: Live so that you can look any man in the face and tell him to go to hell.

And another: Don't become overgenerous on the spur of the moment.

From Ben Hecht: "There is nothing so troublesome to genius as success. It substitutes press notices for dreams and cocktail parties for the pursuit of beauty. Fame is a sort of mummy case in which the creative talents of yesterday lie in state and glitter in mania."

He was interested in success. He made a note that Admiral Halsey became a naval aviator when he was fifty-one. He was more interested in political success. In his notes on the Fulbright resolution he *underlined* the facts that Fulbright was a Rhodes scholar from twenty-five to twenty-eight and became President of the University of Arkansas at thirty-four. He noted that the successful shipbuilder Andrew Jackson Higgins was a profane storyteller of note, that he drank "only when working," that he reduced everything to the lowest common denominator. He noted that Georgia's Ellis Arnall had been attorney general of his state when he was thirty-six, that Ben Hecht had been a foreign correspondent when he was twenty-six and a successful author before he was thirty, that Senator Murray of Oklahoma was profane and played poker and was a millionaire. And he noted that Governor Earl Warren of California was a war veteran, a state employee, had gone into the district attorney's office, had become district attorney at thirty-four, that he had prosecuted rackets, labor killers, bigwigs for conspiracy, that he had become attorney general, and had cracked down on gambling ships, used simple law enforcement procedures, and met all people running for office.

Lieutenant Nixon was also interested in abstractions. "What I Am Fighting For," he noted, picking up a title from a picture in the *Saturday Evening Post*, August 15. "Emphasis on simple things . . . privilege of choosing friends . . . creeds, radio programs, etc. vote."

A note on U. S. Grant. "Time comes in battle when both leaders decide they are defeated. He wins the battle who goes on fighting."

"Summer of Texas on Bureaucracy—favors return of power and independence to state governments. The facility with which a bureaucrat legislates encourages a multiplicity of laws."

On the Federal Communications Commission: "Exercise power over radio—'the composition of the traffic' as well as regulation of financial and contractual practices of the networks (sup. ct.). Clear limitations when power is delegated by Congress is essential to avoid overstepping."

Yet his note-taking was not all confined to practicality.

From Tennyson he scribbled a note: "The most virtuous hearts have a touch of hell's own fire in them."

And from who knows where: "There's a kind of love for permanence. There's another kind that's just champagne bubbles and moonlight. It isn't meant to last but it can be something to have and look back on all your life."

Among the memorabilia that Lieutenant Nixon saved during the South Pacific period was a full-page advertisement ripped from the *Saturday Evening Post*, a public service advertisement in a series called "Thank God I Am an American." This advertisment featured a poem by Margaret Betz, a student at East High School in Rochester, New York. It mentioned: Santa Claus . . . Christmas Trees . . . Thanksgiving Turkeys . . . The Three Bears . . . The Easter Rabbit . . . Tom Sawyer . . . Hiawatha . . . Gone With the Wind . . . The Declaration of Independence . . . The Constitution . . . The Gettysburg Address . . .

Those were things that Lt. Richard Nixon was fighting for.

26
The First
Campaign

The South Pacific meant jungle rot and prickly heat and Spam and many changes in Lt. (J.G.) Richard Nixon. He was transferred out after fifteen months, two battle stars and a promotion to lieutenant.

He went to Alameda naval air station for a time as a transportation officer, then was sent to Baltimore because he was a lawyer. In many ways he was a different man from the young lawyer who had gone away. He was much more worldly, certainly. In Maryland, his job was to help settle contracts with manufacturers that the navy canceled when the war ended.

The work was scarcely scintillating. For example, he investigated a claim of the Furnival Remmer Company, a ball-bearing manufacturer. An order had been placed with the company for five thousand ball bearings, but the war in Europe ended and the bearings were no longer needed, so the contract was canceled after 1336 bearings had been de-

livered. The company was invited to submit a claim for
what its official thought it ought to have. Lieutenant Nixon's task was to sort out such claims, check them for accuracy and then pass on them. The one saving grace of the
work was that before it was through he was promoted to
lieutenant commander. But by the summer of 1945, with
World War II ending altogether, it was obvious that Lt.
Comdr. Nixon would soon have to pick up the threads of civilian life. What would he do?

As the Nixons pondered the question of the future,
back in southern California some of Richard Nixon's constituents were pondering a problem of their own. They were
the Republican party leaders of Whittier, and of the rest of
the 12th Congressional District, who had been looking on
lean times for ten years. The representative from the district
was Jerry Voorhis, the son of a millionaire, a personable
New Deal Democrat. In his ten years in Washington Voorhis had voted for federal control of tidelands oil, for cheap
credit, for cooperatives, and for public power. He had the
backing of organized labor, and until now he had been virtually unassailable in the 12th district. In 1940 and 1942
Voorhis had captured both Democratic and Republican
nominations under the state's cross-filing system.

By 1944 the groundswell of change had been very
much in the air in southern California. The New Deal had
been in office for nearly twelve years, and reaction to it was
growing. Republican businessmen who had been stunned in
1932 and had been licking their wounds ever since were becoming whole again.

Among these was Herman L. Perry, manager of the
Bank of America branch in Whittier. He had been first vice
chairman of the Republican County Central Committee of
Los Angeles, but he was so discouraged by the events of
1932 that in 1934 he dropped out of politics altogether. He
was quiescent until 1944, when a wealthy business friend
(whom he declined to name), a former banker, came to his
office in Whittier and told him he must go to work for the

Republican party again. The country had already traveled too far down the road to socialism, and it was time that someone got down to cleaning up the mess, said his friend.

Perry was lackadaisical. How did his friend hope to do it?

Start with Congress.

Didn't the other know that Jerry Voorhis had the local congressional seat sewed up?

The other knew, but said that if the Republicans got together and organized they could unseat him.

Perry asked his friend if he knew anybody foolish enough to run against Jerry Voorhis. The other said he thought they could persuade Roy P. McLaughlin of South Pasadena to run. They discussed other candidates, but it came back to McLaughlin.

Perry said that if McLaughlin were foolish enough to permit the use of his name, he would go to work. His friend said that was fine and he would put up the money. But there was one proviso: his name must never appear, because his position in the industrial world was such that it might hurt him.

"My friend told me that he expected to assist in financing the cost of the campaign and that it would be my duty to use good judgment in the handling of his funds. The money came in regularly to use as I saw fit," said Perry.

So went the campaign of 1944. For the first time in six years the Republicans captured the Republican nomination, but many Republicans adhered to Voorhis. About three weeks before the election, Herman Perry advised his cautious friend that McLaughlin could not win, and so he refused to spend any more of the other's money. Perry suggested that his friend come in and collect the balance of the unspent funds, but the secret supporter of Republicanism never came and the money sat idle in Mr. Perry's bank.

In the summer of 1945 the movers and shakers of the Republican party in the district were looking, rather hopelessly, for someone to run against Voorhis in 1946. They did not really expect to win, but they hoped to whittle away at the majority once again. They were, in effect, looking for a sacrificial lamb.

It was not an easy job. No Republican in his right mind was going to put himself up against Jerry Voorhis. The Los Angeles central committee and the state committee were not particularly interested in investing money in the coming campaign, preferring to spend where they thought they could achieve victory. So if anything was going to be done, it was going to be done by the Republicans in the 12th district without much help.

A small group of Republican leaders got together and tried to chart a course. They included Earl Adams, a prominent Los Angeles lawyer who lived in the district; Frank Jorgenson and Rockwood Nelson, insurance men; Boyd Gibbons, an automobile dealer; Andrew Dunlap, a broker; and Herman Perry.

At the same time, other forces were at work in the district. Roy Day, Republican district chairman and the manager of the commercial printing department of the Pomona *Progress Bulletin* organized a Committee of One Hundred, whose purpose was to seek a candidate for the party. Day's approach was very direct: he had a flier run off and distributed to all the newspapers in the district. It made a good story, and some papers ran it on Page One so that it looked like (and was often referred to later as) an advertisement:

"WANTED: Congressman candidate with no previous experience to defeat a man who has represented the district in the House for ten years. Any young man, resident of the district, preferably a veteran, fair education, no political strings or obligations, and possessed of a few ideas for betterment of country at large, may apply for the job. Applicants will be reviewed by 100 interested citizens who will guarantee support but will not obligate the candidate in any way."

The press release was very successful and produced results. Four meetings were held at four different towns in the district, and seven applicants appeared. They were a mayor, a smog expert, an assemblyman, a bigot who talked about keeping Jews and Negroes out of the district, a Socialist who would be glad to run as a Republican, and two ordinary citizens. None of them seemed quite right . . .

Meanwhile Herman Perry thought of Richard Milhous Nixon. How he came to think of Nixon has never been precisely established. It has been said that one of Nixon's old teachers at Whittier mentioned the name. It has been also said that Dr. Walter Dexter, the former college president, suggested him. Dexter had been approached but had declined. Actually Herman Perry might well have thought of Nixon by himself, for he knew the Nixons that well. He had been acquainted with Frank and Almira Milhous for forty years, and also Frank and Hannah Nixon, whom he knew as frugal, hard-working customers of the bank. Richard Nixon had gone to school with Perry's son, both at Whittier High and Whittier College. And, of course, Perry had known Richard Nixon when he practiced law in Whittier.

So Herman Perry found out from the Nixons where Richard was and sent him a wire in Maryland, asking two questions. Did Richard want Perry to put him up for Congress in the 12th district? Was Richard a Republican? Nixon was to write, wire, or call Perry long distance.

At nine o'clock that same night, Richard Nixon called. He said he thought he was a Republican—he had voted for Thomas E. Dewey for President in 1944, by absentee ballot. Yes, he was interested in the Republican nomination for Congress.

Perry wanted Richard Nixon to come to California to appear before the Committee of One Hundred. Nixon replied that he would come if they could help him with the cost. Perry agreed to pay half the fare.

After that conversation, Perry telephoned his secret friend and told him he could not now have the rest of the money that was unspent from the 1944 campaign because he was going to use it in 1946. The friend wanted to know if they had a candidate, and Perry said yes, they had several, but that at Whittier they were going to place in nomination the name of Lt. Comdr. Richard M. Nixon. He then identified Nixon.

His friend asked if he knew what he was doing.

Perry certainly did, he said. He was simply following through on the other's insistences of the previous campaign. And not only would he need the money left over, but he would need a lot more.

Perry's secret friend was satisfied. He said he and his friends would supply the money that would be needed for the campaign. (He would also supply funds in 1948, 1950, and 1952.)

Richard Nixon flew back to California, to appear before the Committee of One Hundred. The meeting was to be held on November 2. But first, Lt. Comdr. Nixon lunched with Perry and his group of movers and shakers at the University Club in Los Angeles. There he discussed some of his ideas about government, which were conservative enough to please his potential backers. They assured him, in turn, that they would find the money to finance his campaign.

On the night of November 1, a testimonial dinner was held for Nixon at the Dinner Bell Ranch, and Roy Day appeared, but the movers and shakers were careful not to intrude themselves. Lt. Comdr. Nixon spoke a little about his war experiences, to emphasize his oneness with returning servicemen. He said that the seventeen or eighteen million servicemen and women were tired of regimentation and wanted to return to the American way of life "in its true meaning."

Next evening the Committee of One Hundred met, and several candidates appeared before them. George Knox Roth of Whittier said that he wanted to run, and said he would campaign against unemployment, which could never be solved by socialized government. He pleaded for a return to private initiative in America.

Assemblyman Erwin Geddes of Pomona said he would run if they wanted him too, but he had a big job as assemblyman in the state legislature at Sacramento.

Captain Sam Gist of Pomona had already appeared once and made his views clear. He came again, just to tell the committee that he would devote his whole time and effort to the campaign.

Judge Harry Hunt of San Gabriel spoke against bureaucracy and for government reform. He deplored attacks on the Democrats, and said that people were more interested in what would happen in the next two years than what had happened already. He would conduct a constructive campaign.

Lt. Col. Frank Benedict appeared, and spoke up for collective bargaining as a campaign issue. He also talked about returning the government to the people as soon as was practical.

The movers and shakers had saved Lt. Comdr. Richard Nixon for last. He stood up in his neat navy-blue suit with the two and a half stripes of a lieutenant commander, and was cool, and calm, and very serious. There were two opposite opinions as to what constituted the American system, he said. "One advocated by the New Deal is government control in regulating our lives. The other calls for individual freedom and all that initiative can produce."

Obviously Jerry Voorhis stood for the New Deal. Nixon would stand for the other view.

The meeting adjourned on that high note, and Lt. Comdr. Nixon returned to his navy job. The committee met again on November 28 to select its candidate, and Richard Nixon received 53 of the 77 votes cast.

Back in Maryland he wrote his acceptance of the nomination. It was really unexceptionable. He said he would stand for a foreign policy that would have as its primary purpose the avoidance of all future wars. Who could object to that? He attacked "Old World diplomacy" with its secret personal commitments. Who could object to that? He spoke of opportunities for progress "if the true principles of American constitutional government" were allowed to operate. "The inventive genius and industrial know how which have made America great must not be stifled. . . . Economic dictatorship by irresponsible government agencies must never be allowed to become an accepted principle of our American system of government." He, Richard Nixon, was reflecting his own inside view of the Office of Price Administration, for he had been one of the economic dictators before he became disgusted with government in 1942. Still, anyone—and especially a Republican—could run on that idea and not create much of a fuss.

Indeed, Richard Nixon's acceptance letter was just fine as far as it went, but it certainly would not frighten Jerry Voorhis very much. Nixon's approach to the campaign was representative of his background, it represented a deep interest in modern world history and antipathy to government control of the individual. It betrayed Nixon's youth and inexperience. It was very much like the statement that might be made by a young college debater. He announced to Roy Day that he was going to seek advice from prominent Republicans in Washington, and urged the Republicans to "bring in the liberal fringe Republicans," because, he said, they needed every Republican vote to win.

Pat Nixon was then pregnant, and she was not very much concerned about her husband's decision to enter politics. But once the decision was made, his enthusiasm was infectious. They returned to California, where the baby, Tricia, was born. Within a month Pat had left her in the charge of Hannah, and was out on the campaign trail with her husband.

The family was very much involved. Almira had died in 1943, but Frank and Richard's brother Donald helped from the beginning. They had appeared at the testimonial dinner back in November, and they continued to do what they could. When Richard Nixon rented a small office in an old Whittier building, Hannah donated an old sofa, and

Donald hauled it in the grocery truck. It began as an ama-
teur campaign. Murray Chotiner, a very knowledgeable political professional, was persuaded to take enough time from
Senator Knowland's southern California campaign to help
out on the side. A Pasadena engineer named Harrison
McCall was hired for five hundred dollars a month to manage the campaign.

The first job was to win the Republican primary. Both
Nixon and Voorhis cross-filed; Voorhis was so confident
that he did not even bother to campaign in the district, but
reported that he was too busy representing the people in
Washington. In spite of not even showing up, in spite of
Richard Nixon's energetic appearance at any and every
meeting to which he could wangle an invitation, Voorhis
handily captured the Democratic nomination (4 to 1) and
won the votes of many Republicans (half Nixon's vote), obviously the "liberal fringe Republicans" that Nixon knew
he must have to win.

Voorhis could run—and apparently successfully—on
his record. It was true that there was a groundswell of reaction in the country against the New Deal, but it was not
even very hopeful, on the record of the primary, that Voorhis could be defeated, even though Nixon had polled more
votes than any Republican candidate in the last three elections. Voorhis did not come home to campaign until August
and by that time Richard Nixon found his issue in left-wing
labor. During the 1930s the Congress of Industrial Organizations had developed very rapidly as a labor force in the
growth of the automobile and steel and oil industries. Early
in the 1930s the Communist party had infiltrated various
unions, such as the United Auto Workers, where the Reu-
ther brothers and their allies fought them continuously and
more and more successfully. But the influence of the Communists was a matter of worry to many labor leaders in
1946. The Big Red Scare had not yet begun, but the United
States and the Soviet Union were not getting along well in
the Far East and in Europe. In California, the longshore-

men kicked up a fuss from time to time, so did the oil workers, and there was strong suspicion by the press and some of the public that the Communists were in charge.

The CIO had begun to flex its political muscles through a Political Action Committee, which took sides in national elections and spent money backing candidates in the same manner that bankers and industrialists backed candidates, only with much more hoopla about the procedure.

It would later be said by Nixon supporters that Communism did not play a part in the election campaign of 1946. If that was true, it was only true literally; but it was true that one issue Richard Nixon raised was the radicalism of the CIO Political Action Committee, and Voorhis's relationship to that committee. When all was sorted out, it was shown that Jerry Voorhis had no relationship to the Political Action Committee, except that one of the state PAC organizations had endorsed him without his request or even knowledge.

The general election campaign of the Republicans began with a blunderbuss approach. The theme was generally "Have You Had Enough?" which was to appeal to the reaction of the public against rationing, price controls, and the postwar shortages of automobiles, houses, refrigerators, and other appliances of the good life which had been missing during the war, and which could not be "turned on" overnight.

There was early mention of the Political Action Committee, but it was only one of the issues raised. No one at that time, Richard Nixon included, realized how potent the issue would become.

The realization came in a confrontation of the candidates, and the confrontation came without either candidate apparently really wanting it. Nixon and the Republicans had begun in August on the theme of Had Enough?; and constantly hammered on the idea that Voorhis and Nixon offered two different ways of life: Voorhis offered government control, while Nixon offered to "return the government to the people under Constitutional guarantee."

Concentrating on this theme, Nixon really was not getting anyplace by mid-September, when a nonpartisan Pasadena organization suggested a debate between the candidates. Many of Nixon's advisors were against his accepting the challenge because of his inexperience; Murray Chotiner took the position that Nixon would lose if he did not pull a rabbit out of the hat, and that the rabbit might somehow be produced at this debate. Nixon agreed with Chotiner, and thus accepted the debates.

Why Jerry Voorhis agreed is a little more difficult to understand, for he violated one of the basic precepts of an incumbent in so doing—ignore your opponent, particularly if you are established and he is not. Almost any confrontation between a political champion and a challenger will redound to the benefit of the challenger, because he has no record to defend, and much less to lose. Recalling the matter twenty-five years later, Voorhis said he was running scared. He knew that there was much opposition to the Democrats after all these years in office, and that people were looking for a change, and he said Nixon was shrewd to capitalize on the unrest. But he did not expect the attack that came in the first debate.

Nixon led off the first debate at South Pasadena High School with a series of accusations. He attacked Voorhis for his votes in Congress, for gas rationing, for meat rationing, grain rationing. He accused Voorhis of having once been a Socialist (he was). Then he brought out the charge that Voorhis was backed by the CIO Political Action Committee.

At one point, said Voorhis, Nixon listed a number of controversial measures in which Voorhis had voted along lines recommended by the PAC.

"It took me a month to find out what those bills were, and when I found out I couldn't believe what they were saying," Voorhis recalled years later. "The bills on which I voted were for Social Security, the Tennessee Valley Authority, soil conservation, reciprocal trade agreements and things lots of Republicans voted for. There was nothing sinister." The fact was that Nixon had attacked his opponent at what must be considered at the time to have been his political weak point.

Voorhis came off badly in the first debate. At the end of it, according to William Costello in his "unauthorized" biography of Nixon, Voorhis turned to his campaign manager, Chet Holifield, and asked how it had gone.

"Jerry," said Holifield, "he cut you to pieces. He had you on the defensive all the way. He picked the battleground and you let him fight on his own terms."

Voorhis asked what to do. Holifield suggested that Voorhis either start slugging it out with Nixon, or cancel the other scheduled four debates on the ground that Nixon was using dirty tactics.

Voorhis said he had given his word to debate, so he would debate. And Nixon biographers, pro and con, agree that Nixon won the debates. Voorhis, years later, said he did not believe the debates really made much difference— Richard Nixon had the support of nearly all the newspapers in the district including that of the Los Angeles *Times*. Voorhis tried to defend his record—but since Nixon had no record, there was little to attack except his inexperience.

Jerry Voorhis was a decent, sensitive liberal man who was simply not used to windmill attack, and he did not recover sufficiently to realize what was happening to him. He might have defeated Richard Nixon by ignoring him—although in the face of so much editorial support of Nixon it would have been difficult. Voorhis did have enough money; his campaign advertising in the largest newspaper in the district was almost double that of Nixon. But Nixon had the offensive, and when the votes were counted, Nixon had won by a vote of 65,586 to 49,994.

The Nixon victory was not particularly surprising in 1946; seven Republicans unseated Democratic representatives in the state of California alone, and the Republicans won control nationally of the Eightieth Congress. It was a Republican year, and the "time for a change" argument had won the day; but still the victors had needed campaign issues that could be reduced to the lowest common denominator, and Richard Nixon had used them against Jerry Voorhis. In later years when asked about his conduct in this first campaign, Nixon gave an answer of sorts: "I was very young," he said, which would seem to imply that if he had it to do over again he might have handled matters differently.

When it was over, Jerry Voorhis, who was a moderate man in tone, said he felt that it had not been a fair campaign. Others, not so gentle, charged that Richard Nixon had used acting ability, forensic skills, innuendo, and quotation out of context to create doubts; in other words, that he used the low blow. That was only the first time the charge was to be made. Except by Voorhis supporters, the charge was not made very loudly or seriously in 1946. Richard Nixon had done what he had always done. As Aunt Jane Beeson remarked, he set out to win and gave the game everything he had. It was true that Jerry Voorhis *had been* supported by a branch of the CIO Political Action Committee, and it was also true that the CIO-PAC's political activities were very left-wing and suspect of Communist infiltration. Nixon did not regard it as his responsibility to explain all the circumstances, and it was very nearly impossible for Voorhis to free himself of the unwanted taint. Here Nixon was exploiting an issue. He might have defeated Voorhis on the grounds of "Had Enough?" but he did not know that.

In the future, the liberal press would dredge up some facts about this election, using them selectively as a partisan press does. In southern California, at the end of the election Nixon had the title of Giant Killer. That would change.

27

The Earnest
Legislator

Freshman Congressman Richard Milhous Nixon went to Washington in January 1947, with his wife, while little Tricia stayed in Whittier with Frank and Hannah Nixon until her parents could get settled.

Frank and Hannah now lived in their dream house on Worsham Drive. Frank was sixty-nine and had turned the grocery business over to Donald, who was expanding it into a supermarket operation. Edward, the youngest son, would go to Duke University to study geology, and then to North Carolina State University to get a master's degree. Although to be widely separated, the Nixon family would maintain close ties.

Richard arrived in Washington unknown and unsung. He and Pat stayed at the Mayflower Hotel for a time; housing was very tight in these early postwar years and it was some weeks before they found a two-bedroom apartment in Alexandria for eighty dollars a month. They had about ten thousand dollars in savings from his navy pay, Pat's war work, and the poker games, and a Ford car. Hannah and Frank came to Washington on a trip and brought Tricia with them.

Representative Nixon was appointed to the House Un-American Activities Committee, which he did not ask for, and the House Labor Committee, which he did request. He was far more interested in the activities of the labor committee than the other, but in both he became exposed to the American Communist party. He began to study its relationship to the international Communist movement, and became convinced that Communism in the United States was dangerous because part of its activity was underground, because Communists were involved in Soviet espionage, and because he felt that Communism used any tactics whatsoever to achieve its end of world revolution.

Here, far more than in the election campaign against Jerry Voorhis, Richard Milhous Nixon began to run afoul of the liberal element in the American press. It was a gradual affair.

Before the animosity became developed, Nixon was often described as one of the hard-working young members of Congress. He was a good listener—an attribute he shared with his mother. He joined with other freshman congressmen in a "Chowder and Marching Society," which was their light-hearted way of naming a study club. He worried over the intrusions into the constitutional rights of Americans by the House Un-American Activities Committee. Had he not been involved in that committee (and he considered turning down the assignment) Nixon's political career might have taken an entirely different tack. But as it turned out, almost from the beginning he was involved with Communism and controversy. The Truman administration was very much opposed to the House Un-American Activities Committee, and beginning in 1947 the question of Communist activity in America was allowed to become a partisan issue between Republicans and Democrats, with the Republicans trying to tar the Democrats as "soft on Communism." It was the kind of charge that was difficult to answer, creating frustration and fury in Democratic hearts. (The charge is always easier than the answer and makes better headlines.) It would be at least a generation before the political wounds of the late 1940s and early 1950s would be healed.

Nixon was a member of the Un-American Activities Committee when Gerhard Eisler, a Communist agent, was cited for contempt. Eisler was later deported to East Germany. Then came the committee's war with the American Communist party, which began with a citation of the party for contempt.

During the summer of 1947 Nixon was very busy in Washington with hearings of his committees. Friends wanted him to come home that summer and mend political fences. He refused. He had hearings until September. "I see no reason to spend the government's money to bring me back right after I arrive out there," he wrote Harrison McCall, his old campaign manager. He realized that he must come home and planned to come in October and stay for two months.

The House Un-American Activities Committee began investigating Communism in Hollywood. Nixon was concerned: "Our committee," he said, "is well aware of the ramified and delicate situation with which we are dealing. We are also deeply concerned that in our efforts to combat and break up subversive movements through legislation we do not impair or destroy any of the rights and liberties we hold so fundamental in America."

And yet, in the autumn of 1947, Nixon was not primarily interested in the Communist issue. He had achieved a reputation as a hard-working, quiet young legislator who was very good at his homework. In a labor subcommittee he did groundwork on what would be the Taft-Hartley labor law. He was so highly regarded that Speaker Joe Martin chose him as a member of the Herter committee which was

sent to Europe that autumn to investigate economic conditions—a very respectable assignment. Joe Martin had
promised Republicans back in California to do something
for Nixon, but if Nixon had not shaped up already he would
not have had this plum. And on the European trip Nixon
worked harder than almost any other, and when he came
back to Washington he turned in the smallest expense account of any committee member. He was scrupulous in his
accounts, and unlike many of his colleagues he did not put
his wife on the payroll. (The practice was to be set back seriously in the next few months by a series of exposures of
congressional cupidity by Drew Pearson. Eventually J. Par-
nell Thomas, chairman of the Un-American Activities
Committee would lose his seat and go to jail.)

In the winter of 1947 Representative Richard Nixon
was torn. He cordially disliked many of the methods of the
House Un-American Activities Committee and said so. He
was equally critical of the barrage of charges against the
committee levied by the Truman administration. And he
was growing more concerned about Communism in America. He wrote Harrison McCall, regarding a series of articles by Adela Rogers St. John that had appeared in the
Hearst newspapers.

"In my opinion," said Nixon, "Mrs. Rogers is doing an
excellent public service in acquainting large numbers of
people with the facts of communist infiltration into free
American institutions. I believe she is well informed and
that she does not take an exaggerated view of the situation."

During the Herter committee trip he had a firsthand
view of rioting in the streets of Trieste between Communists
and non-Communists, and saw a young boy whose head
had been blown off by a Communist grenade. That day in
Trieste (September 17, 1947) five people were killed and
seventy-five wounded in the fighting. It was obviously a
traumatic experience, and partly as a result of it Nixon
would cosponsor a resolution to commit the United States to
promotion of defensive alliances and American military aid

to countries threatened with Communist infiltration. He would also that spring have a hand in legislation that would permit the Communist party to function as a political party but called for exposure of Communist fronts. He would even favor teaching about Communism in the schools as a therapeutic measure. His position was jelling.

That winter Richard Nixon was concerned about his political future because he had not spent much time in the district. He came home to Whittier on a brief trip in December, and stayed with his brother Don, while he conferred with McCall and other Republicans. Some were dissatisfied with his record of watching over the interests of the district. He had supported a flood-control project that benefited California, but some said threatened Whittier. He had made weekly radio reports to his constituents—but not all of them listened. He had written a column for papers in his district, but not everyone read it, in fact some papers did not even run it. And some Republicans in his district told him flatly they did not think he could win the nomination in a primary election.

There was another factor, too. He could not expect much help from the movers and shakers this time. "I feel there will be so much emphasis upon the Presidential race," he wrote McCall, "that the Congressional candidates will be completely left out unless they go out and put on their own campaign."

Politicians and press combined late in 1947 and early in 1948 to whip the nation into a frenzy of anti-Communist hysteria. Virtually any public figure who defended any Communist act or even criticized anti-Communists was attacked as "pro-Communist" and the term became very nearly synonymous with traitor in the eyes of a large section of the public. In Whittier there was a frightful stir when a proposal was made to bring a Communist, a Socialist, and a capitalist to the campus for a debate. Many liberals had the deep-seated feeling that Fascism, not Communism, was really threatening the United States, and that big business was trying to pull the wool over American eyes. Those who accepted the reports of the Communist threat at face value thought the liberals were blind. The vast majority of people looked and listened to what was going on around them, and although confused in the maelstrom of publicity, they began to sort out the real charges from the unreal.

By spring, Richard Nixon was thoroughly convinced of the Communist threat, from his personal investigations. He had already been talking with the Rev. John F. Cronin and others who had made considerable study of Communist infiltration into government and labor, and the names of Alger Hiss and others had been mentioned. In 1947 there had been much else on Nixon's mind, but the following year he began to work with the material he had.

The Nixons were still living in the Alexandria apartment. Pat spent most of her time as a housewife, some of it typing for her husband. Richard worked long hours in his office, as he always had, but even harder, as the pressure of public business seemed to demand. He broke his arm in February, which did not help the work schedule. In the spring he was primarily concerned with the affairs of the House Labor Committee, which was involved with coal strike troubles and difficulties with the musicians' union. He and Congressman Karl Mundt proposed a subversive activities control bill; this bill was the result of Nixon's organizational efforts; for two years the House Un-American Activities Committee had investigated and fulminated; now the ambitious young congressman proposed that it legislate.

The Mundt-Nixon bill that followed the proposal was very tough. It called for registration of Communist party members, identification of all material issued by Communist front organizations; denial of passports to Communists; denial of federal employment to Communists; no tax exemptions for Communist front organizations; deportation of aliens convicted of Communist activity; an increase in penalties for peacetime espionage, and creation of a subversive activities control board that would determine whether or not an organization was Communist or Communist front.

The opponents of the bill, including much of the press, said it would control thought, not Communists. The problem was, Who was to make all these determinations? Was it not possible that some homegrown liberals could behave in the manner of "Communist front" organizations? A lot of liberals seemed to be acting that way. Many of them felt that in certain areas of conduct the USSR was right and the United States government was wrong. Did that make them Communist fronters? The issue was to dominate American politics for half a dozen years.

Representative Nixon now rose to a new position of prominence in the House. Freshman though he was, he was chosen floor manager of this important piece of legislation, and comported himself very well. But the bill was opposed by many Republicans, including Thomas E. Dewey, who was then seeking the presidential nomination. (He called it thought control.) It passed the House but went into committee limbo in the Senate.

Whatever else the bill had done (it was later passed), it had helped Richard Nixon's campaign for reelection to the House. That spring and summer instead of campaigning in California he was busy in Washington, but under cross-filing he was lucky enough to win both the Republican and Democratic nominations for reelection, which meant that he did not have to go home to campaign. His congressional record, then, was satisfactory to the people of the 12th Congressional District.

Then came the Hiss case, which made Richard Nixon a national political figure, and increased drastically the national anxiety about Communist activity in high places. Critics of the House Un-American Activities Committee say that in the summer of 1948 the committee was at a low ebb and was looking for headlines. A former Communist agent named Elizabeth Bentley was called on the last day of July and testified to espionage in the federal government in the era of the New Deal. Another former Communist named

Whittaker Chambers, who had become an editor of *Time* magazine since, testified to roughly the same effect and named names, among them that of Alger Hiss, who had been once in the State Department but was now President of the Carnegie Endowment for International Peace, and highly respected in the uppermost American intellectual circles.

Hiss chose to fight back when his name was dragged in the mud. He asked to appear before the committee, and testified that he had never been a Communist and did not know Chambers. Richard Nixon did not believe Hiss, and set out to get at the facts. It was an arduous job and so complex that several books have been written about it; the net result was that Hiss was indicted for perjury for denying his Communist connections, and eventually convicted and sent to prison.

Another result was the rise to prominence of Richard Milhous Nixon, and the polarization of conservative and liberal attitudes toward him. Later, in his critical biography, William Costello would give Richard Nixon credit for having been "thorough but fair." During the whole affair, Nixon was seriously troubled by conscience, particularly aware of his Quaker heritage (Priscilla Hiss was also a Quaker). At one point he tried to get away from it all and take Pat on a cruise to Panama. They went but he was called back; he flew to Washington, and left Pat in Jamaica to find her own way home. Frank and Hannah, having retired, had moved to a farm near the old Nixon country of Washington, Pa., and Nixon later came here during the struggle for a respite.

"He was so exercised about those hearings," Hannah told biographer Bela Kornitzer, "that he wouldn't even come in and eat supper. He just walked from one corner of the yard to the other. I went to him and told him that, if he didn't give up this whole Hiss question, he was not going to be here on earth very long. I will never forget his pale face and gaunt look as he answered: 'Mother, I would give it up, but I am so thoroughly convinced that this man passed our secrets to Russia that I can't quit now. I know Hiss is guilty and I won't surrender.' "

When it was all over, Harry S Truman had been elected President of the United States, which most people considered impossible a few weeks before the election, and Richard Nixon had handily been elected representative of the 12th district. If Nixon needed convincing that his course was the right one, he had it from no less a person than former President Herbert Hoover, who gave Nixon single-handed credit for exposing "the stream of treason that existed in our government."

To a young Quaker lawyer from the small town of Whittier, California, these were heady words, indeed.

28
The National
Figure

Had Richard Milhous Nixon stopped with the Hiss case, and turned his attentions once again to the substantial reputation he was earning as a bright young representative who was interested and knowledgeable about labor reform and foreign policy, he might have disarmed his critics and gone on to a steady slow climb in politics as a hard-working moderate. But now he was a celebrity. At the end of his first term in the House he had been named by the U.S. Chamber of Commerce as one of ten outstanding young men in America. On election night, 1948, the Nixons and the Drowns went to the Cocoanut Grove in Los Angeles for what started out to be a victory celebration, and there the entertainer of the evening, the singer Hildegarde, introduced Nixon as a "great statesman."

Richard Nixon's ambitions could not be bounded by the House of Representatives. Cousin Jessamyn West's father Eldo had once predicted after teaching Richard in

Yorba Linda Sunday school that the boy would some day be President of the United States. Richard Nixon had not yet consciously aimed so high, but in 1949 his ambition led him to aim at the United States Senate. He decided to make an attempt at the Senate the next year.

The seat at which Representative Nixon looked eagerly and anxiously was that of Senator Sheridan Downey, a Democrat. On October 7, he so wrote to Herman Perry back in Whittier, in a letter that was in the way of being a trial balloon. It was marked "confidential," but he advised Perry that the information could be used among friends. He also left a loophole—he was going to make a trip around the northern part of the state and would make no announcement until then.

Perry was in touch with the movers and shakers who had supported Richard Nixon in the first place, and they were appalled at the young man's decision. Here they had wanted a Republican congressman, and had gone to some trouble and expense to get him. And to give Richard Nixon his due he had fitted in perfectly, and with his new national reputation could hardly be dislodged.

Nixon came home to Whittier in November, and held a meeting with the little band of original supporters in Tom Bewley's law office. Almost uniformly they protested. They did not know their congressman very well—in him was the stubbornness of the Milhouses that had led Joshua to buy that organ, and the stubbornness of the Nixons that had led Frank to pick political arguments with his grocery customers, even if he lost the trade. On November 3, Nixon announced that he would seek the Senate nomination.

It *was* a whole new ball game, and not an easy one, either. Late in January he wrote Harrison McCall because he was very much worried lest he fail to get endorsement from an important political meeting in El Monte in February. When the struggle for the support of the Republican party began. He was opposed by Judge Frederick Houser, but he did finally get party support.

On the other side of the fence, the Democrats were squabbling among themselves. Senator Downey withdrew from contention in the spring because he did not like the prospect of "vicious and unethical propaganda" which he said Mrs. Helen Gahagan Douglas had already begun to use against him in her campaign for the nomination. So Mrs. Douglas, who was the wife of the movie actor Melvin Douglas and a former actress herself, campaigned for the nomination against Manchester Boddy, publisher of the Los Angeles *Daily News.* She and Boddy fought it out, and he accused her of being pro-Communist. So did Senator Sheridan Downey. But Mrs. Douglas won the nomination.

Then came the election campaign, and Richard Nixon entered it with the knowledge that he had to put on a very vigorous fight if he was to win.

Nixon believed in no-holds-barred campaigning. Here was the philosophy he later enunciated to biographer Earl Mazo:

"The line I draw between permissible and nonpermissible campaign tactics is a very simple one. The candidate's record is public property insofar as it indicates the position he might take on issues while in the office which he seeks. Now, this means his record in terms of all the votes he has cast if he has held public office, all the speeches he has made, all the organizations to which he has given support. All matters of this kind which bear upon or might indicate his philosophy should be discussed openly and frankly by the candidate and by his opponent. . . ."

He and Pat set out to campaign to win. Pat was an integral part of the struggle; she who had been a Democrat before their marriage now gave everything she had to helping her husband win. She sat in the audience and took notes on his speeches. She manned phones, took care of the office. And the campaign heated up.

The Nixon campaign, run by Murray Chotiner, the old California professional, continued to push the idea that a vote for Helen Gahagan Douglas was somehow a vote for

Communism. It wasn't exactly said, but it was almost said. "Is Helen Douglas a Democrat?" was the question. "The answer is NO." And then the Republican propagandists tried to prove by innuendo that Mrs. Douglas sympathized with the Communists.

On the other side, the Douglas team tried to show that Nixon was the tool of "the interests." Some money for his campaign had come through the office of a notorious Washington lobbyist, and this was used against him. But in addition to Republican backing, Nixon had the left-handed support of Manchester Boddy, and even the declared neutrality of a large number of Democrats. Mrs. Douglas campaigned by helicopter some of the time. The Nixons campaigned in a sound-equipped station wagon. They would drive into a town, playing records on the speaker system to attract attention, stop, and Nixon would get out and speak. Pat would pass among the crowd handing out literature.

There was a debate, which was Mrs. Douglas's mistake, for she did not know of Richard Nixon's skills in that department. He had a whole Democratic administration to attack, and she had her Democratic record in the House to defend.

On election day, Nixon was very gloomy and discouraged, and he would not stay at home and listen to the election returns. He insisted on taking the family to the beach. It was a terrible day, cold and gray with the wind beating in from the shore, and the children did not like it at all, so Pat persuaded them to go home. But Richard could not bear to stay home: what if he lost? He went off alone to the movies. When the show was over, and he drove home through Long Beach, he saw Douglas workers in the street, urging those last-minute voters to the polls—and he returned to the house gloomier than ever, sure that he had been beaten.

But the gloom lifted. He had won by 680,000 votes, and would go to Washington as Senator in January. Actually, he went in December, because Sheridan Downey resigned and Governor Earl Warren appointed Nixon to fill out the last few weeks of the term.

Now they could count on being in Washington for at least six years. No longer would Richard Nixon stand for election in November and have to begin worrying about reelection the following January. They could afford to settle down.

Nixon had received a little money from the old law firm from business that had been begun before he quit to go into the war effort. Pat had received some money from the sale of the Ryan house in Artesia. After Almira's death Richard had received a little money from the Milhous estate, and they had saved a bit and kept their wartime savings. Now they bought a new 1950 Oldsmobile from Richard's old Whittier friend Clint Harris. They bought a two-storey brick house in the Spring Valley section of Washington, near the houses of Senator Kefauver and Senator Sparkman, and they hired a maid, because the demands on Pat as a Senator's wife would increase considerably.

Pat would never become a part of the social maelstrom of Washington. Her days were spent with the children, and as they grew up she would take them to the zoo or for a walk when they came home from school. When Julie was old enough to go to nursery school, Pat began working in the community nursery. Sometimes she went to sewing classes to learn to make draperies and slipcovers for the house, and a blue quilted spread for their bed. Or she was busy helping the maid clean, or she might be making a hat. She had few clothes, mostly tailored, but she did show interest in millinery because hats were the one thing about women's clothes that Richard noticed. And then, of course, there were secretarial chores for him.

The Nixons did not join any clubs, nor did they go to cocktail parties except when necessary, or for that matter luncheons or tea parties. They did not play bridge and they very seldom entertained, because Richard Milhous Nixon was almost totally dedicated to his political life. The Nixons did go out occasionally to small dinners, usually given by one of their close circle of friends, where the recreation took the form of conversation. The election of 1950 marked another change in Richard Nixon's career. He had spent four years of political apprenticeship in the House of Representatives. With election to the Senate his dedication to political life increased.

The Nixon family day began very early in the morning. Pat was up, had the children dressed, and breakfast ready by seven o'clock. At breakfast Richard Nixon would read the Washington *Post*, and thumb through the *Congressional Record*, which was delivered to the house by messenger. By eight, he was kissing Pat and the girls goodbye and getting ready to drive off down Massachusetts Avenue toward Capitol Hill.

He was often the first one in his three-room suite of offices, and he worked there in the morning, unless called to a meeting of the Senate Labor and Public Welfare Committee, or the Committee on Executive Expenditures—which Senator McCarthy was to make infamous, by its ill-conceived assault on the Truman administration for harboring Communists in government.

Nixon had leapt into the public eye with the Hiss case, and he remained there, because his campaign of 1950 indicated to Republicans elsewhere a line of attack that promised victory over the Democrats in coming elections. Nixon was asked to speak a dozen times a month, and he became the champion partisan Republican speaker, setting new sights and new models for other Republicans, in view of the coming presidential election of 1952.

By January 1951, Nixon was laying the groundwork for his attack. That day he wrote Harrison McCall:

"I believe that the desperate position we find ourselves in is due to the failure of our past policies, particularly those which related to the Far East. For that reason, I feel that those responsible for developing those policies must be re-

moved . . . and . . . replaced by individuals who will devote themselves . . . to place the security of the United
States above all other considerations."

Nixon's vigorous attacks on the Democrats brought a
reaction that he quite expected, and he was careful to see
that friends did not become involved in his political struggles. For example, since the days when he had served on the
board of trustees of Whittier College, Nixon had taken a
continual interest in college affairs. When he was elected to
the Senate, the college sought him for many things, including advice on the selection of the new president (he recommended Paul S. Smith, who got the job). In the way of
colleges, in the autumn of 1951, Whittier asked Senator
Nixon if he would not be their commencement speaker for
June 1952. He considered it, then suggested that the idea be
postponed a year. "As you know, we will be in the middle of
a very vitriolic political campaign in June of next year, and
political implications are likely to be drawn by those who
want to find something wrong with the invitation which has
been extended to me." He was showing a sensitivity quite
unremarked by many of his critics.

And, of course, that was one of the qualities of the man.
In his statement of credo on elections, Nixon had also said,
"I draw the line, however, on anything that has to do with
the personal life of the candidate. I don't believe, for example, that a candidate's family is fair game."

He was what his mother and his aunts and his cousins
and his wife all called "a very private person." More than
that, as Jessamyn West said, "It's difficult for Richard to let
his soul show." And the reason, for one thing, was the combination of the strains of Milhous and Nixon in him. The
Nixon element, as personified by his father, was emphat-
ically unrestrained. When Richard was a boy and he and
Merle West used to go swimming in the Anaheim Ditch
that ran between their houses in Yorba Linda, they were
caught from time to time by Frank Nixon, who was constantly "yelling at them" about the dangerous sport. The

boys took to hiding under the footbridge that had been built across the ditch, but this did not always protect them. Once, as Jessamyn watched, Frank saw Richard under the bridge, and came rushing to the bank and caught him. He was furious. "If you like water so much, have some more of it," and he picked Richard up by the nape of the neck and threw him back into the water.

Frank was a hot man with the lid on most of the time, but not always. At one point Frank took offense at the action of a crowd and threatened "to paste somebody."

On the other hand, everyone always knew where they stood with Frank. In spite of his temper, he endeared himself to his in-laws because he also possessed the milk of human kindness. He was a marvelous Sunday school teacher because he did not believe in cant—he attracted young people because he showed them honesty, and advised them to live a Christian life, not just a Sunday school life; he meant in business and civic affairs and, yes, in politics. His position vis-à-vis Richard Nixon's vigorous campaign practices of attacking his opponent for any and everything in the record was that Richard was not doing anything to others that they were not doing to him. He also agreed with everything Richard said about Communism. Frank Nixon had a lively sense of humor and loved to tell stories. On the farm in Pennsylvania he named his milk cows after movie stars so he could startle visitors by talking about "feeding Dorothy Lamour."

The other major heritage in Richard's life was that of the Milhouses. Though Quakers, they were progressive in many ways, and even unrestrained. Among his other worldly faults, Joshua Milhous loved fast horses and was even known to trade in horseflesh, and in his later years Frank Milhous was so overcome by worldliness as to wear a wig when his hair grew thin. True, the Milhouses were of the Western Quaker persuasion, which shocked the effete Friends of the Eastern Meetings, but they were always

mindful of their heritage: Don't make a fool of yourself;
don't stick your neck out; don't give yourself away; don't
expose yourself to criticism. They were admonitions that
would become a part of Richard Nixon's character.

29

Defeat
and Victory

In the 1950s the Nixons and the Milhouses were widely
scattered. Richard Nixon had many cousins in Ohio, where
his father Frank had grown up. He did not know them, but
his father did, and Frank and Hannah stopped off in Vinton county to visit Roy Nixon, who was still farming not far
from the old homestead. They yarned with Roy about
Richard, and Frank could not conceal his paternal pride in
the son who had become so successful.

The Marshburns (Hannah's sister and her husband)
were living in the old Frank Milhous place. Aunt Jane Beeson and her husband were living in Lindsay, where Aunt
Jane was still teaching music. It was a long time since she
had played at the wedding of Frank and Hannah Nixon in
the old East Whittier Friends Church clubhouse and many
years since they had made the rough eight-hour drive in
their old red Ford from Whittier to Lindsay to bring Richard to their home to study music. But Jane Beeson was still

teaching forty youngsters, and still active in the Friends
church. She and Hannah corresponded, using the plain
speech of the Quakers. They used it at home still, too, but
never in public.

P. H. and Edith Timberlake (another of Hannah's sisters), were living in Riverside. Merle West was a successful
rug cleaner in Whittier, and his sister Jessamyn had become
a writer of fiction. She had graduated from Whittier, gone
on to study at Oxford. She had come home, married Max
McPherson, who would be a teacher and later superintendent of schools of Napa, California. Her intellectual career
had come up short when she was stricken, as had been Harold Nixon, with tuberculosis. She spent years thinking she
was going to die, then recovered enough physically and
mentally to begin writing, and began to put together stories
based on the Quaker past of the Milhouses in Indiana. She
really did not expect the stories to sell, but she decided to
write perhaps ten of them, and see what happened. They
were almost immediately successful in the magazine market, and before long she was putting them together in the
book *The Friendly Persuasion* which would make her one of
America's most celebrated writers.

The Milhous tribe was large, and many members had
come to California from the Middle West since the beginning of the twentieth century, so Richard Nixon had literally dozens of cousins in southern California and some in
northern California. The family remained quite close. William Milhous, Jr., for example, a cousin, was working for
Donald Nixon. And Donald Nixon was successful and expanding. He had served on the Board of Certified Grocers
for several years. He had decided to go into the restaurant
business and was going to build a group of five restaurants
in the area. Edward, the youngest Nixon brother, had
finished his education and was in military service in the
navy, where he would go to Officers' Candidate School and
then become a helicopter pilot.

Richard kept in touch, although instead of writing letters by hand he dictated them to a secretary. The family, particularly Donald, now found some pressures on them from people who wanted something from the junior Senator from California. Being related to a rising young figure in politics was not the easiest job in the world. And Richard Nixon, too, was discovering that demands were being made on him, some of which tried his temper. He had a temper problem, obviously Frank's son would have, but he usually could keep his short fuse under control. His office staff would remark on his ability to hold his temper under trying circumstances. Rose Mary Woods, who was now his secretary and would remain so through the years ahead, said he simply did not lose his temper. But he was capable of brusqueness, as when an old Whittier friend, Robert Pellissier, presumed upon their relationship for political reasons. He came to Washington and to Nixon's private office, and laid a bill on the desk—one that would soon come before the Senate.

Nixon picked up the paper and handed it back to Pellissier.

"Would you please give it to my secretary so that it will come through normal channels," he said. And that was that.

Richard Milhous Nixon's temper was obviously an inheritance from the whole Nixon line. The quarrel of old George Nixon, Jr., back in Ohio, over a couple of sheaves of oats that sent him into criminal court is an example. The spicy temperament that caused Frank Nixon to assault the Columbus streetcar company, and to quarrel over politics with his customers in the country store is another. Unlike his father, Nixon learned as a child to keep his temper in check—that was the Quaker. But the temper itself, that was Nixon, and it flared in private from time to time. After the Checkers speech, Nixon exploded, in private. After the Caracas humiliations, Nixon exploded, in private. After the 1962 defeat in the California governorship race, he exploded—this time so that the press saw him. In *Nixon Agon-*

istes, the study of American liberalism that used Richard Nixon as protagonist, Garry Wills has pointed out that even then, Nixon's sense of self-preservation took over and prevented him from saying anything that could later be used against him. But the essence of the explosion was clear, made so by the press itself, and the American public remembered the explosion. After the second Supreme Court crisis of 1971, Nixon exploded, in private, and reporters, who were looking for it later, said they sensed controlled fury in his voice as he explained his Supreme Court nominations of Powell and Rehnquist to the American people on national television.

Politically Senator Richard Nixon was still regarded by Republicans as something of a giant killer. Various factions within the party wanted his association. He had been linked with Harold Stassen in the past; he had admired Stassen. Senator Taft's supporters were talking about a Taft-Nixon ticket. As for himself, Nixon favored General Dwight Eisenhower, who seemed to be deciding to be a Republican that year. When the Republican national convention came in the summer, Nixon was a member of the California delegation, and joined the train at Denver. When Eisenhower was chosen by the Republicans to run for President, they then looked for a young man who would represent the West to be vice-president. The main candidates were Senator Knowland and Senator Nixon, and Nixon was chosen, because he was young, a veteran, he had served in both houses, he was an effective campaigner.

So the campaign began, and with it came another great change in Richard Milhous Nixon. In the beginning, it was what Nixon called a "rockem-sockem" campaign. Eisenhower and his advisors set the tone—they played "holier than thou," accused the Democrats of corruption, and spoke of government by "crooks and cronies." Richard Nixon took up the refrain and in his very effective, emphatic way, he attacked the political enemy without consideration for quarter.

By this time, Richard Milhous Nixon was a controversial figure even in his home grounds of the 12th Congressional District in southern California. Friends and workers in the Whittier campaign secured a list of alumni from the college. They took the position that the interests of Whittier would be served by having one of their members as Vice-President of the United States, and President Smith of the college was a definite, if cautious, supporter of Richard Nixon's. So in the planning of the college homecoming ceremonies, a card was sent out asking alumni to "Walk in the parade and then shake hands with the next Vice President of the United States."

The card drew instant protest from Democrats who were graduates of the college, and one wrote, "Not all Whittier alumni along with I hope sufficient numbers of other persons, share the implied enthusiasm for a man of Mr. Nixon's emotional immaturity. . . ."

Perhaps nothing caused as much controversy as the episode which has gone down in history as the "Checkers speech," which was to have a drastic effect on Richard Nixon's career and on his political style.

A maturing Senator Nixon had grown used to opposition from some of the press. In his first campaign for the House of Representatives he had enjoyed a very positive press in southern California. The Hiss case left what Nixon called "a residue of hatred and hostility" from a substantial segment of the American press. The political campaign of 1950 had cemented the hostility of the left and some of the center.

In the campaign of 1952, then, there were a lot of newspapermen looking for something to hang on Richard Nixon, and besides his enemies, there were newspapermen who loved a good story better than anything else, and many newspapermen who took the highly moral posture that if the Republicans were going to criticize Democratic corruption, they had better be very clean themselves.

After the 1950 election, Nixon supporters in California

started a fund for the young Senator so he could campaign year round. There was nothing secret about it; although the Republicans did not advertise in the newspapers for money, the party leaders toured the state, requesting funds, in amounts not to exceed five hundred dollars a year. The limit was placed so that no scandal could come from this fund, which was to be used for such items as printing and postage and nonofficial trips West from Washington. By the summer of 1952 some eighteen thousand dollars had been thus expended.

Then the press got hold of the story. It could be played two ways—and was. There was a fund, there was nothing wrong with it; other politicians (including Adlai Stevenson, the Democratic candidate for President) had been given similar funds. That was one way. "Secret Rich Men's Trust Fund Keeps Nixon in Style Far Beyond His Salary." That was another way. It was played both ways, one by Peter Edson of Newspaper Enterprise Association, one by Leo Katcher, of the New York *Post*. The *Post* was the attacker. The wire services picked up both versions, and editors of newspapers across the land had their choice, and took it according to their political leanings and their journalistic principles.

The result was an avalanche of fear at Republican National Headquarters and on the Eisenhower campaign train. One reaction was to push Richard Nixon off the ticket as a liability, and put William Knowland on.

As far as the Republicans were concerned the heavens seemed to have opened up to spill out wrath against them. And in a sense it was true: traditionally nothing suits the American press better than a story that turns the tables on the holier-than-thou. Also, Richard Nixon had already proved himself an enigma to the press. A large segment believed that his talk about honesty and individualism concealed a deviousness unmatched in previous politicians; he was regarded as the Machiavellian figure of the day; no one, they said, could surpass him in cynicism. Not only the

Democrats, but many journalists, were eager to deflate the Nixon balloon.

And besides the personalities involved, there is nothing that sells newspapers better in a political campaign than a juicy scandal, particularly if it can be hung on those who have been crying scandal all the time. Even moderate newspapermen felt that the Republicans were going a bit far in their charges against the Democrats for scandalous behavior—and wouldn't it be fitting if the Republicans were hoisted by their own petard?

Frank and Hannah Nixon were in Washington, baby-sitting with Tricia and Julie, when they saw the headlines in the newspaper, and the news on television, with the implication very clear that Richard Nixon was deeply involved in wrongdoing. Hannah was shaken. Her immediate reaction was to worry about her son's health. She stayed by her television set for hours.

Hannah was a Milhous, and Milhouses did not sit by and watch their own destroyed. She wired General Eisenhower, telling him to have faith. She wired Richard, telling him the girls were fine, that she and Frank were thinking of him, and knew everything would be fine.

Richard Nixon, who had reached Portland's Benson Hotel, was completely shaken and despondent. He was also edgy and irritable, and his campaign managers did not know what he might do. It was conceivable that he could blow up. It was not the charge—his thin skin would have been pricked by the charge, but he would have accepted that as the price of doing battle on the terms he had selected for his own political career. It was the small faith of his own party that bothered him.

He cried when he received his mother's telegram, which meant in the private language of the Nixons that she was praying for him.

Nixon wondered aloud then whether the game was worth playing, but of course no other person could answer that question. Also, given his character, it was inconceivable that he could quit the ticket without clearing himself publicly.

The worst of it came on Saturday night in Portland. On Sunday morning, Richard and Pat Nixon went to the Friends church, and he returned in better spirits. He would fight—which meant that he would fight his enemies within the Republican party as well as those outside.

For once the Republicans were in the difficult position of answering an accusation and then finding the difficulty of answering the charge with enough volume to make the impact equal to that of the original charge. The Eisenhower candidacy, the whole Republican campaign of governmental cleanliness threatened to collapse, and many Republican leaders acted as though they had been caught with their fingers in the cookie jar. Nixon, the cause of the trouble, was given the ultimatum that he must either cleanse himself publicly of any suspicion of wrongdoing, or he must get off the ticket.

It was virtually an impossible task. Virtually but not quite.

Richard Nixon did the only thing he could do and stay on the ticket. He bared his soul on national television. He told the story of his life. He exposed the family poverty, in childhood, described his struggles as a young lawyer, revealed his net worth and everything conceivable about his personal finances, down to the size of the mortgage on his house, the amount of life insurance he carried ($14,000 including $10,000 in national service term insurance), the year of his car, and his debts to banks and family. He also described a gift he had received—a little cocker spaniel which the children named Checkers.

The Checkers speech was masterful. How many times are Americans taken behind the front doors of the house of any public figure, and told the cost of everything he owns, how he lives, his prospects and his dreams? It was better drama than any motion picture shown that night anywhere, it was real live drama of a kind never before shown on television, never before presented to the American people.

It was real, and for Richard Nixon it was visceral. When it was over, he had intended to tell Americans who sympathized to respond to the Republican National Committee. He got that far. But before he could tell them the address (Washington) he ran out of time and was cut off. To Nixon, without that address the whole exposure had been a failure. He tossed aside his notes, sank deep into despondency, and tried to send a telegram to Eisenhower announcing his retirement from the ticket. The wire was stopped by campaign manager Chotiner.

Americans responded. It took the Republican National Committee only a few hours to learn how strong the response had been. The responses came in the millions. Much later they were collected in forty-one boxes and presented to Whittier College. Donald C. Brandenburgh, a Whittier student, studied the letters and telegrams for a master's thesis, and he confirmed what the Republicans already knew, that Nixon had appealed to millions of Americans in the Horatio Alger tradition. It was "the pride of we the American people in Richard Nixon" because he represented the common man, and the homely virtues. Americans reacted positively to the presence of Pat in the TV studio when Nixon was speaking, to the feeling he generated that "he is like me," and this cut across monetary and class lines. Nixon brought millions of Americans back to a dream with which they had grown up.

Nixon's Checkers speech was a major political performance, and one of the most successful such gestures in all American history. It probably did not affect Nixon's supporters very much, except to give them a talking point. It probably did not persuade a single enemy. But it exposed to millions of the uncommitted the vision of an Ordinary American—of an Ordinary American Family—who was in the best American tradition seeking the second highest office in the land.

The ability to bare his soul was something Richard Milhous Nixon had picked up along his own way. It did not represent Frank Nixon—he probably would have told Eisenhower to go to hell. It did not represent Hannah. She watched the performance, and feared that she was going to be sick right there in the room as her son exposed his inner being to the people.

"How could I ever forget that evening," she told Bela Kornitzer. ". . . I didn't think I could take it. But I drew courage from my faith. That carried me through."

She then sent General Eisenhower another telegram, a mother's telegram.

> DEAR GENERAL: I AM TRUSTING THAT THE ABSOLUTE TRUTH MAY COME OUT CONCERNING THIS ATTACK ON RICHARD. WHEN IT DOES, I AM SURE YOU WILL BE GUIDED ARIGHT IN YOUR DECISION TO PLACE IMPLICIT FAITH IN HIS INTEGRITY AND HONESTY. BEST OF WISHES FROM ONE WHO HAS KNOWN RICHARD LONGER THAN ANYONE, HIS MOTHER.
>
> HANNAH NIXON.

The personal attacks continued, including a charge that the Nixon family properties were worth more than a quarter of a million dollars, with the implication that Senator Nixon had used his political influence to feather his family's nest if not his own. Investigation showed the charges were totally false: brother Donald's business enterprise was built on rented properties; Frank and Hannah Nixon's house was worth less than twenty-five thousand dollars. Nixon and the family had gone further in exposing themselves than any other Milhouses, certainly, in contradiction to their whole style of life.

The only trouble was, neither Nixon nor his family would ever again be able to affect the public on such a personal level. And much as he and they might try to make themselves available and amenable to the press, it would not quite come off. With the family even more than with Richard Nixon himself there would be a reserve, a resistance to exposure. Compared with the Kennedy family, a comparison that always came readily to mind, the Nixons were aloof and unapproachable. Their reaction to the press and the press reaction to them showed clearly in the coverage of the next few years. With very few exceptions, it was bristling and negative on both sides.

30

Ordinary Family, Once Again

The campaign of 1952 polarized feeling about Richard Milhous Nixon, and that was one reason for the suspicion with which the Nixons came to regard the press. One of his critics complained because he would not release his income-tax statements for ten years. A Whittier College classmate said, "Even in school he was a political slick." Drew Pearson indicated that Nixon had subsidized his brother and parents in business by using the public weal. Moreover, it was claimed that he was antiblack and anti-Semitic because he lived in a segregated section of Washington. And the senior Nixons were hurt by a feeling within the Quaker community of Whittier that Richard Nixon had gone too far in his uncompromising political partisanship and had breached the tenets of the Quaker faith.

Actually, Richard Nixon's religion was now very much his own. During the war years when for a time stationed in New York, he had attended Norman Vincent Peale's Mar-

ble Collegiate Church. He had attended Congregational
services elsewhere. He regarded his religious faith as his own
business, but he maintained his membership in the East
Whittier Friends Church.

His mother, who had once hoped Richard would become a minister, called him "an intensely religious man."
She also said his Quaker heritage was one of the reasons for
the controversies that swirled around him, because he was
stubborn in defending his opinions and ideals, uncompromising in his beliefs.

As for himself, he spoke to biographer Kornitzer about
religion, and the Quaker faith's effects upon his mature life.
His interest in international affairs came from the emphasis
at home on peace and mutual understanding. His interest
in the world's poor came from the Quaker attitude of concern for the unfortunate. "My strong convictions on civil
rights," he said, "came from the family, which was totally
free from any kind of prejudice, racial or religious. All
through my early years, and also at Whittier College, this
whole problem of civil rights was not simply a legal issue,
but above all, a great moral issue."

Yet for some reason, Richard Milhous Nixon was unable to project an image of himself as a tolerant, reasonable
man. His great-grandfather Joshua had certainly managed
that impression—with all his worldly faults. His grandfather Franklin Milhous gave the impression of a man of
great good will. His mother exuded good will and friends
even exaggerated, calling her a saint. So Richard Nixon's
failure here must be at least partly that he took after his
scrappy father in a way unfortunate for a politician.

There were many humiliations in the vice-presidential
years. The town fathers of Whittier planned to name a
street for him, but so much fuss was raised by enemies that
they named the street Mar Vista instead. He did make the
Whittier College commencement address in 1953, as promised, and at the reception following, the college was split;
half wanted to shake Nixon's hand, half would not do so.

Officials at Duke University proposed to give him an honorary degree; the faculty voted it down.

It was hard, how hard is perhaps best indicated by a remark Nixon made to Biographer Earl Mazo: he quit taking the Washington *Post* at home so that his growing girls would not see the Herblock political cartoons, which lampooned him frequently and with almost incredible ferocity. He was uncommonly sensitive for a politician.

The hatred he engendered was harder on the family than on him. Pat had been long-suffering, although she had asked in the heat of the senatorial campaign if it was all worth it to him.

Tricia and Julie were growing up in a loving home, and their mother tried to make up for Richard's many enforced absences. The little girls were extremely well-behaved. Their grandmother was impressed and wrote about them to other relatives. Pat drove them to school in the car pool, she went to Girl Scout meetings with them, and she and Richard attended the PTA meetings when he was free. When the Nixons went on trips and came home there were joyous reunions, and when the girls grew older, they would bake cakes and arrange celebrations whenever they could. Political life was trying for the family nonetheless, and Pat Nixon did not forget the discussions they sometimes had about his retirement. Now, she asked again, more stridently, and Richard promised that when his term of office expired in 1956 he would retire from politics.

One of the worst problems Richard Nixon had to bear was an almost constant accusation of insincerity. Other politicians might make a mistake, contradict themselves, and be forgotten if not forgiven. Nixon was never forgiven or forgotten. It was, of course, the path he had chosen for himself when he campaigned against Helen Gahagan Douglas. He said that every man's public record was his public cross, and the press made the Nixon record just that. If Nixon had a reputation for smearing by innuendo and half truth, he was now himself smeared by innuendo and half truth. But the most cutting blow of all was the charge of insincerity. Murray Kempton made it once in the New York *Post*: "No one can remember him in a display of real indignation." The more moderate Richard Rovere of *The New Yorker* noted that even when Nixon was accusing Democrats of harboring diseased ideas from the Marxist virus "he never managed to convey a sense of outrage deeper than that of a man describing the ravages of Stomach Upset."

Mrs. Eleanor Roosevelt expressed a more hopeful view of Nixon, one that did not have the overtones of journalistic fervor. "He knows the importance of gaining the confidence of the people, and he has worked hard at it and made progress. This still does not make me believe that he has any strong convictions."

During the vice-presidential years the Nixons' life style changed somewhat. He was earning $35,000 plus $10,000 for expenses. They moved to a larger house, a handsome fieldstone building on a dead-end street. They paid $75,000 for it, $25,000 down and a $50,000 mortgage. The Swedish maid was gone, but Pat hired a Negro couple. They joined the Columbia Country Club, and went out to dinner more often. The little girls began to go to Sidwell Friends School.

Richard traveled a great deal, to Africa and Europe and South America and to Russia. Pat went with him; she regarded herself as his "eyes" on these trips—while he performed the services of protocol, she attempted to get information about the places they visited, and in the evenings they compared notes.

Pat was ready to quit in 1956, but it was not to be. Richard Nixon could even have traded the Vice-Presidency for a Cabinet post in a second Eisenhower administration, but he chose to run for Vice-President, and his resolution was stiffened by a move made by Harold Stassen to unseat him. Pat went along, as she always had.

The Nixons were growing away from Whittier now. Disaster had overtaken Donald—his restaurant chain had faltered and failed, just as he was about to "go public," because he did not have the capital or the turnaround time. A desperate attempt to save the business was made when loans of $205,000 were obtained from the Howard Hughes interests. Hannah put up the homestead property as security, and sacrificed it for her son when Donald went bankrupt. Later, the value of the property as security would be questioned and the implication would be clear that had Donald Nixon not been related to an important political figure the loans might not have been made. But Hannah never complained. Soon the old Nixon place and the grocery store would be torn down, and a service station would be built on the spot. Frank and Hannah had sold the Pennsylvania farm—a noble experiment but a life out of a different century for Frank—and come back to live in La Habra. In the summer of 1956, Frank Nixon was very ill. Richard came to see him; he found the old man bedridden, but still lively. The press set up a death watch outside the house, and Frank felt like calling the police to have them run out of the area. Richard Nixon soothed his father—it was just part of their job to hang around when some notable was sick, he said. (Frank died that fall, during the campaign.)

Hannah stayed on. She carried on a correspondence with relatives, and with Frank's relatives in Ohio, mostly keeping them informed of Richard's activities as she knew them. She came East occasionally to visit the Nixons in Washington. But her life was in the Whittier area, wrapped up in the church, and her relatives, and her friends. She kept close track of Richard's doings on the television and in the newspapers. She visited Donald and his family frequently, and they visited her. She continued to cook and bake for others. From time to time Evelyn Dorn, who had been secretary to the Bewley law firm when Richard was a partner, would come to help her with her correspondence. Hannah also collected memorabilia about Richard and the family, and she spent a good deal of time with biographer Bela Kornitzer, who used her as a central figure in his book on Richard Nixon.

In 1958 Richard Nixon and Pat went to South America on a good-will tour that turned out to be not only full of ill will from South Americans, but of actual danger to their lives in Caracas, where they were set upon by mobs. Nixon comported himself with such courage and fortitude, and so sensibly, that he came home a very real hero, even in the eyes of many who had not cared for him before. Also, the old Nixon "rockem-sockem" campaign technique was changing. He was much more statesman now and much less politician in his stance. Obviously, his eye was on the presidential nomination of 1960. Pat's enthusiasm for politics had waned long since; but his mother hoped and expected that Richard Nixon would be elected President of the United States.

Pat's position was that political life—the incessant demands on Richard Nixon—made normal home life very difficult. Breakfast had become the family hour, whereas in most households it was dinner. But only at breakfast could the Nixons be sure that Richard Nixon would be home. He tried to save time for his girls, but the ways he found to do it—a picnic on the rug in his offices, a sudden air trip to California—indicates that it was necessary to make every intimate moment count. That is one of the prices of political life; Pat's willingness to pay it was lessening; but Richard Nixon had become the political man. There were lovers quarrels, and Pat would go into a deep-freeze and not speak to Richard. Once during such a quarrel he called his mother and she came to help settle it. Hannah's way was to move into the house, spend her attention and her sympathy on the girls, listen to Pat, and ignore Richard. She was the best listener the Milhouses had ever produced, the gentlest and most lovable person. It was not long before the quarrel was healed and Hannah went home.

At home in the Spanish-style house off Whittier Boulevard, she would get up at five o'clock in the morning—even though she was now in her mid-seventies—and go about her cleaning, cooking, and gardening. Her concession to advancing age was to hire a man to mow the lawn. She drove an old 1946 Chevrolet automobile (no yielding to worldliness) and she gave regularly to the church. She spent long hours shopping for presents for her grandchildren (Donald's and Richard's children, and then later Edward's). She kept up a lively correspondence that might run to fifty letters a week. And she hoped that Richard would be nominated for the Presidency in 1960, which he was, and elected, which he was not.

The defeat in 1960 was almost more than Pat Nixon could bear, largely because she knew what it meant to her husband. But with the defeat, she felt it was time to get out of politics and begin to enjoy life as a private citizen. Pat Nixon's life had never been easy. As a child she had been poor, as a young woman she had worked her way, as a young politician's wife she had carried the loads of housewife, mother, and political attendant to her husband. She was excellent at her jobs; she controlled herself completely in the political sphere, she became tailored and doll-like in her appearance, she never stepped out of the role of statesman's wife. She did not appear quite real. Jacqueline Kennedy, for example, was known for her flamboyant style, and chic; these qualities enhanced the positive interest of the American people in her. Pat Nixon was known for her iron smile, and she did not come across as real. Norman Vincent Peale once talked it over with a reporter. "You're looking for warts," he said. "There aren't any." If there weren't, the Nixons would have done well to invent them, but Richard and Pat Nixon were intensely personal people, and they could not wear their hearts on their sleeves.

With the political defeat of 1960 still stinging him, Richard Nixon made ready to close up shop in Washington. He devoted his last weeks in the office of Vice-President to a spate of correspondence. He and Pat decided that they would go back to California, where he would practice law. He needed advice and help, so he telephoned Earl Adams in Los Angeles. Adams was the senior partner of the promi-

nent law firm of Adams, Duque, and Hazeltine. Adams was
also one of the original group of Republicans who had met
to promote a candidate for the 12th Congressional District
in 1945, and had chosen Richard Milhous Nixon for the
spot. In various ways, in various capacities, Earl Adams had
worked for Richard Nixon's political career in the years
since, and now he flew to Washington to meet with the
outgoing Vice-President. They lunched and talked, and the
conversation quickly came around to the future. It was not
a political conversation; Nixon wanted to come home to
California and practice law. Adams said he thought that
was easy enough; Nixon could choose his own law firm with
his connections and reputation. The Vice-President seemed
a little surprised; indeed, even a little unsure of himself.
And yet, when they discussed the recent campaign he was
not unsure at all. He was unconvinced—he did not believe
that John F. Kennedy had actually beaten him. He told
Adams that it could probably be proved that the votes in
Texas and Illinois were rigged by the Democrats. But he
also said he had rejected the idea of making a legal case because if the election were turned over, or not, the simple
raising of the issue would thereafter make questionable
every decision of Kennedy's (or Nixon's if he were successful). The press would be impossible to live with. Nixon said
that it was more important that the American people have
a de jure government than a de facto government, more important that the nation have order in a difficult time "than
that Dick Nixon be President of the United States." The
Nixons were sure in the winter of 1960 that they had been
cheated of the election—Pat Nixon was still certain of it ten
years later when I talked to her, a hard gleam entered her
eye and she spoke very bitterly of the purchase of the election by the Kennedys, showing a depth of feeling that
seemed quite remarkable after so many years and the turn-
about of success.

Philosophizing, Nixon could content himself with

statements he gave Bela Kornitzer the year before, when he was considering the Presidency in the future tense.

"What's up today is down tomorrow. Public opinion shifts rapidly, and all a politician can do is to plug away and do the best he can. If it is in the stars that a certain person will be nominated and elected, that's the way it's going to be."

He had a fatalistic attitude toward the Presidency, he said, and he spoke to Kornitzer about figures of the past who had sought the nation's highest office, and failed: Henry Clay, John C. Calhoun, Daniel Webster, William Jennings Bryan, and Robert La Follette, who had been heroes of his father's, and Robert A. Taft, whom he had known well himself.

"A thorough study of past Presidential hopefuls convinced me that the Presidency has seldom gone to men who planned their campaign for the White House methodically. Men who wanted it the most, who tried the hardest, have failed. I believe that the Presidency, almost without exception, seeks the man. The people have a sense, an intuition, about a leader, and, unless a man develops the qualifications that the people believe are needed, he isn't going to be elected."

Those words could have been his valedictory, and Pat Nixon certainly believed that politics was out of the picture.

At that moment in Washington, Richard Nixon was undecided as to whether he would move to San Francisco or Los Angeles. Earl Adams told him he really ought to go to New York or stay in Washington—he could make more money. But Nixon wanted to come back to California.

On Adams's advice Nixon considered several law firms, but finally joined the Adams firm, with a guarantee of $60,000 a year, plus 25 percent of the fees he generated for the firm. His income, it was estimated, could be $90,000 to $100,000 a year. From Nixon's standpoint, Adams said, he could do better elsewhere. From the firm's standpoint it was an excellent bargain. (Adams, Duque, and Hazeltine was still enjoying Nixon business long after Richard Nixon had gone to the White House.)

Then came the problem of finding somewhere to live. Until now, the only aspect of the Richard Nixon career that really differentiated him from his ancestors and relatives was his thrust into politics. He had no financial resources. Even now he only had $35,000 to put down on a house in California. His great-grandfather Joshua Milhous and his grandfather Franklin Milhous had been much more substantial in terms of property than he was. But now, entering private life under the circumstances that he did, the life of Richard Milhous Nixon and his family underwent a remarkable change.

Washington sees politicians come and go, the cave dwellers, some of them immensely rich, regard the politicians in the same terms as the more respectable members of the press—a sort of private zoo for the entertainment of the professional hostesses. Politicians are lionized as long as they are successful, and then dropped by the movers and shakers when they fail.

But a big-time corporation lawyer with the right connections can become a wealthy man in a short time. Fees run into the hundreds of thousands of dollars. And Richard Milhous Nixon was stepping into this heady atmosphere, now to become an equal with people who had supported him from afar in the past. It was time. Pat had watched with interest the fortunes of Jack Drown and his wife, as Drown went into business with his father, and expanded until he owned the most important magazine distribution company in the Los Angeles area. The young Drowns had been poor with the young Nixons. Now the Drowns lived in an expensive house in the horsey section of Rolling Hills and enjoyed southern California life as only the well-to-do can. The friendship had continued unabated; Drown ran campaign trains for Richard Nixon and helped in other ways. Helene invited the Nixon girls for visits; they rode the horses and swam and played with the Drown children.

To begin with, Pat wanted a big, comfortable house, so Richard went to California to find something suitable.

He approached the problem with his usual thoroughness and caution. He looked at Whittier—Whittier would no longer do, for it was a middle-class community and Richard had moved beyond that. He was achieving one ambition, to go into big-city law practice with a big-time firm.

For a prominent politician, looking for a house is not a simple matter. Friends and former political supporters have a tendency to submit all their white elephants at inflated prices. In Nixon's case one contributor wanted three times as much for his house when he heard the Vice-President was looking as he had been asking the week before.

Richard Nixon then sought the advice of a jovial real estate man named France Raine, and after looking at fifty houses or so, in the $100,000 to $175,000 classes, in various districts all over the Los Angeles area, he settled on a lot in Trousdale estates in the new north section of Beverly Hills, largely because Paul Trousdale, the builder, would give him the lot and build the house at cost for the publicity value to him. Still Nixon had to find a place to live while the house was being built. He was staying at the Statler Hotel and Pat and the girls were in Washington. It took time, and to save money he moved from the Statler to the Gaylord, across the street from the Ambassador.

House hunting was hard work. France Raine would pick Nixon up in the morning, and they would search all day, driving hundreds of miles across the freeways, from one end of Los Angeles county to the other. Raine, who carried a good bit of avoirdupois, was deprived of his lunch day after day, because Nixon did not eat lunch. "At least you're going to lose some weight," said the former Vice-President. Raine's laugh was as hollow as his stomach.

They did find a house, in Bel Air, on Bundy Drive, and the Nixons all came to settle down in it.

Nixon was popular in the law firm. Most of the firm was located on the tenth floor, but a suite of offices on the eleventh was done over for Nixon, and he sat up there in splendor—with the pigeons that clustered around his windows and gave him a rash, until Pacific Mutual Insurance Company, the building owner, was persuaded to get rid of the pigeons. Nixon and Pat went to dinner at the homes of the partners. They had trained themselves, they never forgot a name and they never forgot an event, and they were friendly and kindly. On the day of the firm's Christmas party that first year, one of junior partner Robert Volk's children was in the hospital and had just been in surgery. Richard had told Pat Nixon about it, and at the party Pat took Barbara Volk aside "as if she had been her own mother," said Robert Volk.

The Nixon life was now changed, and except for family, Whittier seemed a long way away. He was moving among the powerful, the millionaires and industrialists who belonged to the Los Angeles Country Club and similar wealthy spas, the kind of people who did not eat in restaurants because there was no need. The girls would go to exclusive day schools, because their peers did. When Richard Nixon settled down to write his book, *Six Crises,* some of the work would be done at the private beach home of Mrs. George C. Brock, just beyond Malibu. And then, in 1962, Richard Nixon would have the use of Mrs. Brock's secluded "cottage" again to make an important decision: whether or not to run for governor of California. He was armed with a 3-to-1 vote in the family; Pat voting the negative. And, of course, as almost anyone could have predicted, he would opt to run. He was still the political man.

His defeat in the gubernatorial race in California in 1962 left a very sour taste. For a time, Richard Nixon seemed to have convinced himself that he was really finished with politics. He moved to New York, and to the old, established Republican law firm of Mudge, Stern, Baldwin and Todd, which changed its name to honor him on his entry. He bought an expensive apartment in midtown Manhattan. Pat Nixon, who had once worked in a department store, now began to patronize couturier shops. The girls would follow the pattern of the upper middle class—private day school in New York, and then Tricia would go to Finch College and Julie would go to Smith College. The ordinary American family was ordinary no longer in this generation.

Richard Milhous Nixon, earning perhaps $200,000 a year from his writing and law practice, soon lost the awe he had once felt for people of great wealth. Once he had walked the streets of New York City sick at rejection by the big law firms; now he had all the material success he could hope for, and could meet any lawyer in America on even terms. His daughters would marry very well: Julie would marry David Eisenhower, the grandson of Dwight D. Eisenhower, and who knew what future the political stars would hold for them? Tricia would marry Edward Cox, a promising young law student of an Eastern establishment family.

As for Richard Nixon, he would achieve his own ambition, to become President of the United States, although Hannah would die the year before he crowned his ambition. He would return to California and select a secluded million-dollar retirement estate in lower Orange County, among the very rich with whom he now associated as a matter of course.

Some old Whittier friends would decry his course, and his millionaire friend John B. Reilly, one of the early Nixon political supporters would say that Richard made a dreadful mistake when he assumed the trappings of worldliness, moved among the rich, and bought a big house, instead of choosing the simple life of Whittier. But Richard Milhous Nixon was following the American pattern, even as Joshua Milhous had done. Friends in the meeting criticized Joshua for his music, his organ, his carriages, his horses. But this did not impede his progress, any more than the disapproval of Richard's acquaintances did this.

He would remain true to his old friends of childhood, college, and beyond. He would get together with them and talk football. But there was an unbridgeable gulf now— even the Drowns, intimate as they were, spoke in new tones of Richard Nixon.

Richard Nixon would try to be President of all the people, as nearly every President had tried before him. Politics would get in the way; so would his perennial war with the liberal press, and no one, including the public, would come out the better for that. His ability to antagonize those who did not agree with his conservative philosophy would drive them to extremes. And after more than two years of the Nixon administration, James Reston of *The New York Times* would write that "his record as President is much better than his record as politician and party leader."

As President, Richard Nixon brought the best training and background to the job of any recent President save Lyndon Johnson. Nixon had been congressman and Senator. So had John Kennedy and Lyndon Johnson. John Kennedy had come to the office socially sophisticated, but naïve in international politics; he had underestimated the Russians, which very nearly led him to disaster. Lyndon Johnson was well prepared in terms of government service, but Johnson's major experience, his most useful and powerful years, had been in the Senate. Nixon had spent eight years as Vice-President under General Eisenhower, whose announced intention was to make of the Vice-Presidency a real arm of the administration. If that did not come about, at least Nixon had much experience in Cabinet, national security council, and in traveling abroad. He had met contumely in South America and met it well. He had debated Khrushchev in a model American kitchen in Moscow, and as a result made a good appraisal of the men he would meet in solving the international problems of the Presidency.

Experience leavens. Experience teaches, and sometimes experience causes a man to turn his personal philosophy around. Did this happen with Richard Milhous Nixon? Hardly. It could be said that the Nixon of the 1970s, philosophically, was very much the Nixon who studied constitutional law under Dr. Paul Smith at Whittier College, the Nixon who engaged in debates on the Constitution in college, the Nixon who took an old-fashioned view of the American system as dedicated in perpetuity to the triumph of opportunity over security, of individualism over community effort, the Nixon who took a conservative view of the Constitution and its limitations on federal government.

One could get a glimpse of the essential Nixon by examining the Quaker ethic. When Richard Nixon said that he had absolutely no prejudice against people because of race, color, or creed, his detractors sneered. But why should they? He grew up in an atmosphere that was virtually free of prejudice, which was far more than most Americans could say. In fact, most Americans, black and white, could not even believe it. Grandmother Almira's table was the illustration; not only was it free of racism, but the help ate with the family.

As congressman and Senator he had the opportunity to feather his own nest. Many congressmen and Senators did so, and always had. Lyndon Johnson served in the government nearly all his life, and yet became a multimillionaire; even General Eisenhower's financial dealings were much less able to stand critical scrutiny than Richard Milhous Nixon's affairs had always been. Muckrakers in the press attempted to uncover indications of wrongdoing (*Newsday*'s 1971 "exposé" of Nixon's land dealings in Florida with his friend Bebe Rebozo was a case in point. But the *Newsday* exposé failed to arouse a storm because basically there was nothing to expose: Nixon had been involved in rather minor land speculation, when he was a private citizen, a New York lawyer.) And in the Presidency, although he had earned large sums as a lawyer, Nixon was really not a wealthy man. Pat Nixon said in 1970 that all the Nixons owned was their equity in the Florida property and their equity in the San Clemente villa.

One has to grant that Nixon was as deeply touched by his Quaker heritage as John Kennedy was by his Boston Irish background and Lyndon Johnson by Texas.

Nixon's Quaker heritage has not only influenced his private life but, much more than most people realize, many of his public actions as well. A case in point was the celebrated Nixon attitude toward abortion, which triggered so much liberal fury against him. "From personal and religious beliefs," said Nixon, "I consider abortions an unacceptable form of population control. Further, unrestricted abortion policies, or abortion on demand, I cannot square with my personal belief in the sanctity of human life—including the life of the yet unborn."

One might ask how could any man make such a statement, yet condone and prosecute a war in Vietnam, where thousands of women and their unborn children are killed each year? The fact is that the demands of practical politics and those of religious philosophy were in twentieth-century America quite different. Should Richard Milhous Nixon espouse the totality of Quaker belief, and eschew war, it would make sense—but then he would not be President. No one was saying that Richard Milhous Nixon's philosophy was consistent. Admittedly he changed it, rejected the pure Quaker way when he chose to go to war himself in 1942. But his own change and inconsistency did not wipe out the inheritance and the teaching of the past.

And that inheritance? From the Milhouses came that piety (in him it is often derogatorily called piousness) that would lead him to make the statement on abortion. It would also account for his respect and friendship for Billy Graham, who represented a kind of modern fundamentalism in approach to life and religion. And his respect for Norman Vincent Peale.

Also, from the Milhouses would come the stubbornness of a man of conviction that would lead him into fights as

President that less stubborn men would have avoided. The Hiss case was first. He pursued that when it seemed hopeless, convinced that he was right. His Supreme Court choices and the manner in which he handled them were also indication of this Milhous Quaker stubborn streak. As vacancies occurred in the Court, Nixon did what he had promised: he nominated men whose political philosophy coincided with his own. He was convinced that the Court had swung to an activist interpretation of the Constitution, beginning in the Eisenhower years, and he wanted to make it more conservative. When he was opposed in this, and in his judgment of the caliber of his appointments, it would have been relatively easy to thwart his opponents by appointing a conservative woman—at the very least it would have made the water so hot for his Democratic enemies that they would not wish to be scalded again. He could also have chosen a black conservative, an "Uncle Tom." But instead, he stuck to his guns and called on men who agreed with his philosophy. It was only incidental that one appointee, Judge Powell, was so favorably entrenched in the legal establishment that even the liberals could not gainsay him without attacking the system; the nomination of Rehnquist was much more indicative of Nixon's effort to pick a man for his political philosophy alone.

The Milhous heritage was easy enough to see, although its full significance was probably not understood by any who did not know the Quakers. The Nixon heritage, and its significance in the life of Richard Milhous Nixon was not so readily apparent. Politically speaking, Richard Milhous Nixon's California heritage was thoroughly Republican on both sides, although Hannah sometimes had Democratic leanings, and Frank Nixon espoused the Bull Moose cause of Teddy Roosevelt, and liked Democrat William Jennings Bryan so well that he kept his picture on the wall for many years. Those aberrations can be laid to personality: Hannah was intellectually inclined and a deep believer in peace; and she thought Wilson shared those attributes. Frank Nixon's espousal of Bryan and Roosevelt represented his Western inclinations to some extent; both men attracted Westerners without regard to party lines. But Richard grew up in a socially conservative Republican community, whose attitudes reflected very generally those of the family.

The question was once asked of Richard Milhous Nixon: might he not have become a Democrat if he had gone into politics during the New Deal years. He said no, because he could not accept the New Deal philosophy, due to the strong streak of individualism in the family. "We had drilled into us the idea that we should if at all possible take care of ourselves and not expect others to take care of us."

The principle was brought home in the illness of Harold Nixon. When the doctors discovered that Harold had tuberculosis, they suggested that the Nixons put him in the county hospital "not only so that he could get more adequate care but in order to relieve us of the financial burden." The Nixons were aghast—go on the public dole? Never. That is when Frank sold off part of the land around the grocery store, and even borrowed money to meet the medical bills. Hannah gave up her normal life, and that meant the family gave up their normal lives for five years so that they could take care of brother Harold. That is certainly dedication to principle, and a spirit of independence.

The independence came from both sides. Samuel Brady Nixon, back in Ohio after having spent all his worldly goods trying to nurse his tubercular wife back to health in Virginia and the Carolinas, said "root, hog, or die" as he settled back on Ohio soil without a penny in his pocket. The Milhouses, for six generations, had followed the philosophy that it was not what a man was worth, but what he *did* that was important to the world, and the upbringing and education of every Milhous child was aimed at producing a stalwart independent citizen.

New York Times columnist Tom Wicker would see the case of brother Harold as a philosophical trend that carried into the Nixon attitude toward welfare and public service employment. His family had been stoutly independent; why could not the people on welfare get out and take care of themselves? Perhaps the celebrated Nixon stubbornness, along with the independence, has clouded his vision of the military-industrial-agribusiness state that is now the United States, where such independence as that shown by the Nixons of a hundred years ago is no longer feasible, or even possible (especially for blacks). Nixon's cousin Philip Milhous in Grass Valley, California, illustrates the case. Philip Milhous was self-supporting, if not well-to-do, until 1966, when he suffered a heart attack, which made it impossible for him to work. By 1971 he was receiving $270 a month in payments from Social Security and $57 in state welfare funds, plus payment for a houseworker. The celebrated independence of these Milhouses had come to an end.

In his denial that he could accept the philosophy of the New Deal, Nixon had also hedged to the extent that he said he could not have accepted the "stand-pat philosophy" of old Republicanism, even while he detested what he regarded as the regimentation of the New Deal. When Richard Nixon went to Washington to work for OPA he did not like the bureaucracy or regimentation in which he found himself, but when he was asked outright by Herman Perry in 1945 whether or not he was Republican, his reply was that he "guessed he was." It never was and never would be easy for him to shake off the consideration of conflicting views that is ingrained in a lawyer. He was like many another young American in 1945 in that he was not sure which political party would accommodate his philosophy. Had the incumbent been a Republican, had his friends in Whittier been the Democrats, he might well have taken another road.

No political road would have been easy for Richard Milhous Nixon, particularly when many of the decisions he would have to make would conflict with his basic convictions. Standing for individualism, he still found it proper to appoint, as his second Secretary of Agriculture, Earl Butz, a man who leaned in favor of the big agricultural business enterprises that were able to produce economically, as against the family farm. Earl Butz had once said that there were too many people on the land, that marginal and failing farmers had best seek employment elsewhere. How did that philosophy square with the Nixon spirit of independence? It would not square; one of the problems of the Nixon philosophy in leading the nation was to be that the whole American trend was away from individualism and self-support. A generation before his own, nearly *all* Nixons and Milhouses had made their livings from the land; in Richard Milhous Nixon's generation, *none* of them farmed for a living. Closest to a farmer was Nixon's cousin Roy Nixon, Jr., back in Vinton county, Ohio, who did a little farm work, some carpentry, and other jobs.

The Presidency, where the man is largely the captive of events, had taught Richard Nixon a great deal about the differences between principles and possibilities. Not surprisingly, in midterm he found it easier to state the problem in terms of foreign affairs than domestic. He wanted peace, but "The kind of relative peace I envision is not the dream of my Quaker youth," he told *New York Times* correspondent Cyrus Sulzberger. The dreams of youth vanished, if slowly, replaced by the pursuit of the possible.

For Richard Nixon the presidential years would be the culmination of ambition, tinged, of course, by the hard realization that under the American system politics could never be out of mind. When I met with him in the spring of 1970 in the austere oval room of the White House, the coming congressional elections—and the need for a competitive spirit—were very much on his mind. We talked for some time. He kept coming back insistently to the need to compete in American life.

For Pat, the early presidential years would not be nearly so fulfilling or so happy. It was life in a goldfish bowl—true, a unique and prestigious one—but it was still a goldfish bowl, and if Richard Nixon did not seem to be a prisoner of the White House, Pat Nixon certainly did. Only in the fourth year of the term would Pat successfully step out of her shell. Then, she began the year 1972 with a highly successful public relations trip to Africa, which she made alone. In her role as First Lady she was correct; she listened to criticism and attempted to adjust her "image" to please the American press and public, but underneath there was an indication that it was an ordeal she would just as soon have not undergone.

Back in the West, the Nixon cousins of Vinton county would bask in a certain glow of notoriety during the presidential years, although most of them were Democrats. They would ask for little signs of recognition from their illustrious Richard Milhous Nixon, and he would do his very best to oblige all, for he was an accommodating and kindly man at heart. They would have signed pictures and other mementos from the White House. Since Richard had no sons, the Western line of Nixons would be carried on by Donald's boys, Donald Anthony Nixon and Richard Calvert Nixon. The Far Western family would be scattered, with Edward living near Seattle, and Donald moving away from the Whittier area to the more fashionable Newport Beach.

All the immediate family would become gun-shy of publicity, and even downright cantankerous, in the manner of introverts unused to the responsibilities of those related to persons in high office. This attitude would in turn renew the antipathy of the press to the Nixons. But in time it would all end, and Richard Milhous Nixon would retire to the luxurious villa in San Clemente, and in the manner of Presidents of the twentieth century, would devote himself to clarifying and elaborating on the events of his administration. There would be plaques and libraries and historic sites to commemorate various aspects of the Nixon story—and then life would move on, but the Nixons could never again be another ordinary American family.

Richard Nixon would occupy that strange limbo of ex-Presidents—neither elder statesman nor otherwise actively used by the government he had given so much. Richard and Pat Nixon would be well-to-do, living on their estate at San Clemente. The girls and their husbands would either fade from the public eye or earn public acclaim on their own. But the atmosphere of "royalty" that surrounds the Presidency, while clinging to the Richard Nixons, would not be transferable.

Index

ABOUT THE AUTHOR

EDWIN P. HOYT is a biographer, historian, and novelist who has made a special study of American history as portrayed in the affairs of various families. Before turning to full-time writing, Mr. Hoyt was assistant publisher of *American Heritage*. He has also been television producer (CBS), magazine editor (*Colliers*), newspaper publisher (Colorado Springs *Free Press*), chief editorial writer (Denver *Post*), and foreign and war correspondent (Denver *Post, United Press*). He was born in Portland, Oregon, and educated in the West. He now lives with his wife Olga in Vermont and Maryland.